RED OCTOBER

RED OCTOBER

THE REVOLUTION THAT CHANGED THE WORLD

DOUGLAS BOYD

The History Press

First published 2017

The History Press
The Mill, Brimscombe Port
Stroud, Gloucestershire, GL5 2QG
www.thehistorypress.co.uk

British Library Cataloguing in Publication Data.
A catalogue record for this book is available from the British Library.

ISBN 978 0 7509 8244 3

Typesetting and origination by The History Press
Printed and bound in Great Britain by T.J. International Ltd

CONTENTS

List of Abbreviations and Acronyms   7

Author's Notes   9

Part 1

1. In the Beginning Were the Words   13
2. Who was Lenin?   20
3. Who was Trotsky?   26
4. Who was Stalin?   32
5. Rehearsal for a Revolution   40
6. Russian Roulette   50

Part 2

7. Two Shots – 38 Million Dead   59
8. Arms and the Woman   66
9. The Great Retreat   76
10. Letters from Hell   88
11. God Help Russia!   102
12. White Nights, Red Days   114
13. Peace?   131

Part 3

14. The Struggle for Power   141

15. Enemies at the Gates   150

16. Bloody Murder   165

17. The Enemies Within   176

18. Declaring War on the World   193

19. The Inadmissible Letter   201

    Notes   209

    Further Reading in English   217

    Index   219

LIST OF ABBREVIATIONS AND ACRONYMS

AOK	Armeeoberkomando (Austro-Hungarian Supreme Command in 1914–18 war)
ARA	American Relief Administration
BMO	Bolshevik Military Organisation
Cheka	Chrezvechainaya komissiya (literally, the extraordinary commission – the first Soviet security organisation)
C-in-C	Commander-in-chief
Comintern	Communist International
CP	Central Powers
CPGB	Communist Party of Great Britain
CPSU	Communist Party of the Soviet Union
FBI	Federal Bureau of Investigation (US)
Gensek	Generalny Sekretar (General Secretary of the CPSU)
GPU	Gosudarstvennoye Politicheskoye Upravleniye (Soviet security organisation 1922–23)
HQ	headquarters
KGB	Komitet Gosudarstvennoi Bezopasnosti (last Soviet state security organisation)
LSR	Left Socialist Revolutionary (Party)
NCO	non-comissioned officer
NEP	Novy Ekonomicheski Politik (New Economic Policy)

NKVD	Narodny Komitet Vnukhtrennikh Del (Soviet state security organisation 1934–46)
NRZ	Neue Rheinische zeitung
OGPU	Obyedinonnoye Gosudarstvennoye Polititicheskoye Upravleniye (Soviet state security organisation 1923–34
OHL	Oberste Heeresleitung (German Supreme Command in 1914–18 war)
Okhrana	Otedleniye po Okhraneniyu Obshchestvennoi Bezopasnosti i Poryadki (Tsarist secret police)
Orgburo	organisational office of the CPSU
Politburo	governing body of CPSU Central Committee (literally policy office)
POUM	Partit Obrer d'Unificació Marxista (Catalan Marxist Party in Spanish Civil War)
POW	prisoner of war
PR	public relations
RSDLP	Russian Social Democratic Labour Party
RSFSR	Russian Soviet Federative Socialist Republic
SDLP	Social Democratic Labour Party
SIGINT	signals interception
Sovnarkom	Soviet Narodnikh Komissarov (Council of National Commissars)
SR	Socialist Revolutionary (Party)
Stavka	Stavka Verkhovnovo Glavnokomanduyushchevo (Russian Supreme Command 1914–18)
Tseka	Tsentralny Komitet (Central Committee of CPSU)
US/USA	United States of America
USSR	Union of Soviet Socialist Republics (1922–91)

AUTHOR'S NOTES

1. All translations by the author, unless otherwise attributed.
2. With the exception of the last Tsar, referred to throughout by the English form of his name as Nicholas to distinguish him from all other Russians called Nikolai, Russian first names are in their transliterated form of e.g. Yevgeni A. Tchaikovsky, with the middle initial standing for the patronymic.
3. Until February 1918 Russia used the Julian calendar, which by then was thirteen days behind the modern or Gregorian calendar introduced under Pope Gregory in 1582 and subsequently used elsewhere in Christian countries. This is why the October Revolution took place in November 1917. Dates here are according to the modern calendar, except where noted otherwise.
4. Russian being gender-sensitive, the wife of Mr Ranevsky is Mrs or Madame Ranevskaya, etc.

PART I

IN THE BEGINNING WERE THE WORDS

Karl Marx's *Manifest der Kommunistischen Partei* was published in German in 1867 and subsequently translated into a number of other languages. Its English title was *The Manifesto of the Communist Party*. In the original, it began *'Ein Gespenst geht um in Europa'* – 'a spectre is haunting Europe, the spectre of the communism.' It continued with the assertion that all the governments in Europe were afraid of a virtually non-existent political party, ending with the exhortation, *'Proletarier aller Länder, vereinigt Euch!'* – which is commonly rendered in English as, 'Workers of the World, Unite!' The manifesto did not include the formula *'Jeder nach seinen Fähigkeiten, jedem nach seinen Bedürfnissen'* – 'From each according to his ability, to each according to his need'. Outside of a few religious communities this utopian formula has never been known to work for very long. Marx quoted it in his 1875 *Critique of the Gotha Programme*, but it had previously been used by French socialist Louis Blanc in 1839, whose version of communist philosophy was named Blanquism. In less succinct form, it can be traced back as early as 1755 to express the *ideal* of communism, not its practice.

The year 1848, in which Marx began to write the Manifesto,[1] was the Year of Revolution throughout Europe. It began in Sicily in January, followed by France in February and spread to more than fifty other countries in Europe and elsewhere. There were many factors in this coincidence, which included the dissatisfaction of the rapidly growing working class employed in the vast factories of the time and badly paid, fed and housed in slums of towns whose expansion was too rapid for a proper infrastructure of paved streets and sanitation. Their anger was often harnessed and given direction by middle-class educated leaders like Marx, himself raised in a prosperous German-Jewish family, and his collaborator Friedrich Engels, who came from a rich German Protestant background. Engels had contributed to the drafting of the manifesto, but was not credited as co-author or contributor on publication.

The March revolution of 1848 in the thirty-nine states of the German Confederation – it was not a united country until 1871 – was followed by an uprising in Denmark and Schleswig-Holstein at the end of the month. Further north in Sweden, the riots collectively called *Marsoroligheterna* were suppressed in Stockholm by mounted police troops. The breakaway cantons in Switzerland were brought to heel in the Swiss Confederation. Poland, the Danubian principalities, Wallachia, Moravia and Ukrainian Galicia all saw riots in the streets and damage to property. The Great Irish Famine led to an uprising by the Young Irelander group, which ended in bloodshed. The Austrian Empire was riven by various revolutionary movements of socialist and nationalistic character, trying to break away from Vienna's hegemony. In Hungary, it seemed that the self-determination uprising had been successful, until it was put down, with concessions, by Russian and Austrian troops. In that one year, tens of thousands of strikers and demonstrators were killed across the continent; many others were obliged to flee into exile, with France the destination of choice because of its tradition of welcoming political refugees since the revolution in 1789. For several years thereafter, echoes of the 'spirit of '48' inspired uprisings in many countries across the world.

It seemed to Marx that all this unrest proved the time had come to demolish the bourgeois-industrial society created by the Industrial Revolution, which had enticed into the cities and factories millions of workers and their families whose forebears had been free wage-labourers or serfs under feudalism. As far as Russia was concerned, although Catherine the Great had issued the *nakaz Kateriny Velikei*, or Instruction of Catherine the Great, in 1767, envisaging a Russia in which all men were equal and banning capital punishment, torture or serfdom, in fact feudal serfdom was still widespread in Russia in 1848, and was only abolished there nearly a century after the *nakaz*, in 1861.

On the land, working alone or in small groups, the widely dispersed labouring classes had been unable to organise themselves into a position of power, from which to negotiate better terms for their labour. Once herded together in those temples of nineteenth-century industry that were the factories – the largest employing several thousand men and women in one place – ease of communication made possible the organisation of all who shared a common resentment at the conditions of their lives: long hours, sometimes dangerous work, poor pay, accommodation in slums, no health care, high infant mortality and inadequate clothing and diet. The growth of a free press also contributed; while most newspaper owners and editors supported the moneyed classes, some socialist periodicals were also published cheaply for the working masses.

Marx was a classically educated man approaching his fiftieth birthday when the first edition of his verbose and slightly confusing manifesto was published. In it, he traced the development of human society from the first cities to the feudal period when hereditary nobles had absolute power over the common people, and from there to the medieval guilds that empowered the burgesses of independent cities to form a new class, the bourgeoisie of artisans, merchants and speculators that became the driving force of the Industrial Revolution. In nineteenth-century Europe, he argued, the time was ripe for the next massive upheaval in social relations: the vast majority of workers or proletarians[2] should seize power from the numerically inferior members of the bourgeoisie that exploited them. Private property, inheritance and ownership of land must be abolished; the means of production must be vested in the workers who should all share equally in the wealth this produced. However, since the bourgeoisie controlled the forces of law and order, it would not easily relinquish its monopoly of power, which would therefore have to be seized by violent revolution.

Considering the millions of people who have suffered and died under various forms of applied Communism, it is worth comparing the utopian aspirations of the political philosophy with the lifestyle of its originator. Born in Trier, Prussia, in May 1818, Marx attended a *Gymnasium* or grammar school and was subsidised by his prosperous family during his extended dilettante student years after being exempted on the grounds of poor health from Prussia's obligatory military service for young men. Although descended both maternally and paternally from generations of rabbis, his father Heinrich[3] was a lawyer, who had converted to Protestantism and ran a successful practice that financed the purchase of several vineyards and a prestigious ten-room residence near Trier's still extant Roman town gate, known as Porta Nigra. Frau Marx, who had not converted to Christianity and remained in every sense a Jewish mother, came from a Dutch business family related to the founders of the Phillips electrical empire. While still a student of eighteen, their son Karl began a seven-year engagement to Jenny von Westphalen, a girl from an aristocratic family that strongly disapproved of her choice, partly because he was Jewish although baptised in a Protestant church, but also because he showed no inclination either to work at his studies or to earn money to support a wife and family. He was, and remained throughout his life, totally self-obsessed, many times accepting money from the Dutch relations of his mother, which he knew came from what revolutionary socialists called 'the exploitation of the workers'.

The other 'name' in early Communism was Friedrich Engels. In 1842, at the age of 22, his parents sent him to Manchester, to work as a clerk in one of his affluent family's several textile mills. This was done in the hope that their son would 'come to his senses' and settle down to serious work. Instead, Friedrich met there a radical young working woman named Mary Burns, who did her very adequate best to ensure that he did not identify too closely with the cause of the bosses by showing him the sordid underside of Manchester's prosperity. As the eponymous poet Robert Burns might have said, the best-laid plans of parents 'gang aft agley'. Although never marrying because they despised the bourgeois institution of marriage, the couple produced under Engels' name *Outlines of a Critique of Political Economy*, which was sent to Paris, to which city Marx had moved shortly after marrying Jenny von Westphalen in 1843. Heading a group of young German émigré socialists, he edited a periodical titled *die Deutsch-Französische Jahrbücher* or German-French Yearbooks – not that French contributors were very evident. Engels' critique was published, as were three later articles by him exposing the evils of child labour, industrial pollution and the overworked and underpaid labour force in Britain. These articles were incorporated into his first book *The Condition of the Working Class in England*, published in German in 1845 and in English in 1887.

Marx's magazine in Paris ceased publication when his single patron became disillusioned and withdrew his financial support, but when he met Engels there in 1844 – they both shared a predilection for reading the Russian newspapers free-of-charge in the fashionable bistro Le Dome – a rather unequal partnership was born. After Engels left to pursue his political career in Germany, Marx was expelled from France in February 1845. He and his family moved to Brussels, where Engels joined them, both he and Marx becoming involved for three years in an undercover dissident organisation calling itself the League of the Just, which later became the Communist League. During this period, Engels contributed to Marx's thought and writing, although Marx did not acknowledge this publicly. Expelled from Belgium for giving money to arm anti-government extremists, he moved back to Cologne, obsessed with his theory that the bourgeoisie of his homeland would cast off the feudal monarchies of the several German kingdoms and principalities so that the proletariat could then in its turn overthrow the bourgeoisie. Using a legacy from his father's estate, he edited and published a new left-wing daily *die Neue Rheinische Zeitung* (NRZ). Although there were other contributors to the paper, even its nominally joint editor Engels had to admit that the tyrannical 30-year-old chief editor of the NRZ was an absolute dictator. Unsurprisingly, Marx was several times put on trial for disturbing public order and insulting public functionaries. Expelled from Germany with a pregnant wife who had already produced three children, he returned to Paris, to find the City of Light[4] in the throes of a repressive counter-revolution and a cholera outbreak. Deprived of his Prussian citizenship in 1849, he immigrated to London in June, where he would fall out with most other members of the Communist League, which had transferred its headquarters there.

Although Marx occasionally wrote articles for the leftist *New York Daily Tribune* and other socialist newspapers, after the move to England his family lived for several years in abject poverty in a three-room Soho slum, while he spent long hours every day in the warmth and comfort of the new, centrally heated British Museum reading room. On at least one occasion in 1850, Jenny and the children were evicted for non-payment of rent and their belongings thrown into the street – not that there was much to throw. A visitor commented on the disorder, squalor and filth in which they lived with broken furniture, inadequate clothing for the children and a near-starvation diet, confirmed by Marx, who wrote in the summer of 1851:

> My son is ill, little Jenny is ill, Lenchen is ill … I cannot call the doctor because I have no money for medicine. For the last eight to ten days I have been feeding the family on bread and potatoes.[5]

Lenchen was the family nickname of Helène Demuth, a servant employed by the von Westphalen family, who was sent by them to put some order into the chaotic living conditions of their daughter's household. Helène soon gave birth to an illegitimate son christened Frederick Lewis Demuth, an embarrassment who was put out to a working-class foster family shortly after birth. Marx and Engels tried to convince Jenny that Engels was the father, but it seems likely that the unwanted boy child was fathered by Marx himself.

To prove that he was a man of action, as well as a gentleman at ease in several languages and a lover of literature, art and music, Engels actually took up arms in anti-government uprisings in Germany, so alarming his parents that they threatened to terminate his allowance unless he emigrated to America for his own safety and to avoid disgracing the family. Escaping into Switzerland one step ahead of an arrest warrant, he negotiated a compromise whereby he was not cut off from their financial support in return for returning to England, to manage a family textile enterprise in England. Turning up in London, he lived in a pleasant house in Primrose Hill, very unlike the Marx family's sordid accommodation, and siphoned money from the family coffers to subsidise his impoverished friend, while himself enjoying fox hunting with people of his own leisured class and hosting generously catered Sunday parties, which lasted into the small hours of Monday morning.

Somehow caring for her husband, Lenchen and the children, despite the chronic shortage of cash, Jenny lived through the deaths of three of the children in infancy and a still birth in 1856 – all partly caused by malnutrition and lack of medical treatment. In 1856 the family moved to less insalubrious quarters in Kentish Town, and moved up-market again in 1864 after Jenny came into a family inheritance of £1,600.

The year 1871 saw France's defeat in the Franco-Prussian war produce the short-lived Paris Commune,[6] which raised the hopes of European revolutionary socialists until it was brutally suppressed by French government forces with Prussian assistance after two months with 30,000 executions and 40,000 *communards* imprisoned, many to be deported to penal colonies overseas.[7] Although ending in tragedy, it may have been the Commune that connected in Marx's and Engels' minds the idea of a disastrous national defeat producing the chaos necessary for a revolution in Germany, a country at the stage of social development which they considered ripe for a radical socialist revolution. As early as 1853, they also talked of a revolution starting in St Petersburg that would unleash a civil war across Russia, despite this contradicting the premise in the manifesto that a period of bourgeois society was necessary before the workers' revolution could take place; the bourgeoisie in Russia was a small minority living mainly in the few big cities that were dotted widely apart across the vast Romanov empire.

Caused largely by his irregular sleep pattern, excessive use of tobacco and unsuitable diet, Marx suffered increasingly from insomnia, which he self-medicated with narcotics that could then be freely purchased over the counter. He had always fallen out with his collaborators, with the exception of Engels. As painful boils and other skin problems, and abscesses that prevented him sleeping or even sitting comfortably, eye trouble and neuralgia contributed to his increasing irascibility, he alienated even his closest admirers.[8] In 1881 his long-suffering wife died and a decline into worse health brought Marx's death on 14 March 1883. His sociopathic attitudes were the reason why just nine mourners attended the burial of the great prophet of Communism in Highgate cemetery.[9] In 1956 the Communist Party of Great Britain (CPGB) paid for the present grand tombstone, under which his remains were reinterred, to make a shrine to which a dwindling throng of left-wing tourists flocks every year. The only happy note on which to end, is that Friedrich Engels on his death in 1895 provided reasonably generously for Marx's two surviving daughters out of his estate, worth roughly in the region of £120 million in today's values.[10]

2

WHO WAS LENIN?

The city of Simbirsk was founded on the western bank of the mighty Volga river in 1648 some 555 miles south-east of Moscow at what was then the fringe of Russian territory. Its function was to implant several thousand settlers and to serve as a military base for troops to keep at bay the nomadic tribes living across the Volga and to the east. Looking for it on a modern map is fruitless because it was renamed Ulyanovsk in honour of its most famous son after his death in 1924. He was born to Ilya Nikolayevich Ulyanov – a respectable teacher and school inspector – and his wife Maria Alexandrovna Ulyanova, who ranked as minor nobility in the strictly hierarchical tsarist society due to Ilya's position in the administration. The Ulyanov family's impeccable record was irretrievably blotted just a year after his death when his eldest son Alexander was arrested in March 1887 for plotting with other members of the Narodnaya Volya, or People's Will, terrorist group at St Petersburg University to assassinate Tsar Alexander III on the capital's famous Nevsky Prospect. Ten of the conspirators were saved from the gallows by the Tsar's clemency, but 21-year-old Alexander Ilyich had not only used his knowledge of chemistry to make the 'infernal machine' or bomb they were intending to use, but was also arrogant enough to make a defiant political rant in court instead of pleading for his life. He and four of the other students were hanged in the grim fortress-prison of Shlisselburg on an island in Lake Ladoga – the Alcatraz of St Petersburg.

Alexander Ulyanov's 17-year-old brother Vladimir had hero-worshipped him, but returned to his studies and graduated one month later as the Simbirsk *Gymnasium's* best pupil. Further education should have been barred to him as the brother of an executed terrorist, but his school's director had been named guardian of the family in Ilya's will. He vouched for Vladimir's good behaviour so that he could commence studies at Kazan University in the autumn of 1887. Once there, the formerly 'best pupil' gravitated to the company of extremist students, a group of whom protested in December at the expulsion of some professors who expressed liberal political views and demanded a new and more relaxed regime. At the confrontation between the student activists and the dean, Vladimir Ilyich and forty others were briefly arrested and then expelled.

Internal unrest had seen the tsarist secret police reorganised in 1881 – the year Alexander II was assassinated – as *Otdeleniye po Okhraneniyu Obshchestvennoi Bezopasnosti i Poryadki*, or the Department for Defence of Public Security and Order. Under the acronym of Okhranka or Okhrana, this forerunner of the KGB was tasked with infiltrating and subverting trade unions, political parties and discussion groups – and generally spying on the whole population, for the last generations of Romanovs were fatally intent on maintaining the quasi-feudal old order. Schools and universities excluded the lower classes and the judiciary was brought back under central control; Russian was imposed as the sole official language throughout the Empire; and other branches of Christianity were disadvantaged vis-à-vis the Orthodox Church. Under the 'Temporary Laws', Jews were more strictly confined to the Pale of Settlement.

Thanks to his mother's persistence in lobbying for her problem son, although banned from Kazan University Vladimir Ulyanov was permitted to complete his law studies at St Petersburg University, where he graduated with honours. Going through the motions of starting a law practice in the city of Samara, where Maria Alexandrovna and her younger children were then living, he actually devoted more energy to reading the writings of Karl Marx and disseminating them clandestinely. This was tolerated initially because the Okhrana considered the Marxists likely to draw support away from Narodnaya Volya, already responsible for many assassinations, and judged their publications too boringly abstruse to influence many people anyway. 'Nothing will come of them for at least fifty years,' remarked the Samara chief of police in 1894.[11]

At 24, Vladimir I. Ulyanov was already called 'the old man'. With his bald head and slit eyes that rarely gave away what he was thinking, that was understandable. All work and no play made this Jack an ill boy. After nearly dying of pneumonia early in 1895, he did what middle-class Russians did to recover their health, going abroad for a European tour – in his case to meet influential extreme socialists living in exile, including the so-called fathers of Russian Marxism, Georgi Plekhanov and Pinchas Borutch, who had taken the Russian name Pavel Axelrod. Both were impressed by a week of debate with Ulyanov, which demonstrated his unshakeable belief in the need for revolution.

Returning to St Petersburg in September 1895 Ulyanov joined Julius Tsederbaum, who used the Russian name Jules Martov, and other revolutionary socialists in *Soyuz Borby za Osvobozhdenie Rabochevo Klassa* – literally, the Union for the Struggle for the Liberation of the Working Class. Tracked by Okhrana agents and informers, they were arrested on 20 December. Conditions in the prison were far from the repressive regime that Lenin would impose after the revolution: young Ulyanov was allowed visits twice weekly, when relatives might bring in books and other publications. When leaving, they were not checked for outgoing messages, so that Ulyanov's mother and sister Maria Ulanova acted as postmen for his intensive correspondence with comrades outside. During his fourteen months' incarceration, Ulyanov managed to organise from his cell at least one major strike involving 35,000 workers.

The sting in the tail of his sentence was a three-year exile to Shushenskoye, a village on the mighty Yenisei river in the Siberian province of Krasnoyarsk, more than 2,000 miles east of Moscow. With a weekly allowance[12] that was adequate for his needs, he used the time and lack of civilised distractions for studying, thinking and writing. Although this may be partly Soviet propaganda, the record is that the local people respected and liked him after he gave free legal advice based on his law studies and even the gendarmes charged with watching the exiles came to treat him with respect. Love – at least in one direction – entered his life when a female comrade from St Petersburg arrived in Shushenskoye. Nadezhda Konstantinovna Krupskaya had been exiled to Ufa. Although also in Siberia, it was still 1,500 miles away, but the tolerant tsarist authorities accepted her story that she was Ulyanov's fiancée and allowed her to join him in May 1898. Married in a local church, Krupskaya, as she was generally known, settled down to married life as Ulyanov's tireless confidante and secretary for his extensive correspondence with other extreme socialists both at liberty in Russia, in internal exile all over Siberia and abroad. It was a busy life. During this period, the manuscript of one political text by Ulyanov was smuggled back to St Petersburg for publication there under a pseudonym and another – *The Aims of Russian Socialism* – was published in Switzerland under the name of Lenin, a name he took from the Siberian river Lena, and under which he would achieve worldwide fame.

The period was also crucial as it marked his absolute rejection of revisionist Marxist factions and the beginning of a war of words with them first evidenced in a periodical titled *Iskra* – meaning the 'spark' that Lenin intended to ignite worldwide revolution. The first edition, printed in Leipzig on thin onionskin paper in December 1900, was stored in Berlin by the German Social Democratic Party and inserted into small parcels sent to addressees near to the Russian frontier, then passed on to professional smugglers for onward transmission into the Russian Empire. Krupskaya, having been left behind in Ufa to complete her exile, and released at its end, did not find it easy to track down her absent husband, who used many aliases, changed his address frequently and did nothing to help her. Eventually catching up with him in Munich, she became again his maid-of-all-work, writing to his mother in August 1901:

> Volodya [affectionate diminutive of Vladimir] is working diligently. I am very pleased with him. When completely engrossed in a certain work, he is in excellent spirits. His health is very good, no trace of his cold remains, nor does he suffer from insomnia. He invigorates himself every day with a cold water rub-down. In addition we go bathing almost every day.[13]

It reads like a message from the overprotective mother of a fragile child. By the following spring, the political risks of publishing *Iskra* had frightened off two printers. Among the expat revolutionaries, Plekhanov and Axelrod chose to move to Switzerland, while Lenin and Krupskaya opted for London, where he used the Reading Room of the British Museum as his office, as Marx had done, to produce another book titled *Chto dyelat'?* – *Nabolevshie voprosy nashevo Dvizheniya*, in English *What is to be done? Urgent problems of our movement.*

The revolution, as Lenin emphasised in the book, would have to be led by a single omnipotent leader, i.e. himself, controlling a rigid party structure. Also rejecting Marx's philosophy of a classless society, Lenin was already more like Orwell's Napoleon in *Animal Farm*, believing that the most important people in post-revolutionary society should be better treated than the mass. Equally intransigent on land ownership, although some colleagues considered that agriculture should be left to the peasants doing what they did best – growing food and raising beasts – Lenin insisted that all land be nationalised and collectivised, which was to prove a disastrous policy when put into force, condemning millions to death by starvation, since the political commissars who made all the decisions had no idea what they were doing.

Although *Iskra* and *What is to be done?* had focussed the attention of many revolutionary socialists inside Russia on what Lenin considered the right way to apply Marxism to existing social problems, his elders like Plekhanov and Axelrod were still stuck in the nineteenth-century intellectual style of writing and thinking – unlike Lenin whose style was that of the demagogue, hammering away at a few simple slogans, as he would later do to win over live audiences. A split in the editorial board between Lenin in London and the others in Geneva led Lenin to move there in April 1903, swiftly alienating even the comrades who admired his thinking and wished to work with him, but could not accept his demand for total, unquestioning obedience. One of them named Alexander Potresov summed up the problem, as did many others, by saying, 'It is impossible to work with him.'[14] But Lenin refused to deviate from his blueprint: a corps of lieutenants controlled with military discipline by their unquestioned leader, i.e. himself.

On 30 July 1903 an *Iskra*-organised conference of Russian and expat revolutionary socialists began in Geneva, but so heated were the debates that the Swiss police ordered the expulsion of four delegates, after which the venue was moved to London. Of the forty-three participants, only three or four were workers; all the others were what the police of the time termed 'professional revolutionists', whose socialist philosophies differed widely. Since they refused entirely to bow down to Lenin and the *Iskra* group, the Jewish Socialist Bund members and the Economists all walked out when Plekhanov demanded a coherent party structure. A new word for the world's political vocabulary was coined after Lenin's *Iskra* group won the debate of a slight majority of the motions tabled at the conference and grabbed the name *Bolsheviki* from the Russian *bolshinstvo*, meaning majority. By implication, their opponents were labelled

Menshiviki – the minority. From then on, these two labels divided the movement. Essentially, the Bolsheviks were prepared to destroy every vestige of social infrastructure in Russia to achieve their ends, while the Mensheviks considered that socialism could be implemented by building on, and modifying, the framework of bourgeois society. Before long, the mere label Menshevik was enough to see thousands of sincere socialists executed for the crime of failing to agree with Lenin.

One of Lenin's most enthusiastic supporters, a Belorussian doctor and political theorist named Alexander Alexandrovich Bogdanov, visited Finland in 1906 to meet Lenin, who already had a cast-iron vision of what a revolutionary socialist party should be: the ordinary members should pay dues, which would support himself and a few other important full-time activists. He had, in fact, a cast-iron opinion about everything, refusing to accept anyone else's ideas, which made it very difficult for Bogdanov or anyone else to work with him for long. Initially regarded by Lenin as his political 'favourite son', well versed in the history of revolution, Trotsky later agreed with Plekhanov that: '[Lenin is] a despot and terrorist who sought to turn the Central Committee of the party into a Committee of Public Safety in order to be able to play the role of Robespierre.'[15] *Le comité du salut public* was Robespierre's tool for dictatorship during the bloody months of the Terror 1793–94. It was a pertinent comparison that caused Lenin, in a fit of pique, to resign all his offices and sever all connection with party colleagues, isolating himself totally. Instead of bringing the others to their senses, as he had hoped, he found himself without supporters, comrades or even friends except the ever-loyal Krupskaya. A man who sees himself obsessively as a leader is no good to himself, or anyone else, when he has driven away all his followers. The result was a disabling neurasthenia, as a severe mental breakdown was then called. His therapist was, as so often, the adoring and ever-faithful Krupskaya, who took him away for a month-long walking holiday across Switzerland staying in small, cheap country inns with nothing but rucksacks, in which to carry the barest necessities. The remote Swiss valleys were a wonderful sanatorium and health spa where he could forget the ungrateful world. Krupskaya wrote to Lenin's mother on 2 July 1904:

> Volodya and I have made a pact not to discuss [political] affairs. We sleep ten hours a day, swim and walk. Volodya doesn't even read the papers properly.[16]

3

WHO WAS TROTSKY?

Leiba Davidovich Bronstein[17] was the fifth of eight children born to a family of prosperous Jewish farmers near the city of Kherson in the Pale of Settlement. His parents were discreet about their non-observance of religious ritual, not wishing to alienate their Sabbath- and diet-observant neighbours, whose Yiddish they understood, although themselves preferring to speak the local dialect, which was a mixture of Ukrainian and Russian, and in which they could also converse with their non-Jewish labourers on the farm. The Pale – a vast area that stretched from the shores of the Baltic all the way south to the Black Sea across stretches of modern Latvia, Lithuania, Poland, Belarus, Ukraine and Moldova – was Catherine the Great's solution for keeping the Jews of her empire out of Russia proper, and most certainly out of the cities, where only a few very rich or socially useful Jews were tolerated, and the only single Jewish women allowed were registered prostitutes or schoolteachers.

An academically bright child, at the age of 9 Leiba was sent 200 miles away to be schooled at a German *Gymnasium*, or grammar school, in Odessa, where he lodged with a family of older cousins as a paying guest. The town-dwelling cousins taught the farm boy about personal hygiene and careful dressing, to the point that he became rather a dandy, liking to be neatly dressed and keep his fingernails trimmed. In childhood, and sometimes in later life, he suffered from fainting fits, which he seems to have inherited from his mother. To complete his schooling, he was sent to the riverine port city of Nikolaev,[18] constructed on a peninsula in a bend of the mighty Southern Bug river, 50 miles from the Black Sea. This was already an important shipbuilding centre and had been the homeport of the Russian Black Sea fleet when the sea was demilitarised after the Crimean War.

Leiba abandoned the study of mathematics after becoming embroiled with a group of radical socialist students at the Nikolaev *Realschule*. At first using the *nom de guerre* Lyov, he moved out of the comfortable lodgings for which his father was paying in order to live in a student commune, where he participated in the production of revolutionary publications. None of the students seem to have realised that they were being watched by the Okhrana. Getting himself arrested at the age of 18 in 1897, Leiba was locked up with the others in Nikolaev prison before being transferred to prison in Odessa, where they languished for a year until transported to Moscow Transit Prison. There, he married a fellow student political detainee named Aleksandra Lvovna Sokolovskaya, so that they would not be separated when exiled to Siberia under the reasonably humane tsarist prison regime of internal exile for political prisoners.

In the summer of 1900 they were transported by rail some 3,000 miles eastwards to Irkutsk in distant Siberia, where the temperature then touching 40°C gave no idea what life would be like when it would plunge to −50°C in winter. Aleksandra, already pregnant, then had to endure a slow voyage of 400 miles northward along the mighty Lena river. Lodging in a remote village in the house of a Polish cobbler and later allowed to move to another town, where they had exiled friends, the young couple had an intermittent income from Leiba's articles and book reviews written for the Irkutsk magazine *Vostochnoe Obozrenie (Eastern Review)*. In 1902 Alexandra gave birth to their second daughter. There is no evidence of the father's profound dissatisfaction with life until in 1902 when he started receiving, hidden in the binding of some books, copies of Marxist publications printed on thin paper abroad, as well as a copy of Lenin's recently published book *What is to be done?*.[19]

He already knew that he had a talent for writing and always wanted the largest possible stage on which to perform. Reading Lenin's book gave him the idea of escaping from Siberia to join its author in attacking 'revisionists' of Marx's doctrine in front of an international audience. On 21 August 1902, having bought a passport in the name of Lev Trotsky from a free local resident, he abandoned his birth identity, his wife and their daughters in Verkholensk, travelling with a female fellow-Marxist on the first of many clandestine stages of the journey back to Irkutsk, where political sympathisers equipped him with clothes and money for the long journey back to European Russia. From there, the fake Mr Trotsky travelled via Vienna and Geneva to London, where Lenin co-opted him onto the editorial board of the revolutionary newspaper *Iskra* – the Spark – which was also the name of Lenin's group of young Marxists. By March 1903 Trotsky had become the 'favourite son' of Lenin, in the face of the hostility of mistrustful older expat socialists like Plekhanov.

Revolutionaries are essentially dissidents: the characteristics that impel them to fight established authority, by illicit or illegal means, also cause them to disagree with each other. Although the revolutionary socialists and the anarchists in the émigré Russian population all shared the Marxists' interest in getting rid of the tsarist regime, they also spent much energy in demolishing each other. While in London, Trotsky outmatched two important anarchist speakers in a debate and then travelled to Paris to attack the revolutionary socialists there with similar success, in spite of the fact that some veteran Marxists thought his grasp of political essentials was sketchy – to put it mildly. From the City of Light, he wrote to Alexandra, telling her what a success he had been in the West, omitting to inform her that he had also found a younger woman named Natalya Ivanovna Sedova to share his bed. Aleksandra ended her life in a Soviet labour camp in the far north of Siberia in 1938.

The next stop on Trotsky's travels was Brussels for the Second Party Congress of the Social Democratic Workers' Party in July 1903. Founded in 1898, the party was already split into two main factions: Lenin's Bolsheviks and the Mensheviks. Despite the implication of the labels – which referred only to the motions carried at the congress – their numbers were equal, not exceeding a *total* membership of approximately 8,400 people in each faction. Three-quarters of the active members were under 30 years old and Lenin himself was only 35. Some of those attending the Second Party Congress changed sides during the meeting. These included Georgi Plekhanov, who distanced himself from Lenin's hardliners, as did Trotsky, in a split from his formerly admired mentor that was to last for fifteen years.[20]

In 1903 Trotsky married Natalya Ivanovna Sedova bigamously and formed a close political partnership with Israel Lazarevich Gelfand[22] in Munich. Although born of Jewish parents in Russia, Gelfand had joined the German Social Democrats and wrote articles in the Left press under the pseudonym Alexander Parvus – *parvus* being the Latin for 'poor man'. Belying the nom de plume, he was to make a considerable fortune dealing in armaments during the Balkan wars of 1912–13. Siding with the Mensheviks, in 1904 Trotsky turned on Lenin personally, accusing him of clinging to an outdated political philosophy and failing to realise that the essential dynamic element of militant Marxism was the mass of workers, not the few educated theoreticians. His own writing did not bring in enough to support himself and Natalya, so from time to time he accepted money from his father, whose way of life he despised. Some people close to him at that time had reason to believe that undercover Okhrana agents helped out with anonymous contributions, to fuel the dissension between him and Lenin.

Although it was not obvious then, Lenin and Trotsky were to be the two key players in the 1917 revolution. One man who knew them both was Robert Bruce Lockhart, then the British Consul in Moscow. He summed up Lenin thus:

There was nothing in his personal appearance to suggest the super-man. Short of stature, rather plump, with short thick neck, broad shoulders, round red face, high intellectual forehead, nose slightly turned up, brownish moustache and short stubbly beard, he looked at the first glance more like a provincial grocer than a leader of men. Yet in those steely eyes there was something that arrested my attention, something in that quizzing, half-contemptuous, half-smiling look which spoke of boundless self-confidence and conscious superiority. Later I was to acquire a considerable respect for his intellectual capacity, but at that [first] meeting I was more impressed by his tremendous will-power, his relentless determination and his lack of emotion.[22]

Of Trotsky, Bruce Lockhart wrote:

[He has] a wonderfully quick mind and a rich, deep voice. With his broad chest, his huge forehead, surmounted by great masses of black waving hair, his strong, fierce [blue] eyes and his heavy protruding lips, he is the very incarnation of the revolutionary. He strikes me as a man who would willingly die fighting for Russia, provided there was a big enough audience to see him do it. He is neat about his dress. He [wears] a clean soft collar and his nails [are] carefully manicured.[23]

A St Petersburg politician named Roman Gul compared the public speaking techniques of Lenin and Trotsky, considering Trotsky the master:[24]

> In his manner of speaking Trotsky was the polar opposite of Lenin. Lenin moved around the platform. Trotsky stood still. Lenin offered none of the flowers of eloquence. Trotsky showered the public with them. Lenin did not listen to himself. Trotsky not only listened to himself but also surely admired himself.[25]

Like Bruce Lockhart, Gul also commented on Trotsky's sartorial vanity: a revolutionary who dressed like a bourgeois professional and who would, after the revolution adopt a military cap and greatcoat for his role as creator and commanding general of the Red Army. Another Marxist militant named Lunacharsky wrote: 'Trotsky had practically no wholehearted supporters at all; if he succeeded in imposing himself on the party, it was entirely though his personality.'[26]

In short, Lenin was a cold, disciplined theorist, Trotsky a flamboyant performer. Meeting both men together after the revolution, Bruce Lockhart wrote:

> [Lenin] furnished a complete antithesis to Trotsky, who was all temperament – an individualist and an artist, on whose vanity even I could play with some success. Lenin was impersonal and almost inhuman. His vanity was proof against all flattery. The only appeal that one could make to him was to his sense of humour, which, if sardonic, was highly developed. During the next few months I was to be pestered with various requests from [the government in] London to verify rumours of serious dissensions between Lenin and Trotsky. I could have given the answer after that first meeting. Trotsky was a man of immense physical courage. But morally, he was as incapable of standing against Lenin as a flea would be against an elephant. In the Council of Commissars [after the Revolution], there was not a man who did not consider himself the equal of Trotsky, yet regarded Lenin as a demi-god, whose decisions were to be accepted without question.

I remember [Georgi] Chicherin[27] giving me an account of a Soviet Cabinet meeting [sic]. Trotsky would bring forward a proposal. It would be violently opposed by another commissar. Endless discussion would follow, and all the time Lenin would be writing notes on his knee, his attention concentrated on some work of his own. At last, someone would say, 'Let Vladimir Ilich [Lenin's first name and patronymic] decide.' Lenin would look up from his work, give his decision in one sentence, and all would be peace.[28]

4

WHO WAS STALIN?

Few people alive today can recall Trotsky, fewer still Lenin, but millions have personal and very painful reasons to remember Stalin, the third man of the triumvir who used the October Revolution to impose a vice-like grip of terror on the inhabitants of the vast Union of Soviet Socialist Republics (USSR) that lasted through three decades until his death in 1953.[29] Indeed, so deeply imprinted was Stalin in the minds of the 241 million Soviet citizens, the leaders of the Communist Party of the Soviet Union (CPSU) and the hundreds of thousands of foreign Communist Party members that his successors for the three decades after his death failed to dismantle the paranoid internal repression and external hostility to the West that were his legacy. Like everything else in the Soviet Union, his death was a state secret until all the ramifications had been discussed in a closed session with the survivors of the Politburo. One of the first confirmations of his death to arrive in the West was the SIGINT interception during the Korean war of a clipped VHF transmission from a Soviet Mig-15, whose pilot muttered to his wing man when he thought they were out of range of their ground station, *'Stalin umer!'* – Stalin is dead. But it was a case of 'Stalin is dead. Long live Stalinism!' Apart from possibly Adolf Hitler, no other single person caused so much misery and so many deaths during the twentieth century. On occasion, Stalin personally signed hundreds of death warrants in a single day.

Stalin was born on 18 December 1878 to Mingrelian-speaking parents Ketevan Geladze and her drunken husband Besarion Dzhugashvili in the town of Gori, some 50 miles to the north-west of Tiflis, the capital of the state of Georgia that is now called Tbilisi. His mother, Ketevan, was a cleaning woman; Besarion a cobbler. Although born Ioseb Besarionis dze Jughashvili, as Georgia had just been annexed into the Russian Empire by force of arms, their son was christened in the Russian fashion Josef Vissarionovich Dzhugashvili. The boy's early home life was complicated by his father sliding deeper and deeper into alcoholism and eventually being told to get out of town after one violent episode involving damage to property and injury to the police chief, by which time his successive business failures and inability to pay rent had caused the family to move home several times before the boy was ten. Josef was a sickly child. Among other childhood ailments, he caught smallpox at the age of seven and was left with a pockmarked face for life, necessitating airbrushing of all his official portraits. A minor physical anomaly was two webbed toes on the left foot.

Growing up in a slum area with little police presence and spending much time in the street while his mother was working, Josef became a *kinto* or street urchin, brawling with other neighbourhood kids and witnessing adult gangs settling accounts more bloodily from time to time, the lawlessness of poverty being exacerbated by the Georgian tradition of blood feuds. In fact, Gori was nearer both in spirit and geography to Teheran and Baghdad than to Moscow or St Petersburg. Able to hold his own in the street, Josef was also precociously intelligent. At the age of 6, he started attending a church school run by the local priest Father Charkviani – who, some neighbours suspected, was the boy's true father. There Josef's intelligence enabled him rapidly to teach himself to read the ancient Georgian script and even help the priest's 13-year-old daughter with her learning problems. He did not begin studying Russian until two years later, and never lost his thick Georgian accent.

Just as today many children are injured by motor vehicles, then large animals – particularly horses – and wagons injured many victims in country and town alike. One such victim was young Josef, whose left arm was broken and never mended properly. A second street accident at the age of 12, when one of his legs was run over by a steel-rimmed wagon wheel, gave him a lifelong limp.

Aged 16, this prize pupil was awarded a scholarship to Tiflis Theological Seminary, where postulants for the Orthodox priesthood were prepared, exclusively in Russian. He was at first an exemplary student, attending services and singing enthusiastically in the choir. The Georgian and Mingrelian languages being forbidden in the seminary, he showed hidden rebelliousness by writing poetry in Mingrelian and was guilty of many other disciplinary offences, and was eventually expelled in 1899 for refusing to sit the final examinations, which he despised. His first professional job was as a low-grade meteorologist but most of his mental energy went into organising strikes and demonstrations as a member of the Marxist-orientated Social Democratic Labour Party. Discovering the writings of Karl Marx, Josef took to the clandestine world of terrorists and revolutionaries of all political hues like a fish to water. Narrowly avoiding arrest by the Okhrana in April 1901, he borrowed the name of the hero in a popular Georgian novel of the time and went underground using the name Koba and a succession of other false identities. By 1900 the former *kinto* from Gori was fomenting industrial unrest all over the Caucasus with such callous disregard for the workers in the front line who were the targets of police bullets and the sabre slashes of mounted Cossacks that even his fellow conspirators were sometimes appalled.

Six months later he was employed in a Rothschild-owned oil refinery in Batumi, Georgia's second city and largest port, where he was suspected of sabotage when a fire broke out. Organising an armed attempt to rescue some comrades from prison, Josef caused the death of thirteen of the would-be rescuers and the injury of others, while he stayed in the background as would become his method throughout his clandestine years. However, the Okhrana infiltrated virtually all the dissident movements and, thanks to an informer, Josef was arrested in April 1902. Lack of proof that he was the instigator of the attempted jailbreak saw him merely sentenced to exile in Novaya Uda, a Siberian village 180 miles north of Irkutsk. So many revolutionary socialists were exiled in the region that the split between Lenin's hard-line Bolsheviks and the more moderate Mensheviks under Jules Martov was well known. Having decided to join the Bolsheviks – at least superficially – Josef bought a new identity and was back in Tiflis by the end of January 1904. He had no money, or means of earning any – not that he ever showed much interest in working for a living. He lived on the generosity of his Marxist friends, with some of whom he fell out over his idea of a Georgian Social Democratic Party that conflicted with their internationalism. One who managed to stay on good terms was Lev Rosenfeld, later to Russify his surname to Kamenev.

On 8 February the Japanese sneak attack on the harbour of Port Arthur opened a fourteen-month war, which Russia lost. Georgia and other non-Russian provinces took advantage of the war to weaken the bonds that tied them to St Petersburg while the Russian armies were engaged elsewhere. When tsarist provincial governors ordered mounted Cossacks to attack the separatist demonstrators and strikers, as many as 200 unarmed men were hacked to death with sabres in the streets during one riot. As ever, Josef did not lose sight of the long-term objective. Although raising funds by protection rackets using a small gang of enforcers and robbing banks too during this period, he was also publishing lies and intrigue to undermine the Mensheviks, who at that time were the leading revolutionary socialists in Georgia. It was his ruthlessness that commended him to Lenin. At the same time, Josef was not above collaborating with Menshevik terrorists in assassinating a police official. It was about this time that the protection mobster and political activist began a liaison with a fellow tenant, in a house where he was staying, named Ekaterina Svanidze – known to her friends as Kato.

A fateful meeting took place in Tampere, Finland, on 7 January 1906 when the Caucasian bandit Dzhugashvili met the cold intellectual Tatar Ulyanov, each warily working out how he might use the other. This was followed by their presence at the fourth congress of the SDLP with Kliment Voroshilov, Grigori Zinoviev and the sociopathic minor Polish nobleman Feliks Dzerzhinsky,[30] later head of the Cheka, which replaced the tsarist Okhrana as the organ of state terror after the revolution. Despite the presence of these powerful hardliners and their leader, Lenin, the congress expressed its disapproval of criminal acts like bank robberies – a setback for both Lenin, who needed the cash, and the Georgian, whose image of himself as a man of action would have suffered. The other way of proving his manhood was by getting Kato pregnant immediately after their wedding in July. Nine months later, on 31 March 1907, she gave birth to a son, christened Yakov. The presumably proud father did not hang around to change the nappies, but departed to the fifth congress of the SDLP, held in the safety of London, at which Lenin managed to garner the majority of votes. While there, Dzhugashvili came face to face for the first time with Trotsky, whose dapper appearance and silver tongue did not impress him. To differentiate their concepts of revolutionary socialism, on return to Georgia Dzhugashvili pulled off his biggest bank raid yet.

Mid–morning on 26 June a stagecoach carrying nearly 350,000 roubles,[31] followed by another coach full of armed soldiers and surrounded by mounted Cossacks, halted at the Imperial Bank in Tiflis. A bomb thrown from a rooftop killed forty of these men and shattered windows for up to a mile away. Emerging from hiding, Dzhugashvili's gang shot survivors and made off with the loot.[32]

There was a price to pay. Fleeing the Georgian capital, he took his wife and infant son to Baku, where she contracted typhus, which was rampant in the Caucasus and even in Moscow, and died. Abandoning his son for her family to raise, Dzhugashvili went on a tour of industrial agitation mixed with robbery and extortion, which led to his arrest in April 1908. As before and after, the Okhrana's prisoner had concealed his master role in the list of crimes and was merely exiled to Solvychegodsk, 800 miles north of Moscow in the Archangel province. Like so many other internally exiled politicals, he purchased a free local citizen's passport and escaped, dressed as a woman, seven months later. It was during this period, perpetually on the run from the Okhrana in and around Baku, that he abandoned his true identity for good and was known to revolutionary comrades from then on as Stalin – from the word *stal* meaning steel. Trapped once again by an informer, in early April Comrade Stalin was arrested and sentenced to complete his exile in the Far North, leaving behind a second son by his landlady in Solvychegordsk.

Judging that too many Bolsheviks were followers of the Belorussian doctor and political theorist Alexander Bogdanov, in 1908 Lenin published a book titled *Materialism and Empirio-criticism*, in which the double-talk disguised the fact that this was intended as a verbal assassination of Bogdanov. When it failed, Lenin unsuccessfully tried to have him expelled from the Bolshevik movement and set up the first publication, in Vienna, of what would be the most famous Communist periodical of all. Since *Izvestiya* already existed, the title of the new paper *Pravda*,[33] meaning 'the truth', allowed uncommitted Russians to pun, '*Nyet pravdy v Isvestiye, nyet isvestiyi v Pravde*' – 'there's no information in *Pravda* and no truth in *Isvestiya*'.

The internecine squabbling of the expat revolutionaries continued, stirred by undercover agents of the Okhrana in both Bolshevik and Menshevik groups, until Lenin found himself unable to control the Bolshevik leadership. In January 1912 the Bolsheviks organised an exclusive assembly in Prague, declaring themselves a separate party called the Russian Social Democratic Labour Party (RSDLP). The idea was not greeted with much enthusiasm inside Russia, although in the Fourth Duma, or national parliament, of 1912, there were six Bolshevik deputies, who kept their political distance from the Menshevik members. The RSDLP's perpetual problem was finance, partly due to Lenin's frequent travelling and his insistence on salaries for himself and a few close supporters. A theme constantly hammered out was that socialists of all hues should refuse en masse to answer summons for conscription in any international war and instead take up arms against their own national governments.

In January 1912 Lenin finally separated the Bolshevik faction from the parent body of the RSDLP at a party conference in Prague, but several of its leaders were arrested after returning to Russia. This created an opening for Stalin on the Central Committee and as editor of the new party's weekly *Zvyozda*, meaning 'star', which he used the party's secret funds to convert into a new-look *Pravda*. Heady with his new position, in a feat of political arm-wrestling, he rejected article after article submitted by Lenin, who was then living in Kraków, Poland. Summoned there to account for himself, Stalin talked his way out but was less successful in avoiding yet another trap set by the Okhrana on his return to Russia. Exiled this time to Narym, an unpleasant small town in Siberia surrounded by mosquito-ridden swamps in summer and very cold in winter, he escaped again, to be re-arrested on 8 March 1913, when he was sentenced to four years' exile in Turukhansk, an absolute nowheresville 1,000 miles north of Irkutsk, from where escape would have been more difficult. His isolation here was made more bearable by the body warmth of a neighbour's 13-year-old daughter, who bore him two children. Whilst in Turukhansk a childhood accident, when his left arm was broken, saved him from conscription for the army in the First World War, as it had during the Russo-Japanese war.

Exiled to Siberia seven times, Stalin escaped so easily each time that many Old Bolsheviks suspected he was an undercover agent for the Okhrana. Intelligence officers, and especially those who defect, are all habitual liars, which makes their memoirs suspect. With that caveat, an odd light was thrown by NKVD defector Alexander Orlov on this lingering suspicion among Stalin's original comrades whom he had executed on trumped-up charges after seizing total power for himself. Orlov told the FBI in his debriefing that an NKVD researcher had found an Okhrana file dating from before the revolution, in which were numerous denunciations of fellow Bolsheviks, written in Stalin's very distinctive handwriting. Of a small circle of trusted friends who saw this, only Orlov was still alive two years later – and that was because he was safely in the West. Among the others, Marshal Tukhachevsky was one of the first executed in Stalin's otherwise unexplained purge of the Red Army in June 1937. He was shot within twenty-four hours of being sentenced, in defiance of the Soviet law requiring a delay of seventy-two hours to permit an appeal.

Orlov made this public in an article for an April 1956 edition of *Life* magazine. In the same issue Russian-born journalist Isaac Don Levine wrote about a letter dated 12 July 1913 from Okhrana headquarters in Moscow to its Yeniseisk station that had allegedly been brought secretly to the US by a Russian émigré. The letter outlined Stalin's role as an informer beginning after his arrest in Tiflis in 1906, continuing through 1908 with his reports to the Okhrana in Baku and later in St Petersburg. Tests of the paper and the typewriter that had been used confirmed the authenticity of the letter. Under his revolutionary name of Stalin, Dzhugashvili directed for three and a half decades a regime of state terror that held in thrall a population of 250-plus millions – a third of whom were not ethnic Russians – by ruthlessly eliminating any rival, killing millions of his innocent subjects and exiling many other millions to forced labour in inhuman conditions for no crime at all. Yet, because he was elevated by the professedly atheistic Communist Party to the status of living god, it used to be said by his long-suffering subjects that all the crimes committed against them were the work of his minions, acting without the personal knowledge of the man they called 'the little father of his people' or simply '*vozhd*', meaning exactly the same as *der Führer*.

US diplomat George Kennan, whose US Foreign Service years included periods in Moscow both before and after the revolution, and who knew Stalin personally, wrote:

Stalin's youth is shrouded in the mists of underworld revolutionary activity – largely in his native Caucasus. From that he graduated into the Dostoievskian atmosphere of revolutionary conspiracy in European Russia. His life has known only what Lenin called 'the incredibly swift transition from wild violence to the most delicate deceit'. The placid give and take of Anglo-Saxon life, in particular the tempering of all enmity and all intimacy,

the balancing of personal self-respect, the free play of opposing interests –
these things [are] incomprehensible, implausible to him.[34]

Later, when the Second World War was nearing its end in autumn 1944,
Kennan described Stalin for Washington's guidance as:

courageous but wary; quick to anger and suspicion but patient in the
execution of his purposes; capable of acting with great decision or waiting and dissembling as circumstances may require; outwardly modest and
simple, but jealous of the prestige and dignity of the state he heads; not
learned, but shrewd and pitilessly realistic; exacting in his demands for
loyalty, respect and obedience.[35]

Reading between the lines of Kennan's tempered diplomatic language,
he could have been describing such despots as Ivan the Terrible or Peter
the Great. Yet, Kennan was far from being hostile to the Russian people.
An astute observer of them and their leaders, he was later to make himself
unpopular with his masters in Washington at the height of the Cold War
by arguing that the tendency of Western political leaders and especially
the Western military to demonise the whole Communist bloc was dangerous because it failed to take into account that decisions and actions
taken in London, Paris, Bonn or Washington affected the other side's
moves in the great confrontation of the twentieth century that threatened
to exterminate all human life.

5

REHEARSAL FOR A REVOLUTION

In the early years of the twentieth century most people inside Russia were unaware of the expatriate revolutionaries' internecine manoeuvrings because their lives had more pressing concerns, including the war with Japan. Ever since 1860, when Tsar Alexander II founded a military/administrative base on the Pacific coast and dubbed it Vladivostok – meaning, Lord of the East – the Japanese government in Tokyo had feared the Russian presence on the Pacific littoral and therefore watched every move in the construction, with foreign finance and foreign technology, of the longest railway line in the world: the *Transsibirskaya magistral* or Trans-Siberian main-line railway.

Count Sergei Yulevich Witte was appointed Minister of Finance in August 1892 by Tsar Alexander III. Introducing many Western financial systems to give a new dynamic to industry in Russia, he launched a programme of modernisation that included a state bank to make capital loans to industry, savings banks, joint-stock company law, convertibility of the rouble and promotion of technical education. He also astutely floated huge loans in Western Europe to finance Russian industrialisation and railway construction – of which the most important project was the Trans-Siberian, which, it was hoped, would stimulate the economy of the eastern provinces, make Russia the interface between Europe and the Far East, and unite the otherwise unmanageably vast empire, spread across eleven time zones and covering one-sixth of the planet's landmass.

To connect Russia's former medieval capital Moscow with Vladivostok required nearly 6,000 miles of rails. The difficulties of the terrain – major rivers, high mountain ranges and the vast sprawl across Central Asia of Lake Baikal, the largest freshwater expanse in the world – stretched construction from 1891 to 1916, but the length of the line already constructed in 1904 alarmed Tokyo because it meant that European armies would soon be able to travel across Siberia and arrive on Japan's doorstep by train, fresh and ready for battle, with the advantage of being re-supplied by rail with everything from blankets and bread to big guns and ammunition of all calibres.

In 1895 a war between Japan and China had ended with Japan the clear victor. Under the Treaty of Shimonoseki, China recognised the independence of Korea – coveted by Japan for its mineral resources and for strategic reasons – and ceded Taiwan, the Pescadores Islands and the Liaotung Peninsula in south-eastern Manchuria – a wedge of land jutting out into the Yellow Sea. China also paid a huge indemnity and gave the Japanese certain trading privileges on Chinese territory. Russian fears of this Japanese expansion onto the Asian mainland were supported by France and Germany, who joined forces in what was called 'the triple intervention', which forced Japan to hand back the Liaotung Peninsula in return for an additional indemnity from China. Russia's expansionist imperative[36] now prompted Tsar Nicholas II to conclude treaties with China that included Russian occupation of the Liaotung Peninsula and the right to build a branch line connecting the Trans-Siberian main line with the port of Lushün on its southern tip. This deep-water harbour, ice-free throughout the year, was swiftly converted into the heavily fortified naval base of Port Arthur, and a civilian port was established nearby at Dalian.

All this did not go down well in Tokyo – or in London. With Russian military columns progressively pushing eastwards through Central Asia and tsarist agents inciting unrest among the tribes on the Northwest Frontier as a way of weakening the British Raj in the Indian subcontinent, Queen Victoria's government had no intention of helping the ruler of Russia anywhere – never mind that the *Tsarina*, née Princess Alix of Hesse-Darmstadt – was one of her many granddaughters. In 1902, therefore, Britain signed a treaty with Japan, under which each side agreed to support the other's interests in China and Korea. This was a warning shot against Russian expansionism in the Far East.

At the beginning of 1904 Tokyo decided to launch a pre-emptive attack before the Tsar's Far Eastern forces could swiftly be reinforced

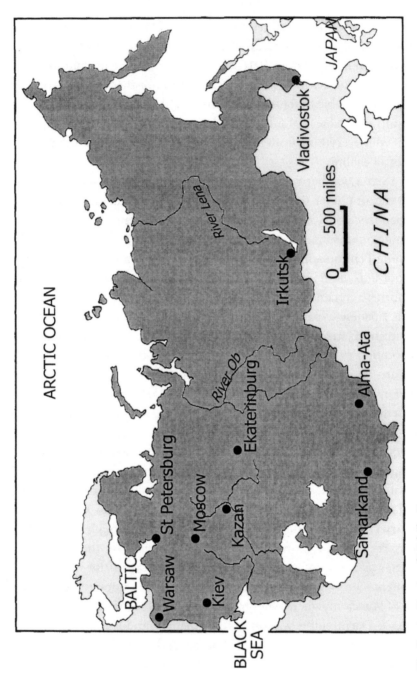

The Russian Empire of Nicholas II.

from European Russia over the new railway, once it was completed. On 8 February a surprise torpedo attack on the Russian naval squadron at Port Arthur was followed up by the sinking of blockships loaded with cement on 27 March to interdict use of the harbour, plus a naval blockade, to prevent supplies or reinforcements being brought in by sea. In the same month, a Japanese army landed in Korea and rapidly occupied that peninsula. In May, a second Japanese army landed on the Liaotung Peninsula, cutting off the Port Arthur garrison from reinforcement by the main body of Russian forces in Manchuria and then pushing northward to win pitched battles at Fu-hsien and Liaoyang before the Russians finally fell back on Mukden (now Shenyang), where they lost another 80,000 men. The torpedo attack on the Russian warships in harbour at Port Arthur before any declaration of war should have been a clear warning to the US Navy thirty-seven years later because, among the junior officers wounded at Tsushima was Ensign Isoroku Takano. Under his adopted name of Yamamoto, he was the US-educated commander-in-chief of the combined Japanese battle fleet and architect of the surprise attack on Pearl Harbour that brought the USA into the Second World War against Germany, Italy and Japan.

In October 1904, strengthened by reinforcements transported most of the way along the new railway, the Russians went over to the offensive. On the other side of the world, Admiral Zinovy Rozhestvensky set out with the Russian Baltic Fleet from the Latvian port of Liepāja to relieve the blockade of Port Arthur. On the way, he nearly provoked war with Great Britain by attacking British trawlers fishing on the Dogger Bank in the North Sea after Russian lookouts mistook the fishing boats for Japanese torpedo boats! Compensation was paid to the families of the trawlermen killed and a memorial to them can still be seen in their homeport of Hull. On the Liaotung Peninsula, the Japanese siege of Port Arthur continued. On 2 January 1905, after the last seaworthy ship in harbour was scuttled, Port Arthur's commander surrendered in an act of gross incompetence or corruption despite having 10,000 combat-worthy men under his command and three months' food and ammunition still in hand.[37]

Fortunately for European historians, official Western observers were present with both belligerents. Major Marcel Cheminon, who spent the whole war as a bilingual French observer with the Russian army, returned to Paris with maps and detailed accounts of all the major battles, bringing with him two beautiful Russian sisters, whom he married one after the other.[38] We also have the observations of the official British mission to the Japanese armies and of General Sir Ian Hamilton, who went out at his own expense and left an interesting 'scrapbook' of his observations during the war. The Western observers on both sides noted that, while both the Japanese and Russian soldiery were largely conscripted peasants, the Japanese, trained by German instructors, were better drilled and more disciplined than their opponents. General Hamilton, for one, was professionally shocked by the Tsar's C-in-C General Alexei Nikolaevich Kuropatkin's profligate waste of his soldiers' lives, and by the way his officers exposed themselves at the front from bravado, thus revealing their men's concealed positions to Japanese artillery observers.

The London *Times* had several correspondents in the theatre, one of whom transmitted radio despatches to his editor in London via a relay station in a British treaty territory on the Chinese mainland. Telegraphed from London to Russia, news of the colossal loss of life caused by the disastrous generalship on the Russian side fuelled protests in St Petersburg, where troops fired on unarmed protestors on 22 January – or 9 January under the Julian calendar – known thereafter as *Krovavoye Voskresenye* or Bloody Sunday, heralding the start of the 1905 Revolution. Exactly why the guards opened fire on the crowd is still disputed, but the day ended with some 200 demonstrators lying dead according to Count Witte and 1,000 killed according to the organisers.

Commenting on the event, British Ambassador Charles Hardinge confirmed that the victims were unarmed peasants and workers, marching to the Winter Palace peacefully to present a petition to the Tsar. Like the ignition along a powder train, demonstrations spread throughout Russia, supported by soldiers who blocked the transportation of reinforcements along the Trans-Siberian main line and also strikes in factories and mines. In Russian-occupied Poland, Finland, the Baltic States and Georgia nationalist independence movements took advantage of the disorder. In retaliation, the fanatically reactionary *chernyye sotni* launched pogroms against socialists, students and Jews. Although usually literally translated as Black Hundreds, these independent groups without overall command waving banners proclaiming '*Pravoslaviye, Samoderzhaviye i Narodnost*' – authodoxy, autocracy and (Russian) nationalism – would better be understood as Black Squadrons. Blessed by the priests, they tortured and slaughtered perceived enemies without fear of retribution.

In the Japanese home islands there was a growing anti-war movement, with the Emperor's Chief of Staff proposing that the conflict, the costs of which had nearly bankrupted Japan, be brought to a speedy end, after which the cabinet debated peace terms while covertly funding the purchase of weapons for the revolutionaries in Russia. The final land battle of the Russo-Japanese War was fought at Mukden at the end of February 1905 between Russian armies totalling 330,000 men and Japanese forces totalling 270,000. The Russians lost 89,000 men against 71,000 Japanese dead, which indicates that the Japanese generals were more careful of human life than their European opposite numbers. Russian care for the wounded not having improved since the Crimean War, tens of thousands of casualties died unnecessarily, the chief medical officer of the Second Russian Army committing suicide in despair. After several days of conflict, Kuropatkin disengaged and withdrew northward in a blinding dust storm, leaving Mukden to the Japanese.

On 14 April Rozhestvensky's Baltic Fleet at last anchored in Vietnam's Cam Ranh Bay to re-group. Four weeks later it belatedly set course for the surviving far eastern Russian naval base at Vladivostok, Port Arthur having already surrendered. Rozhestvensky was apparently unaware that Admiral Tōgō Heihachirō's more modern battle fleet was waiting in ambush at the Tsushima Strait between Japan and Korea. In the long and bloody battle of Tsushima on 27–29 May the Russian fleet lost over 200,000 tons of shipping, against Heihachirō's losses of 300 tons, with 4,830 Russian sailors killed and 6,000 taken prisoner, including the admiral, while Japanese casualties totalled less than 200.

When the news of the debacles at Port Arthur, Mukden and Tsushima reached St Petersburg, there was a public outcry and bitter criticism of the government, followed by numerous mutinies among returning survivors of the Far East campaign. Sailors on a battleship in Odessa harbour refused to report for duty as a protest against their weevil-infested food. A firing squad refused to shoot these mutineers, providing Soviet filmmaker Sergei Eisenstein with the best scene in his 1925 Soviet epic *Bronenosets Potemkin – Battleship Potemkin*.[39]

The Japanese victories brought the Russian government to the peace table in the ignominious position of the first major European power to be vanquished by an Asiatic enemy during the long years of clashes between European imperial armies and the peoples they sought to exploit.[41] At the peace conference held in Portsmouth, New Hampshire, between 9 August and 5 September 1905, US President Theodore Roosevelt acted as mediator. The Treaty of Portsmouth gave Japan everything it wanted: control of the Liaotung Peninsula and Port Arthur, the South Manchurian railroad leading to the port – and also half of Sakhalin Island. Russia agreed to evacuate southern Manchuria, which was to be handed back to China, and Japan's right to occupy Korea was recognised.

Humiliated, the Tsar and his ministers turned their attention to the internal problems that threatened to shake the very structure of Russian society to the core. There were plenty of precedents. Russian history consisted of 1,000 years of expansionism,[40] each invasion of neighbouring territory being accomplished by savage attack and equally savage repression of any resistance. Throughout this time, any internal resistance in the duchy of Moscovy that became the tsarist kingdom and in turn the Russian Empire was punished equally harshly. In 1667, with Tsar Alexis I on the throne, the son of a prosperous Cossack family named Stepan, or Stenka Razin, gathered together on the upper reaches of the Don river a band of escaped serfs who literally had nothing to lose but their lives. For three years they raided Russian and Persian towns around the Caspian Sea. A popular Russian folk song tells of Stenka falling in love with a beautiful Persian princess he had captured. When taunted by his men, *tolko noch' s'nei provozilsya, sam nautro baboi stal* – that after one night with her he had become as soft as a woman himself – Stenka proved his manhood by drowning her in the river Volga and setting out in 1670 to attack fortified Russian cities along the Volga.

Principally motivated by the prospect of loot, rape and torturing captured officers and nobles, his undisciplined army of, initially, 7,000 ragged rebels attracted twice their number of recruits in a bloody progression up the Volga – mainly serfs and peasants rebelling against the nobility and bureaucracy, but not their quasi-divine ruler. Alarmed at the insurrection's spread into central provinces of the Russian state, Tsar Alexis sent an army to put down the rebellion. Trained by Western European instructors, the army easily defeated Stenka's rabble in October 1670. Betrayed by Cossacks in the resultant chaos, he was brought to Moscow and tortured, then executed by beheading and quartering, after which Alexis' forces savagely reduced the rebel strongholds and executed their leaders. By December 1671, it was all over.

A century later in 1773 the country was certainly ripe for rebellion again. The man of the moment this time was an invalid Don Cossack officer named Yemelyan Pugachoff, who claimed to be the assassinated Tsar Peter III and led the greatest uprising Russia had so far seen, culminating in the capture of the city of Kazan, only 500 miles from Moscow. By June 1774 Pugachoff's ragged army of serfs was ready to march on Moscow, when the current war with Turkey – there were many throughout the centuries – ended in a Russian victory, allowing Tsarina Catherine the Great to divert troops to crush the rebels by savage reprisals. Before the end of September, betrayed by his own Cossacks as Stenka Razin had been, Pugachoff was confined in a metal cage for transport to Moscow and public execution there in Bolotnaya Square by beheading and quartering.

Closer in time to 1848, in which year none of the widespread European rebellions achieved fully its original objectives, in December 1825 one indirect result of Napoleon's Grand Army invading Russia in 1812 and being followed by Russian troops all the way back to France was a revolution led by officers returning home from Western Europe convinced that their still largely medieval society must modernise. When the Decembrist rising failed, five ringleaders were hanged, thirty-one were sentenced to long terms of hard labour by the newly crowned Tsar Nikolai I, and the lesser participants exiled to Siberia, taking their wives and families with them.[41] The most important achievement of the Decembrists was forcing the creation of a Ministry of State Domains, which operated an administration down to the level of each group of villages, or *volost*, governed by a mayor elected by male householders. The laudable intention was to introduce medical services and stockpiling of food in case of the crop failures that produced regular famines and to build schools and improve traditional methods of agriculture, but the programme foundered because the ministry's central and provincial staffs were as corrupt and inefficient as the rest of the tsarist bureaucracy.

The 40 million-plus serfs remained unable to marry or leave their estate without permission from their owners – this long after serfdom had ended in most European countries. For minor offences both men and women were viciously flogged with the *knout* – a multi-thonged whip similar to the Roman *flagellum* and the later cat o' nine tails. Nikolai I did attempt a radical overhaul of the civil service, but since his provincial governors exercised authority through *ispravniki*, or magistrates, who were elected by the local landowners, the abolition of serfdom was abandoned because it would have meant them losing a self-renewing unpaid labour force. The opposition to serfdom grew slowly, with the emancipation in 1861 coming about not from liberal political pressure on the government but because the growing middle class of entrepreneurs found this medieval institution that tied peasants to the land an obstacle to the urgent need for a labour force of many thousands of freely mobile wage-earners to operate the machines in the new factories.

Six weeks after the Treaty of Portsmouth, red flags were everywhere in the streets of Moscow and other cities. Industrial action by railway workers turned into a general strike that rapidly spread to most major cities. In Ivanovo, north-east of Moscow, the first *soviet* or workers' council was formed, followed by others in St Petersburg, Moscow, Odessa and other cities. The Russian word *soviet* means both a council and counsel, but it is more helpful to translate it here as 'self-elected committee'. Originally set up to manage the strikes, these committees swiftly acquired the character of an alternative administration and were the models for the *soviety* that would be formed in 1917. The Bolsheviks had no great role in all this but Trotsky and Natalya, using various aliases, returned to St Petersburg, where she was betrayed by an Okhrana informer and jailed for six months. Not for the only time, Trotsky crossed the nearby frontier into Finland, concentrating on writing for *Iskra* and putting forward Gelfand's ideas on government by the workers, not by theorists of bourgeois origins like Lenin and himself.

Throughout that summer, industrial unrest in Russia paralysed the country and mutiny was rampant in the armed forces. The man who seemed most likely to pull Russia into the modern European world was Count Witte, who negotiated at the Portsmouth conference the best possible deal for Russia. The causes of the people's discontent were legion. Although emancipated four decades earlier, the peasants did not have the right to sell the land allotted to them, nor to raise money by mortgaging it, nor to renounce their entitlement to it. So, they had to pay a kind of tax for many years to claim their property, which they might not have wanted. Although some rose to the occasion with an entrepreneurial spirit and raised finance to purchase land and launch business enterprises, many fell into arrears with the redemption tax. Lacking the money to buy the food their families needed, they took to the roads in search of paid work, resorting to petty crime on the way. Desperate peasants looted the property of prosperous landowners and set fire to crops and houses until troops were sent in. Government committees of enquiry into the causes of the problems blamed a lowering of agricultural productivity even in the *chernozem* or fertile black soil area of southern Russia at a time when peasant numbers were on the increase. A major famine in 1891 had led to many deaths, particularly of the elderly and children.

It was estimated that the nobility had mortgaged as much as a third of its extensive lands and sold off another third. Anton Chekhov's last play *Vishnyovy Sad* – the cherry orchard – which was premiered in 1904 at the Moscow Arts Theatre, depicts the personal relationships and social changes obliquely but well. In short, the Ranevsky family forfeits its estate because Madame Ranevskaya refuses to sell off her famous cherry orchard, which would enable the mortgage on the rest of the estate to be repaid and the family's life to continue, more or less as before. Probably no other theatrical masterpiece better interweaves the playwright's personal experience with the spirit of those times when the landowning classes were wallowing in regret for their vanished traditional way of life. The obstinate head of the family, the bewildered ex-serf, the ex-peasant turned self-made entrepreneur – they are all there. The moral of the play is in the off-stage sound effect at the end: the noise of axes chopping down Madame Ranevskaya's beloved trees anyway.

6

RUSSIAN ROULETTE

The millennial expansion of the Russian Empire had absorbed many nationalities and religious minorities, who were disadvantaged by comparison with Orthodox Russians, but national independence movements were gradually gathering strength. The Jews of the empire, who then had no country of their own, were similarly discriminated against, few having the right to purchase land outside the Pale and all having limited rights to education – which partly accounts for the disproportionately high numbers of dissident Jewish students in the revolutionary socialist movements.

Witte's modernisation programme had accelerated a vast population movement from country to town – from working the land to earning a wage in factories, where the workers picked up political ideas that they, in turn, fed back to their relatives still in the country. There were laws in place to forbid the employment in most factories of children under 12; adolescents under sixteen were not supposed to work on Sundays or feast days; eleven-hour days were the norm, although many were forced to work longer hours and trade unions were banned, as were strikes, with any attempts at labour organisation resulting in arrests and imprisonment. All this repression produced a corresponding reaction; one strike that began in 1902 affected nearly a quarter-million workers by the summer, encouraged by students, who had the education to publish their demands, risking arrest, internal exile to Siberia and conscription for military service.

In April 1902 a career civil servant named Vyacheslav von Plehve was appointed Minister of the Interior, and used Okhrana undercover agents to infiltrate and eliminate a number of the Narodnaya Volya terrorist groups. Having survived one assassination attempt in 1903 and two early in 1904, he was finally assassinated on 28 July 1904 by a Jewish member of the Socialist Revolutionary Combat Group Boevaya Organizatsiya, who threw a bomb into Plehve's open carriage outside St Petersburg's Warsaw station.

There were repeated calls for the end to tsarist autocracy and its replacement by a constitutional monarchy, while more radicalised protesters organised and led larger and larger strikes in many major cities. Prince Pyotr Kropotkin, who at the age of 12 had discarded his title, forbidding friends to use it when addressing him, had become a respected anarchist philosopher and clearly saw the disaster ahead. In December 1905 the Moscow city council or Duma was demanding freedom of the press, freedom of religion and the establishment of a national legislature. Nicholas II reacted with the publication on 24 December of a manifesto that acceded to some of these demands, but not the establishment of an elected national parliament. Wildfire strikes and protests in St Petersburg paralysed the city, climaxing in the massacre of Bloody Sunday.

Whatever the actual number killed by the Tsar's troops, the massacre was the spark that ignited the 1905 revolution. Within a week, more than half of all the industrial workers in Russia were on strike, and the proportion was much higher in those provinces where independence movements sought the right to use their own national languages and free themselves from tsarist rule. Sailors and soldiers, some of whom had fought in the war against Japan, also mutinied while loyal troops suppressed the demonstrations with bullets and spontaneous pogroms by the black squadrons targeted students and the Jewish population. Tens of thousands of political prisoners were released in an endeavour to calm the situation, but this had the reverse effect because many of them joined the protesters. In March universities were closed, which added numbers of radicalised students to the mobs demanding change. Trotsky had already fallen out with Lenin; now he attacked the Mensheviks and every other political faction and party, gaining a reputation for insufferable arrogance. Alexander Bogdanov wrote to Krupskaya, 'Trotsky came to see me. I very much dislike him. He's utterly unpleasant.'[42] Veteran socialist revolutionary Jules Martov called Trotsky a dilettante. Like Lenin when discarded by the comrades he had alienated, the result in Trotsky's case was a breakdown, signalled by one of his periodic blackouts. In the end, about the only comrade who had not severed all connection with him was Gelfand/Parvus.

Terrified that he was going to be left out of the start of a world revolution, in February 1905 Trotsky had his distinctive appearance altered by a close-cropped haircut and acquired false identity papers before following Natalya to Kiev, which was safer than arriving in St Petersburg directly from abroad, since he was on the Okhrana's instant arrest list. In London, Lenin had now decided that a two-stage revolution was required, the first stage incorporating much of what Witte and other liberal political figures were effecting without revolution. Moving back to the Russian capital in May, Trotsky's wife Natalya was betrayed, arrested and sentenced to six months' imprisonment after police and troops surrounded a clandestine gathering in some woodland outside St Petersburg. To save his own skin, her husband fled across the frontier to the town of Rauha, where he felt reasonably safe in the more easy-going, although Russian-occupied, grand duchy of Finland.

On 19 August Nicholas II signed a decree creating a national parliament with advisory functions but no legislative power. This toothless tiger enraged the people it was supposed to placate,[43] and led indirectly to more strikes – of typographers, bakers, telegraph and postal employees – and rioting in the streets. Without any central direction, strike committees liaised with one another and in mid-October 1905 the chaos gave birth to the Soviet of Workers' Deputies. Trotsky bombarded the left-wing papers with articles under his own name. With Gelfand, he started a new newspaper titled *Nachalo* – 'The Beginning' – for which he claimed there was an exponential increase in circulation from the very first issue. Addressing the St Petersburg Soviet at its third session, his eloquence sidelined its first leader effortlessly, placing him at its head. When the Soviet ordered all shops to close, the shopkeepers obeyed from fear of violence, as did factory owners. The Soviet published a new daily paper *Izvestiya*, meaning 'Information'. Appointed prime minister by Nicholas II on 22 October, Count Witte advised the Tsar to liberalise his autocratic regime because the Romanov regime was only likely to survive this crisis by converting Russia into a modern state – or a military dictatorship. Nicholas lacked the intelligence to understand the situation even when his chosen military dictator, his uncle Grand Duke Nikolai, threatened to blow his own brains out on the spot if the Tsar did not liberalise the government. Reluctantly,

Nicholas II agreed to sign the 'Manifesto for the Improvement of the State Order', known as the 30 October Manifesto, which promised basic civil rights to all citizens, universal male suffrage, elections for a national parliament and creation of a sole legislative body called the *Gosudarstvennaya Duma*, or state parliament. Unfortunately, Nicholas II and his closest advisers saw this merely as a temporising trick, and had no intention of carrying out its provisions long term. Trotsky wrote of this:

> [On] the day after the Manifesto's publication, many tens of thousands [sic] of people were standing in front of St Petersburg University, intoxicated with the joy of their first victory. I shouted to them from the balcony that a half-victory was unreliable, that the enemy was irreconcilable, that there were traps ahead. I tore up the Imperial Manifesto and threw the pieces to the winds.[44]

Reading the manifesto abroad, Lenin and the other émigré revolutionaries were emboldened to return, using false identity papers and keeping a low profile. Desperate not to be left out of a nationwide uprising, Lenin returned to Russia under a false identity, to lead the country in the name of the Bolshevik Party, now completely divorced from all the other revolutionary groups. He had the gall to accuse the in-country Social Democrats, who had lived through this tumultuous year, of failing to act for the previous six months, and now exhorted them to throw bombs into police stations, assassinate Okhrana agents, rob banks to obtain funds and beat up ordinary policemen. As to the Soviet, he was furious that this spontaneously formed body had usurped what he saw as the proper role of the Bolsheviks led by himself. He therefore shed no tears when its leaders, including Trotsky, were arrested on 3 December.

By the end of October the strikes had brought St Petersburg to its knees. On 8 November there was a massive mutiny by the garrison of the important offshore naval base and fortress on the island of Kronstadt, built there by Peter the Great to interdict foreign access across the Baltic to his otherwise exposed new city of St Petersburg. The hitherto loyal army now wavered in its allegiance. Witte appealed to the city's soviet, addressing its members as 'brothers' and claiming to have their welfare at heart, but his ploy was immediately rejected. On 15 December the executive committee of the Soviet issued a call to cease payment of taxes, overthrow the Romanov regime and summon an Uchreditelnoye Sobranie or Constituent Assembly. Next day, the executive was arrested and all newspapers reporting its call suppressed by government order.

The Bolsheviks were dividing their forces into *boyeviki* or 'combat groups' of not more than twenty-five armed men. With St Petersburg stunned, Lenin directed his attention to Moscow, the former capital, whose population seemed more favourable to insurrection. Barricades were erected in the streets. The combat groups were ordered to split into small groups and fight a guerrilla war, striking at the forces of law and order but melting away before retribution came. After a week of indecision, the government sent the elite Semyonovsky Guards to put down the uprising but Lenin was nowhere to be found. He had again placed himself in safety across the Finnish border on 24 December, accused by some of his followers of rash opportunism. As far as he was concerned, the abortive rebellion had taught the masses the lesson that they could not win an armed confrontation with the government unless he was in total charge.

Paying the price for placing himself in the forefront of the revolt, Trotsky spent the next fifteen months in jail under the relaxed regime for politicals, allowed reading material and able to smuggle out articles for clandestine revolutionary publications. Conjugal visits by Natalya Sedova resulted in her becoming pregnant again. Something of the tolerance showed by the authorities was evident when the discovery of some tools secreted for an escape by Gelfand were dismissed by the prison governor as probably planted by the Okhrana. On 19 September 1906 the trial opened and lasted until 2 November when a verdict of not guilty to the charge of insurrection was handed down, but they were judged guilty on lesser charges and sentenced to loss of civil rights and exile for life. A fortnight later, Natalya gave birth to a son.[45]

On 5 January 1907 Trotsky and thirteen others were escorted from the prison to a railway carriage with barred windows for a journey of 2,000 miles to Tobolsk in Siberia and from there 700 miles to the north by sledge, right into the Arctic Circle in the middle of winter, where they were decanted in a nomadic settlement of *yurty*[46] without a permanent house or hut in sight – except that Trotsky was not with them, having faked illness on the way. Purchasing a false passport and clothes for the journey, he did not take the easy route back to civilisation, fearing recapture, but rode on reindeer sleighs under a pile of furs from one Siberian

nomad encampment to the next all the way to the slightly more civilised
Archangel province, where it was possible for Natalya to join him, with
help from sympathisers in St Peterburg, and travel back to her temporary
home and their infant son at Zelenogorsk[47] 50 miles north-west of the
capital and conveniently near the Finnish frontier. After a few days' rest
for Trotsky to recover from the arduous journey, they crossed into Finland
and found a temporary haven near Helsingfors – modern Helsinki –
before travelling on to Vienna, where the Austro-Hungarian authorities
were tolerant of Russian dissidents, since they regarded tsarist Russia as a
potentially hostile state.

Nicholas II had received no useful education or training from his
father – and had no knowledge of physics. His empire was a powder keg
that needed only a spark to explode and *Iskra* already existed as the name
of Lenin's Marxist group. Instead of lessening the pressure on the turmoil
of volatile social elements in Russia to dissipate the force of the eventual
social explosion, Tsar Nicholas applied more repression, suspending the
Duma several times and tamping down the unrest, so that when the
explosion did eventually come, it would shatter the entire infrastructure
of Russian society. In this, his unlikely ally was Lenin, whose hostility
to the Duma was tolerated by the Okhrana agents infiltrated into every
Bolshevik group because their bosses considered that the real danger to
the autocratic rule of Nicholas II was the Duma.

It seemed for a while that the 1905 revolution had exhausted the
potential for rebellion in Russia and something like normal life returned
as the Third Duma under Nicholas II's Prime Minister Pyotr Arkadyevich
Stolypin permitted more personal freedom, allowed legitimate trade
unions to function and authorised some socialist publications to appear.
Abroad, even the expatriate Bolsheviks distanced themselves from Lenin,
with the exception of Zinoviev and Kamenev – with whom he consti-
tuted the Bolshevik Centre and who would pay the supreme penalty for
this closeness when they were both executed by Stalin in 1936. Lenin
went through another black period, tormented by headaches and insomnia, remarking to Krupskaya on a walk through the streets of Geneva, 'I
feel as though I've come here to be buried.'[48]

In the autumn of 1909, they moved to Paris, sharing an apartment
with Krupskaya's mother and one of Lenin's sisters. In summer 1910
Lenin attempted to extend his control over the Socialist International in

Helsinki, but nearly all the other delegates were alienated by his arrogance and bored with his perpetual harping on the imminence of a revolution, which, for the moment, seemed off the cards. To regain power, Lenin organised a congress in Prague of revolutionary socialists who would accept his authority. Of the thirteen voting members, it later transpired that two were undercover Okhrana agents. In early 1912 the leaders of a strike by miners in the Siberian goldfields were arrested and a protest meeting was gunned down by troops without warning. Reportedly several hundred were killed. When the news spread back to European Russia 250,000 workers went on strike in sympathy. In July Lenin, Zinoviev and Kamenev moved from Paris to Kraków, in Polish Galicia, to be nearer the main cities of Russia.

PART 2

1

TWO SHOTS – 38 MILLION DEAD

The first shots of the First World War were fired on Sunday 28 June 1914 in Sarajevo, the administrative capital of the restive province of Bosnia-Herzegovina, which had become an Austrian protectorate at the Congress of Berlin in 1878 and was annexed into the Austro-Hungarian Empire as recently as October 1908. In a monumental failure of close protection, Archduke Franz Ferdinand, heir presumptive of Austria–Hungary, and his consort Countess Sophie Chotek von Chotkova und Wognin died shortly after being shot by Serbian terrorist Gavrilo Princip.

In Vienna, court protocol forbade Countess Sophie to ride in the same carriage as her husband because she was by birth only a Czech countess. The marriage was a love match, to which the ageing Emperor Franz Joseph had consented after long delay on condition that any children would have no right of succession – as was normal with morganatic marriages. Since the visit to Sarajevo was not a court function and that Sunday was their wedding anniversary, Franz Ferdinand wanted for once to be seen in public with his beloved and pregnant wife at his side. This gesture of affection, respect and consideration for her was to prove fatal. Sarajevo had been chosen for the courtesy visit because Franz Ferdinand was nearby, observing the annual manoeuvres of the imperial army, but the choice of date was ill-advised, for this was the 525th anniversary of the Battle of Kosovo, in which the army of neighbouring Serbia was defeated by a Turkish army, ending Serbian independence for more than four centuries – and memories have always been long in the Balkans.

This was the heyday of assassins. In peaceful, prosperous Britain, Queen Victoria survived no less than seven known attempts on her life. In 1861 Russia's Tsar Alexander II was killed in what was the fifth attempt on his life. The French president had been assassinated in 1894, along with two prime ministers of Bulgaria in 1895 and 1907, Austro-Hungarian Emperor Franz Joseph's wife, Elizabeth, in 1898, the king of Italy in 1900 and King George I of Greece only fifteen months before the fateful day in Sarajevo. Just across the border from Sarajevo, the king and queen of Serbia had been murdered in their bedroom by a clique of their own officers in 1903. They were shot several times, hacked at by sabres and an axe and the queen's partly dismembered body was tossed over the balcony into the garden below. The list of European royalty, politicians, high officers of state and other public figures who succumbed to assassins' bullets or to 'infernal machines' – meaning bombs, many of them improvised by amateurs – was long indeed.

Among the crowd lining the route of the procession from the railway station to Sarajevo town hall were five armed terrorists, sent from neighbouring Serbia to murder the royal couple. A local notable had warned Countess Sophie that the royal visit on that particular day invited trouble, but she had brushed off his warning because all the people she had previously met in Bosnia-Herzegovina had been friendly. Yet, the five young men waiting for her as the motorcade drove along the embankment of the river Miljacka, known as the Appel Quay, were not Bosnians but members of a Serbian undercover revanchist group. As the royal car drew level with the first of the terrorists positioned along the route just after 10 a.m. on that balmy summer morning, he lost his nerve and failed to throw his 2lb 8oz bomb made in the Serbian state armoury in Kragojevac. The others also had revolvers from the same source and were all carrying poison, with which they were supposed to commit suicide, if arrested.[49]

The royal couple were riding in the second car of the cortège, a 1911 Gräf & Stift luxury limousine with the hood down, which was owned by Lieutenant Colonel Count Franz von Harrach, who was sitting in the front passenger seat. At the wheel was Harrach's best driver, Leopold Lojka. Seated in the jump seat facing the imperial couple was General Oskar Potiorek, military governor of the province, whose responsibility it was to protect the royal couple. Further along the quayside, a second terrorist did throw his bomb at the car just opposite the main police station, but his aim was faulty. It bounced off the folded canvas roof, to explode beneath the following vehicle, wounding a dozen passengers and bystanders, some seriously. Lojka attempted to accelerate away from the scene, but stalled the engine because the throttle lever on the steering wheel was set to a slow processional speed.

The bomb-thrower swallowed his poison, which burned his throat but failed to kill him, and then leapt over the balustrade, hoping to escape by swimming across the river. Due to the summer drought, the water was only a few inches deep, so he landed in the thick mud of the riverbed 26ft below the embankment and was quickly seized and bundled away by two civilians and two policemen, after being relieved of his unused automatic pistol. After re-setting the throttle and climbing down to turn the engine over with the starting handle at the front of the vehicle, Lojka drove on with the other undamaged cars past three other conspirators, none of whom took any action.

At that point, Governor Potiorek should have aborted the visit. Instead, Franz Ferdinand was driven to the town hall, as planned, where he quietly protested to the mayor, Fehim Effendi Čurčić, 'I come on a friendly visit and someone throws a bomb at me.' However, in the rigidly protocol-ridden society of the time, the reception passed with an exchange of polite addresses, after which Franz Ferdinand and Countess Sophie left about 11 a.m.

The archduke decided, with nineteenth-century courtesy, to visit and console the injured victims of the terrorist bomb in the hospital, despite Countess Sophie wanting to leave Sarajevo as fast as possible in case another attempt might be made on their lives. Leaving the hospital, Governor Potiorek got back into the car with them, to make his point that there was nothing to fear. Because his adjutant was lying injured in a hospital bed, no one else thought to tell Lojka of a last-minute change of route. Halfway along the return journey to the railway station, Lojka followed the leading car into a congested narrow street that led to the medieval bazaar. It was a wrong turn. Too late, Potiorek shouted at him to stay on the main street. Having no reverse gear, the car had to be pushed back around the corner with the gear stick in neutral.

By sheer coincidence, this happened just 5ft away from where one of the terrorists was eating a snack on the pavement. Dropping his food,

19-year-old Gavrilo Princip whipped out his Belgian-made Browning FN 7.65mm automatic pistol and fired two shots at point-blank range, hitting the pregnant Countess Sophie in the abdomen and wounding Franz Ferdinand in the neck, severing his jugular artery. The time was about 11.30 a.m. Either Count Harrach or Potiorek seized the stricken heir to the imperial throne by his uniform collar to support him in his seat. Franz Ferdinand could hardly speak, although Harrach afterwards said he had murmured to Sophie that she must live for the sake of their children. Princip was hustled away by police to prevent him being lynched by the crowd. On arrival at the governor's residence, thought to be safer than the hospital, Countess Sophie was found to be already dead, as was the child she was carrying. Her husband died shortly afterwards.[50]

The time was midday. In two short hours, the fate of millions had been decided, although nobody was aware at the time. London newsrooms were quiet that Sunday afternoon when a Reuters telegraph message arrived with the first news of the double assassination. In Vienna, the rigid court protocol prevented it reaching Emperor Franz Joseph's ears for several hours. Since the four assassins who had been caught were Serbs who had been trained in Serbia, the Austro-Hungarian Foreign Minister sent a harsh ultimatum to Belgrade, but two weeks passed before *The Times* printed a report from Vienna that at last indicated possibly serious repercussions for Princip's act:

> A feeling of uncertainty … is affecting the Vienna Bourse most adversely. Very heavy falls of prices were noted all round yesterday.[51]

Yet, one week later the *Manchester Guardian*'s correspondent in the Austrian capital was calm: 'Vienna is notoriously the most jumpy capital in Europe, and talk about war between Austria and Serbia is surely not to be taken seriously.'[52]

Otto von Bismarck, the statesman who had united Germany in 1871 was rumoured to have said on his deathbed, 'One day, the Great European War will come out of some damn foolish thing in the Balkans', but to most British and French people and their politicians, Austria's ultimatum to Serbia after the assassination was – as Prime Minister Chamberlain would famously put it in 1938 – 'a quarrel in a faraway country between people of whom we know nothing'.

Historian Christopher Clark summed up the general failure to foresee the consequences of the increasing tension in the Balkans in the title of his 2013 book *The Sleepwalkers: How Europe Went to War in 1914*. Eventually, *The Times* sounded the alarm that should have awoken all Europe:

> War fever in Vienna. French pessimism. Germany the key to the situation. British naval manoeuvres. Orders to First and Second Fleet.[53]

'Manoeuvres' was a euphemism for placing armed forces on a war footing, and 'orders to the fleet' yet more menacing. Still the *Manchester Guardian* declared that its readers cared nothing for the tension between Vienna and Belgrade. The *Daily News* and *Yorkshire Post* declared that there was no reason why British lives should be put at risk in a quarrel that was not a British concern. Only *The Times* was talking of British intervention, but Foreign Secretary Sir Edward Grey thought that the French government was allowing itself to be drawn into a Balkan war, which Britain had always avoided and would continue to do so. He was convinced that the matter could be resolved by gentlemen like himself talking to other gentlemen and no one getting excited.

Exponential inflation of the tax base in the preceding century, due to rapidly increasing industrialisation, meant that the Continental powers had large standing armies to protect their land frontiers – a problem that did not exist for sea-girt Britain. A flurry of ultimata flew by telegraph between the continental foreign ministries throughout July, resulting in the escalation of military preparedness as pre-existing treaties ranged the combined might of the German and Austro-Hungarian empires against the Triple Entente of Britain, France and Russia, with Italy hovering on the sidelines. The Triple Entente had 9.5 million men, against 8 million in the combined German and Austro-Hungarian imperial armies, but was at a tremendous strategic disadvantage in that nearly 1,000 miles separated the Western Allies from the nearest Russian troops; whereas the German Supreme Command – Oberste Heeresleitung (OHL) – could switch its forces from east to west or vice versa over modern railways in just a few days. Just six weeks after those two shots in Sarajevo, on 3 August Germany declared war on France, having demanded the right to move troops across neutral Belgium, to whose defence Britain was committed by treaty. The following day, Britain declared war. A week later, all Europe was divided into two armed camps.

As the continent hurtled into the greatest war the world had seen, which cost an estimated 38 million casualties in the following four years, there was at first on both sides a wellspring of misguided patriotic fervour with General Kitchener in Britain proclaiming that he needed just 100,000 men in uniform to sort out the 'Huns'. As another 100,000 men and another and another were mown down by water-cooled, gas-operated Maxim machine guns, or blinded, crippled for life or blown to pieces by modern explosives in the unheroic slaughter of twentieth-century battle, the gung-ho mood of the Tommies' 'For King and Country', the French slogan '*Pour la Patrie*' and the motto on the belt buckles of the Kaiser's soldiers '*Gott mit uns*' rapidly lost their magic. For the politically uninvolved, the innocent optimism of 'It'll all be over by Christmas' was replaced by a fatalistic hopelessness in the trenches of Flanders and the vast forests, mountains, swamps and plains over which the war of movement on the eastern fronts raged. Most of the front-line soldiers had no clear idea where they were, or why. It was all summed up by the Tommies' dreary dirge 'We're here because we're here because we're here because we're here ...'

In the mounting chaos of preparations for war in the summer of 1914, in addition to the armaments manufacturers – whose factories rapidly moved into top gear, eventually to make them obscenely huge profits – and the military officers on both sides enjoying rapid promotions, a very different group of Europeans saw the outbreak of war as the chance for which they had been waiting. By now, the many revolutionary socialist parties of Europe agreed only on one thing: that only 'violent' revolution could destroy what they called 'bourgeois capitalism' and impose 'the dictatorship of the proletariat' in its stead. But the various movements did not collaborate, each viewing the others with paranoid suspicion. No single movement – nor even all of them – had the financial means to launch a revolution because uprisings, as covert operations officers know, cost money.

In summer 1914 few people would have guessed that *the* revolution would take place in tsarist Russia. On 7 August 1914 Lenin had been arrested in the Polish city of Kraków by the Austro-Hungarian authorities as a suspected Russian spy, but was released two weeks later when it was realised that he and his followers had the potential to produce severe agitation among both the Russian tsarist armies and the workers in the essential Russian war industries. At some point later came the idea of using Lenin to provide the Central Powers – as the German and Austro-Hungarian alliance was known – with what was later called a fifth column, if they could get him back to Russia.

Lenin was reported as saying at this time that he had no idea what to do after taking power because the important thing was to seize power and work out what to do with it later. If true, it was a rather disingenuous statement for a man who had spent his entire adult life scheming for this moment. From the safety of a Swiss retreat, he called for all revolutionary socialists to transform the imperialist war between the Triple Entente and Central Powers into civil wars in their own countries, arguing that the true enemy of the worker was not the worker in the opposite trench but the capitalist at home, and that rank-and-file soldiers should turn their weapons on the vulnerable members of the bourgeoisie and aristocracy wearing officers' uniforms who exercised the power of life and death over them. By killing all the officers, they could seize this chance of destroying the capitalist system that was plunging the world into the greatest carnage ever known.

A number of ultra-rich German businessmen, like millionaire industrialist Hugo Stinnes and banker Max Warburg, chose to ignore his revolutionary rhetoric and double-talk, equally hostile to the Central Powers as to tsarist Russia, and prepared to use their own wealth as subsidy that could turn the Russian dissidents into the fifth column that would stab the Russian armies in the back.

8

ARMS AND THE WOMAN

Field Marshal Helmuth Karl Bernhard Graf von Moltke was Prussian Chief of Staff 1857–71 and German Chief of Staff 1871–88, after Otto von Bismarck engineered the political unification of the German nation. A great military thinker, Moltke summed up the difference between staff college war games or pre-war plans and the reality of a shooting war in his dictum: 'No plan of operations extends with any certainty beyond the first contact with the main hostile force.' Often paraphrased, this remains true, even in the age of smart bombs and drones.

The outset of the First World War illustrates Bismarck's dictum perfectly – on both sides of the lines. Germany's Schlieffen Plan called for a rapid encirclement of Paris to decapitate France, but the modified Schlieffen Plan, launched in August 1914, failed to take into account Schlieffen's deathbed warning to 'keep the right flank strong'. The resultant failure at encirclement produced the four-year slogging match in the trenches of Flanders. Had the plan gone according to his blueprint, after the collapse of France OHL could have rushed battle-hardened divisions eastwards across Germany's excellent internal rail network to mount an attack against the vulnerable tongue of Russian-occupied Poland, known as the Warsaw salient, while its Austro-Hungarian allies launched an offensive into Russian-occupied Poland from the south-west.

Less than a decade after the humiliating defeat that ended the war with Japan, the Russian General Staff – Stavka Verkhovnovo Glavnokomanduyushchevo, usually abbreviated to 'Stavka' – was staffed by generals who counted on the western marches of the tsarist Empire,

The Warsaw salient.

for the most part devoid of railways or even roads, as a considerable deterrent for any invader. The lack of communications was, of course, equally an obstacle for Russian forces deployed to meet any invasion. Offensive strategies were the Top Secret Plan 19A, to be rolled out if Austria was the main enemy and Plan 19G, to be used if Germany was the main threat. Plan 19A posited concentrating the major part of the imperial forces against the weaker Austro-Hungarian armies in central and southern Poland, swiftly breaking right through the Carpathian Mountain passes to strike across the Hungarian Plain to Budapest and knocking Austro-Hungary right out of the war after a short campaign. That plan called for leaving just enough men in East Prussia to contain the German forces there until Austro-Hungary was defeated. As a strategy, it might have worked. However, in warfare, the devil is often in the allies one has chosen. The French government desperately needed to divert German divisions from the attempted encirclement of Paris and persuaded Stavka to launch a diversionary pincer movement against the German forces already in East Prussia. The Vilna Army, commanded by General Paul von Rennenkampf, was to attack from the east, to meet up with the Warsaw Army, commanded by General Alexander Samsonov, driving into East Prussia from the south.

A pincer movement over hundreds of miles requires precise geographical coordination and a strict schedule. Yet, although all sides were intercepting and/or jamming each other's diplomatic radio traffic, the brains at Stavka were locked into the nineteenth century and Russian military radio communications were transmitted in clear language. They were thus easily intercepted by front-line German wireless interception units, which were so efficient that Marshal Joffre's 'Order of the Day for the Battle of the Marne' in September 1914 was intercepted and read by OHL before it had reached the French front line.[54]

Worse, between the two prongs of the Russian attack, there was no direct radio link because von Rennenkampf and Samsonov had fallen out during the 1904–05 war with Japan – each accusing the other of being responsible for the defeat – and still refused to speak to each other or to let their staffs communicate directly. Communications between the two armies therefore had to be sent via radio link with Stavka, giving the German interceptors two bites at each apple. As a result, the Germans were able to attack and annihilate the Warsaw army before it was anywhere near linking up with the Vilna army. At the Battle of Tannenberg, 26–30 August 1914, Russian losses were 92,000 men taken prisoner and 50,000 casualties. Two weeks later, Russia had lost 250,000 men; two and a half years later 1.3 million Russians had died in combat, from wounds or from disease, with 3.9 million taken prisoner.

With out-of-date commanders like Samsonov ordering mass attacks of infantry against the terrifying power of twentieth-century firepower, it was inevitable that war on the several Russian fronts would cause millions of casualties, most of them for no military gain. The fitting end of the appallingly inept generalship in East Prussia came when, after Tannenberg, Samsonov's small party of aides-de-camp, lost in the forests without maps or compass, heard a single shot ring out, as he rightly committed suicide.

Russian researchers have criticised uneducated peasant conscripts for trying to describe the horrors of being marched forward into an artillery barrage by using such similes as 'thunder', 'earthquake', 'hell' and so on, but is this so different from images used by educated westerners, like Wilfred Owen's 'monstrous anger of the guns', 'the stuttering rifles' rapid rattle' and 'shrill, demented choirs of wailing shells'?[55]

Because of the vast distances over which combat ranged in this war of movement,[56] individual one-on-one physical violence was more common than in the West. When the artillery had yet to be moved into the line, or the gunners had no shells to fire or infantrymen had no compatible cartridges for their rifles – as happened all too often in the Tsar's armies – killing was often face-to-face with bayonet, sword, lance, sharpened spades and blunt instruments. The Germans and Austro-Hungarians had an advantage in this area, with a better-developed rail network and many good roads to their rear. This compared with the paucity of roads behind vast stretches of the Russian lines, deliberately left as a wasteland, to deter, or at least delay, any invasion from the west. This theatre of war tied up 2 million Austro-Hungarian troops and about a quarter of all the German armies. An estimated million Austro-Hungarian soldiers and three-quarters of a million Germans, plus nearly four million Russians, died and were buried there – or had their bodies scavenged by animals if comrades had no time to dig a grave before retreating or advancing elsewhere. And then there were the uncounted civilian casualties of all ages and many nationalities as the fluid fronts advanced and receded and advanced again and receded again …

In the history of warfare, no greater contrast may be found than that between the static trench warfare of the Western Front and the slaughter on the Russian fronts, which spread over thousands of miles, creating enormous logistical problems for both sides. In this war of movement, simply ensuring food, clothing and ammunition reached the millions of men, plus fodder for millions of draught and cavalry horses and officers' mounts, was an insoluble headache.

One British observer with the Russian armies was Colonel Alfred Knox, referred to by Winston Churchill as 'an agent of singular discernment, whose luminous and pitiless despatches' were of great use to the British government in following developments there.[57] Knox knew the Russian mind. He spoke German, Russian and French – the last being the second language of the Russian educated classes – and was personally acquainted with many senior officers of the several Russian armies and with Tsar Nicholas, also the handsome and charming Russian Commander-in-Chief Grand Duke Nikolai Nikolaevich who, at seven feet tall, towered over the slightly built Tsar. Knox also knew personally the Tsarina and the four princesses Olga, Maria, Tatiana and Anastasia as well as the Tsarevich, or crown prince, Alexei. As a man of his time, never once did Knox display any lack of courtesy to the royal family, although Nicholas was known to his intimates as an ignorant and indecisive man totally unfit to exercise autocracy, who had inherited the title of Tsar on the death of his father, Alexander III, complaining that he did not want to rule. It was true that he had never been given any instruction by Alexander, who thought him too stupid to waste time on, but the greatest of his many personality flaws was that of a weak man who mistook stubbornness for strength. On being given the advice, before taking any decision always to consult his uncles the grand dukes because they had older and wiser heads, Nicholas had reluctantly accepted the crown, but gradually stopped consulting his uncles in favour of his bride, the dominating Princess Alix of Hesse-Darmstadt. Beautiful and elegant, she was also cripplingly superstitious and prone to influence by the 'Siberian priest and horse-thief' Rasputin who was apparently able to stop by hypnosis the potentially fatal internal haemorrages of Crown Prince Alexei, who suffered from haemophilia.

Knox's book entitled *With the Russian Army, 1914–1917*, being chiefly extracts from the diary of a military attaché,[58] begins with a modest observation:

> The writer can at any rate claim to have enjoyed greater opportunities for observation of the Russian army [sic] than any other foreign observer, both previous to the war [when he was] Military Attaché to the British Embassy at Petrograd [sic] and during the war as a liaison officer at the front.

On one occasion, Col Knox accompanied a Russian officer to the nearest railway station to see why no mail was being delivered by the *polevaya pochta*, or field postal services. They found enormous piles of mailbags addressed to men at the front, weighing a total of 32 tons. Taking the stationmaster to task, they were told that the regional governor had not provided enough carts for onward transport, so nothing could be done. Knox commented: 'A man like this [station master] should be hung [sic] when one remembers how poor fellows at the front long for news from home.'[59] That other eyewitness of Russian events, British Consul Robert Bruce Lockhart, wrote of Knox: '…no man took a saner view of the military situation on the Eastern [sic] front and no foreign observer supplied his government with more reliable information.'[60]

Knox recorded that, although the Tsar's uncle Grand Duke Nikolai had reluctantly accepted the position of commander-in-chief on the approach of war, he had formerly been inspector-general of cavalry and commander of the St Petersburg military district – and thus had no prior knowledge of Stavka's plans, which had been made two or three years earlier. He was in any case somewhat of a figurehead, surrounded by his own courtiers and usually preferring 'not to get in the generals' way'.[61]

On Saturday 15 August, Col Knox was on board the grand duke's train and noted in his diary its good but simple cooking with a glass of vodka or wine and cognac with the coffee.[62] His host occupied himself on the journey in rubber-stamping Plan 19G. He would have done better to reflect on the impossibility of executing it with a problem identified by Col Knox as the overwhelming preponderance of Russian guns on many fronts being rendered useless because no shells were available at the batteries for the gunners to fire.[63]

In July and August 1914 Russian mobilisation was faster than the Germans had reckoned possible because of a clandestine call-up during the diplomatically termed 'Period Preparatory to War'. By the end of the year, 5 million men were wearing the Tsar's uniforms, of which 2.2 million were front-line troops. Yet Knox commented that this was 'a poor performance, for the adult male population [theoretically] liable to military service in the vast Russian Empire on 1 January 1910, was 74,262,600 men'.[64]

Thanks to corruption and privilege, millions of men simply did not serve. Knox also remarked that 75 per cent of recruits were drawn from the peasant class, which made poor soldiers. The Tatar-Mongol domination of Russia and the subsequent institution of serfdom – which had only been abolished a half-century before – had robbed them 'of all natural initiative, leaving only a wonderful capacity for patient endurance'. As to their training, he wrote:

Since 1911, when I was appointed in St Petersburg, I had always attended the annual manoeuvres of the Military District, where accredited foreign officers were invited as guests of the Tsar. We lunched and dined at his table, used his motor-cars, rode his horses, and attended with him nightly performances at the local theatre. We saw much martial spectacle, but very little serious training for modern war.[65]

Russian conscripts looked like the illiterate peasants most of them were in civilian life, wearing baggy drawstring trousers under a short, belted smock with soft uniform cap. In summer, to save carrying a greatcoat – little wheeled transport was available or, indeed, usable in the roadless wastes – the soldier's blanket was rolled up with ends tied together and worn bandolier-style over the left shoulder, leaving the right arm free for the rifle – if he had one. The output of the state rifle factory at Tula in 1914 was five – repeat, *five* – rifles per day although the factory was tooled up to produce 5,000 a month. Many conscripts had to drill with a broomstick and were ordered into battle with a pocketful of bullets and instructions to pick up and use the rifle of the first dead man they stumbled over. In retreat, Russian officers tended to sacrifice men to save artillery, which was considered more valuable than peasant lives.

As to infantry weapons, most of the issued rifles were Vintovka Mosina – a Russian design, but made in Belgium with a magazine holding five rounds.[66] It was wildly inaccurate when used by raw recruits. There were also single-shot black-powder rifles dating from 1870 that had been re-machined in Belgium to use smokeless ammunition of the same calibre as the Mosin-Nagants and accept the same bayonets. There were also 450,000 obsolete French single-shot black-powder rifles, a half-million M1891s from the Manufacture Nationale, 400,000 obsolete three-shot Italian repeating rifles, 800,000 Arisaka rifles from Japan, plus 3.5 million rifles ordered from Remington and Westinghouse in the USA and 300,000 model 1895 Winchester repeaters, of which total some 1.6 million were delivered before the Treaty of Brest-Litovsk. Given the inefficiency of re-supply, such a wide variety of different bores meant that infantry units often received the wrong ammunition and could not fire a shot.

In all the Russian armies there were only 4,000 machine guns, many lacking wheels for rapid movement in advance or retreat, when they had to be carried. The situation of the artillery was almost as chaotic. Russia's backwardness in heavy engineering had obliged War Minister Vladimir Sukhomlinov to purchase from the German firm Krupp its 120mm quick-firing light howitzers and 150mm howitzers from the French company Schneider-Creusot,[67] but the seven divisions of heavy artillery had not finished training on them when the war began.

In contrast, each German division on the Russian fronts had its own heavy and medium artillery and Austro-Hungary had the benefit of excellent guns produced in the Škoda Iron Works in Bohemia. There was similar disparity in shells; OHL issued 3,000 shells per gun, but Russian ordnance provided only 1,000 shells per gun at the declaration of war and could manufacture only 1.5 shells per gun per day thereafter – a grotesquely inadequate situation when artillery bombardments prior to a major offensive could exceed 700 rounds per gun per day. As historian Timothy Dowling points out in a very comprehensive examination of the situation, two out of every three shells emerging from the barrel of a Russian gun were imported – as were two-thirds of the bullets fired by Russian small arms. Both Col Knox and French Ambassador Maurice Paléologue commented that the 5 million men mobilised were equipped with only 1.2 million rifles in the front lines and 700,000 in reserve. The shortage of armaments was echoed in the insufficiency of just about every kind of ancillary equipment. Typically, Samsonov's 150,000-strong 2nd Army disposed of just ten motorcars, four motorcycles and twenty-five telephones. For the first months of the war Russian artillery brigades had no telephones, so that requests for their supporting fire arrived by Cossack despatch riders on sweating ponies. Morse operators and their transmitting sets were in short supply. Russian military transportation was also inadequate. Officers rode everywhere; the soldiers had to march, in some cases for hundreds of miles from the nearest railhead to the front, where they were thrown immediately into combat.

Summing up that disparity in training and equipment of the two sides on the Russian fronts, that coolly detached observer of the Russian war machine Colonel Knox reported: 'For a long war, Russia was outclassed in every factor of success except in the number of her fighting men and their mollusc-like quality of recovery after severe defeat.'[68]

Israel Gelfand had swallowed whatever socialist beliefs he held to make a fortune as an arms dealer in the Balkan wars[69] and was now writing

73

for German left-wing periodicals under the sobriquet Parvus. Persona non grata in both Russia and Germany, he wrote a memorandum dated 9 March 1915 setting out at considerable length the methods of using the expatriate Russian dissidents to create the maximum social and political unrest in their homeland, leading to an early withdrawal of the Romanov empire from the war.[70] To convert the Bolsheviks' minuscule membership into a forceful powerbase required what would today be called 'spin' in a very expensive public relations campaign. Back in Berlin, Stinnes and Warburg had been talking with the politicians, with the result that, in January 1915, Germany's Under-Secretary for Foreign Affairs, Arthur Zimmermann, was arranging a German passport for Gelfand, his strategy considered so urgent that on 26 March Zimmermann 'requested' from the Imperial Treasury a subsidy for the Bolsheviks of 2 million gold marks, as negotiated by Gelfand/Parvus. Arrangements were made to pay this via deniable middlemen to subsidise the Bolsheviks and Mensheviks inside Russia.[71] In May Gelfand met Lenin to compare notes but although Lenin, as usual, rejected anyone else's ideas, Gelfand pressed on with his design.

On 9 July Zimmermann's boss Gottlieb von Jagow upped this budget to 5 million marks. In talks with Gelfand and other intermediaries, Stinnes reportedly offered 2 million roubles of his own money to subsidise anti-war propaganda in Russia and Warburg also allocated substantial funds for 'publishing activities' there.[72] The Bolsheviks sought these generous subsidies because they needed to bombard the uncommitted 99 per cent of the Russian population with propaganda if they were to have anything like sufficient support to stage a coup d'état. Despite the high cost of scarce newsprint in Russia, their covert financial backing enabled them to produce no less than forty-one daily and periodical publications that promised land to the dispossessed, food to the hungry and peace to those yearning for an end to the killing. In a massive PR campaign to make themselves respectable and popular, they commenced hammering away at public opinion with the simplest of slogans – none of which were overtly Marxist.[73]

A 27-year-old English governess working in Moscow, Florence Farmborough volunteered to serve as a *krestovaya sestra* – a Red Cross nurse in a *letuchka* or field dressing station. In those days when delay in treating any wound often meant death from infection, the *letuchki* were set up very near the front lines, moving frequently to keep up with advances and retreats. After a few weeks' training in a civilian hospital, she spent a whole month travelling by railway to reach the south-western front in the Carpathian foothills early in 1915, and kept a diary whenever she had time to write. Her first base was in a well-built house with several pleasant, airy rooms, where the nurses' first task was to scrub every surface clean and paint or whitewash the walls. An operating theatre was set up and a pharmacy stocked with medicines and surgical material. They were told not to think they would be there long: the stay might be six months or six hours, depending on the movement of the front. By chatting with the wounded men, she gained insights into the cares and preoccupations of the ordinary Russian soldier:

> Lately, ammunition had been sent in large quantities to our Front, but little of it has been any use. Out of one consignment of 30,000 shells, fewer than 200 were found to be serviceable. Cartridges were sent in their hundreds of thousands and distributed among the men in their trenches, but they were of a foreign cast [sic] and would not fit the Russian rifle. Large stores of Japanese rifles had been despatched to neighbouring divisions, but the Russian cartridges [supplied there] failed to fit them.[74]

9

THE GREAT RETREAT

Three days after Florence's arrival, there was a sense of foreboding in her entry for 28 April, which recorded the arrival of a first batch of fifty wounded men, whose wounds had to be dressed before they were sent on to hospital in Yaslo. Against the booming of enemy cannon fire growing continually closer, the soldiers voiced their dismay that German troops and heavy artillery had been sent to this section of the Front. 'We are not afraid of the Austrians,' they said, 'but the German soldiers are quite different.'[75] Two days later, the new nurse of Letuchka No. 2 was shocked by a colossal influx of seriously wounded men after Russian 3rd Army was cut to pieces and 61st Division – to which the *letuchka* was attached – lost many thousands of men. By the end of April the reality of a combat nurse's exhausting life had sunk in:

We were called from our beds before dawn on Saturday 1 May. The Germans had launched their offensive. Explosion after explosion rent the air. Shells and shrapnel fell all around. Our house shook to its very foundations. Death was very busy, his hands full of victims. Then the victims started to arrive until we were overwhelmed by their numbers. They came in their hundreds from all directions, some able to walk, others dragging themselves along the ground. We worked day and night. The thunder of the guns never ceased. Soon shells were exploding all around our unit. The stream of wounded was endless. We dressed their severe wounds where they lay on the open ground, first alleviating their pain by injections. On Sunday the terrible word retreat was heard. In that one word lies all the agony of the last few days. The first line troops came into sight: a long procession of dirt-bespattered, weary, desperate men. Orders: we were to head east without delay, leaving behind all the wounded and the unit's equipment! '*Skoro, skoro!* Quickly! The Germans are outside the town!'[76]

Again and again, the surgeon, orderlies and nurses of Letuchka No. 2 fled eastwards out of towns and villages as the German spearheads entered them from the west. The arrival of a Cossack despatch-rider on his mud-flecked pony brought an order to pack up the instruments and tents if there was still time, always to head further east. Sleep-deprived, the nurses nodded off to get whatever rest they could in the jolting horse-drawn carts bumping over unmade roads. This was the Great Retreat of 1915. The joint German–Austrian attack continued its momentum, driving the Russian forces back to the river San just over a week after that. By the end of the month, the front had shifted more than 100 miles to the east. Knox also noted in his diary that the field hospitals were so overloaded with wounded men that most had to be left lying on stretchers or the ground outside, exposed to the weather.

By 15 June Letuchka No. 2 had moved so many times as the front collapsed that it was back inside Russia, but the retreat was not over yet. Asleep on their feet, the nursing sisters collected up all the equipment and packed again and again as the temporary haven of care for the suffering where they had worked the previous day fell into the hands of the enemy. Bumping along the bad roads in unsprung carts, two of the nurses were ill – partly, Florence thought, from the sustained anxiety. Trying at night to sleep on a carpet of pine needles in the forest, she heard the nurse lying beside her crying quietly. When dawn came, they merged again into the stream of humans and animals, all moving eastwards. Entire herds of cattle were being driven by their owners, as were droves of sheep and pigs. And always behind them black clouds of smoke rose into the sky as the scorched earth policy that had been used against Napoleon's Grande Armée a century before required all the peasants' hayricks and barns full of straw to be fired in order to deny them to the enemy. She wrote:

It was said that the Cossacks had received orders to force all the inhabitants to leave their homes so they could not act as spies. In order that the enemy should encounter widespread devastation, the homesteads were set on fire

The great retreat of 1915.

and crops destroyed. The peasants were heart-rending. They took what [livestock] they could with them but before long the animals' strength gave out and we would see panting, dying creatures by the roadside, unable to go any farther. One woman, with a sleeping infant in her arms, was bowed almost double by a large wicker basket containing poultry, which was strapped to her back. Sometimes a cart had broken down and the family, bewildered and frightened, chose to remain with their precious possessions, until they too were driven onwards by the threatening knout of the Cossack or the more terrifying prospect of the proximity of the enemy.[77]

Further north, near Lublin in the Warsaw Salient, 5,000 Cossack cavalry and Russian artillery wiped out two crack Austrian cavalry regiments, mostly killed in medieval manner by sabre or lance. Knox described one Austrian officer taken prisoner after having the whole of his lower jaw carried away on the point of a lance.

Like all fit Czech men of military age, Joseph Bumby was conscripted into the Austro-Hungarian armed forces – in his case on 2 August 1914 in the Bohemian town of Kroměříž. Transported in a cattle wagon to a position south of the salient, Bumby described in his diary his officers trying to find the regiment's designated position, which turned out to be just a few hovels to accommodate several hundred men – a confusion familiar to the Russian soldiers facing them.

At Kielce, midway between Warsaw and Kraków, the regiment was dug in when attacked by Cossack [cavalry]. We had to attack a burning town and run the gauntlet in crossing a bridge 150 feet long over the river under intensive shrapnel bursts. The bridge was blown up. Men died around me. We slept that night on the ground under a cold rain. After lunch we had to retreat to a village with three churches.[78]

We asked the [Polish] peasants for wood to make a fire and dry our clothes. They wouldn't give it, so we broke down their fence and burned that. We bought some milk and eggs, so that was okay. One night we slept in a school, on the benches or under them. Alcohol was forbidden us in Russia, but we found vodka the Cossacks had left in the cellar, and drank that. But we didn't have any bread, nor did the local people. There was no field kitchen, so we killed some geese with sabres, for which the peasants wanted us to pay.[79]

Bumby later described his capture as follows:

> I was left alone in front of the Russian trenches with six dead men on my
> left and the forest on my right. The Russians were 200 paces behind me
> when I was shot in the neck. In the evening when the firing died down,
> some Russian soldiers came close and called out to me. One escorted me
> to a house in the village of Něgartova where they gave me bread, tea and
> cigarettes, but they stole my gloves and some canned goods I had. Then
> they gave me some straw to sleep on.[80]

Prisoners always recall the first night in captivity, after which it all becomes
a blur. Further north again, on 7 July Russian forces took thousands
of POWs on the northern front and pressed on to take the key fortresses at Königsberg and Allenstein before being driven back. Florence
Farmborough's mobile surgical unit was then attached to 5th Caucasian
Infantry Corps on this front. Her diary records that, of 25,000 men originally in the corps, only 2,000 had survived so far.[81]

To the Russian General Staff the Warsaw salient of occupied Poland
was of double strategic importance. The western extremity of the salient lay only 200 miles from Berlin and its northern border was a mere
fifty miles from the Baltic coastline, theoretically offering the possibility
of a swift drive to cut off the German garrisons of East Prussia from
reinforcement by land, forcing them to surrender. Yet, the salient was
itself vulnerable to the German forces in East Prussia to the north and
Austro-Hungarian forces in Polish Galicia to the south, which would
trap tens of thousands of Russian troops deployed there. Thus, on the
maps in Berlin, Vienna and Petrograd, the salient represented a threat
that needed to be dealt with at the outset. On the German side of the
lines, because of the priority given by OHL to the invasion of France,
only General Maximilian von Prittwitz's 8th Army was allotted for the
defence of East Prussia and had little chance of driving into the salient, where two-fifths of Russia's peacetime army was located around
Warsaw in Russian-occupied Poland, making the salient a huge reservoir
of men and materiel poised for action at short notice. Of these, roughly
half was allocated by Stavka for an attack on Austro-Hungarian forces
to the south because Plan 19A stationed just a holding force along the
East Prussian border to contain the German garrisons there while first

concentrating on destroying the Austro-Hungarian forces south of the salient, largely composed of men from vassal states who had no love for Emperor Franz Joseph, no loyalty to the government in Vienna and often no common language with their officers.

Knox recorded the start of the third battle for Warsaw in July. After a feint along the river Vistula, the Germans opened up a hurricane barrage on 12 July, which showed that they had no shortage of shells. The weather had been dry and the dirt roads were at their best, so one corps of Russian 1st Army had to oppose forty-two large-calibre enemy guns with only two of its own, with the result that an entire Siberian division was wiped out amid widespread panic. When the German infantry attack came in on 13 July, the Russian troops withdrew from the front line without pausing to defend a second defensive line that had been prepared. The majority of Russian conscripts being of peasant origin, when retreating, they routinely implemented the scorched earth edict by driving off live-stock instead of slaughtering them, also looting other possessions from civilians. This slowed down their retreat, with the result this time that German cavalry caught up with them and broke through in the centre of the line, attacking the slow-moving and vulnerable transport columns. The term 'scorched earth' itself requires clarification. It seems that poor peasants lost everything, as did the Jews. But noble estates belonging to rich Polish landowners who had connections with German, Austrian and Russian high commands, could 'arrange' for their lands and property to be left intact.[82]

By the time Warsaw fell to General Mackensen on 4 August, Russian losses in the war totalled 1.4 million casualties with nearly a million officers and men taken prisoner. What Russians called 'the black summer' continued, but the German advance – in places up to 125 miles from the nearest railhead – was fraught with problems. Cavalry commanders complained that fodder for horses was impossible to obtain in sufficient quantity. Worse still, as they drove through primeval forest and hit the Pripyat marshes, there was ironically no drinkable water for men or horses until it had been boiled.

There was already trouble brewing in the subject nations on both sides of the battle lines. A Czech independence faction wanted to use the war to break away from Austrian domination. The Slovaks wanted independence from Hungary. The Russian government was aware that the

Finns, Poles, Estonians, Latvians, Lithuanians, Ukrainians, as well as the Caucasian nations subdued in the nineteenth century, were all waiting for the right moment to escape from Russian hegemony. In a feeble attempt to purchase the loyalty of the vassal races, the tsarist government promised post-war reforms – which stopped short of independence – to the Baltic nations, the Finns, the Poles and Ukrainians – and to the Jews, although Nicholas was an unabashed anti-Semite.

Probably no one in Russia was aware on 30 September 1915 that an Estonian nationalist called Aleksander Kesküla had informed Berlin of the conditions under which Lenin would be prepared to sign a peace treaty with the Central Powers in the event of a revolution in Russia bringing the Bolsheviks to power. He relayed to Berlin Lenin's programme, which included Point 4 – 'Full autonomy for all nationalities of the Russian Empire' – and Point 7 – 'Russian troops to move into India, forcing Britain to withdraw troops from the Western Front for the defence of the Raj'. Whether the latter point was sincerely intended as a replay of the Great Game that tsarist agents had been playing for decades, or was simply included in the programme as bait to loosen the German purse strings, is unclear.

There has never been any proof that Kesküla was Lenin's agent, or that the two men ever met. It seems rather that Kesküla's motives were those of an Estonian nationalist, who foresaw that a Marxist revolution destroying the Russian Empire from within presented the best chance for his country to gain its independence during the resultant chaos. He may also have been influenced by Lenin's writings, which included mentions of national self-determination for the minorities of the Empire – a promise he never intended to fulfil.

Russian losses swiftly climbed to an estimated 3.8 million men killed, wounded and taken prisoner, although German C-in-C General Hindenburg later wrote:

In the Great War ledger the page on which the Russian losses were written had been torn out. No one knows the figure. Five millions or eight millions? We too have no idea. All we know is that sometimes in our battles with the Russians we had to remove the mounds of enemy corpses in order to get a clear field of fire against fresh assaulting waves.[83]

On the day following the Russian surrender of Warsaw to the Germans, Colonel Knox lunched about 1,000 yards from the firing line with the commander of the elite Preobrazhensky Guards Regiment, founded by Peter the Great. They ate from a camp table covered with a clean white cloth and all the officers seemed in excellent spirits. When Knox asked about strategy, one of them joked, 'We will retire to the Urals. When we get there, the enemy's pursuing army have dwindled to a single German and a single Austrian. The Austrian will, according to custom, give himself up as a prisoner, and we will kill the German.' There was laughter all round.[84]

Stavka was convinced that the hundreds of thousands of Poles, Czechs, Slovaks, Croatians and others Slav soldiers in Franz Joseph's armies would rather surrender to their brother Slavs in Russian uniform than fight and die in the service of their Austrian and Magyar overlords. Yet, the officers and senior NCOs of Austrian General Conrad's predominantly Slavic units were ordered to shoot any men preparing to give up without a fight – as did British and French NCOs and military police on the Western Front. Secondly, unless all the men in a particular group were agreed about surrendering, there was always the possibility of an informer giving away the plan. And what were their prospects, if they did surrender?

Ferdinand Filáček was an 18-year-old Czech metalworker from Litomyšl who was called up in August 1914. Arriving at the front in mid-November, he was taken prisoner near Novi Sad on 5 December. It is true that he was temporarily out of danger, but the next year was spent in three different POW camps, ending at Semipalatinsk (now Semeï in Kazakhstan), a sparsely inhabited area 2,000 miles east of Moscow, where the Soviet Union would explode hundreds of nuclear devices during the Cold War.[85] At his second camp, he crossed paths with another Czech, František Tomek, who wrote in a letter home much later:

Dear friends, dear sisters and brothers!
It was 30 July 1914 when I left home, as they said, to fight for the emperor and my country. I reported to my military unit, Č.K. Infantry Regiment No. 21 in Čáslav. Fortunately, I was posted to the Russian front and not Serbian, where I was originally supposed to go. I will not recount the hardships of war, for I have decided not to remember evil things. On

3 November I was happy to be taken prisoner. The first Circassian soldier I saw did indeed want to kill me, but the second was a friendly Cossack, who saved me and took me to the prisoner assembly point, where we were about a hundred in total. As he was leading us to the rear, a general kindly waved his hand and called 'Bohemia, Bohemia!' [This was a Czech independence slogan.] A band played Czech marches and we cheered him. For some days we were marched around Galicia before being transported to Kiev. On the twenty-first day of captivity we arrived in Novo-Nikolayevsk in Central Siberia, on the river Ob.

We were marched for the best part of an hour through the night out of the city and up a hill where there was *voyenny gorodok* – a military camp. The snow was already about one meter deep and still falling [but we consoled] ourselves that we should be staying in what we thought were empty barracks. No such luck! Marched through a gate into the forest, we found ourselves staring at dugouts with steps leading down into the earth and some smoke coming out of a hole – except it was not smoke, but steam from men's bodies.

Our quarters were in a dugout eight or nine metres across, with plank-lined walls and a roof which rose only half a meter above the ground, with small windows just below the eaves, all covered with snow. There was no floor, so our feet sank into the mud floor and the foul air was almost unbreathable. At the entrance hung a small kerosene lamp, by the light of which I made out three-tier bunks occupied by POWs, which took up so much floor space that there was hardly room for two men to squeeze past each other between them. As late-comers, we had to take the top bunks, climbing up makeshift ladders to get there. Up there the smell was worse and occasional drops of melting snow fell from the roof.

I lay down on a filthy bunk, using my cap as a pillow and wondering what to do. A batch of Czechs was already there and one of them told us that the dugout camp held 3,000 POWs – Czechs, Germans, Turks, Hungarians, Bosnians and Croats, all in dirty rags, sick and ill, but segregated by nationality.[86]

In some POW camps, the death rate from malnutrition, exposure and disease – particularly typhoid fever – reportedly reached as high as 80 per cent until a tall, blonde, blue-eyed Swedish Red Cross worker named Elsa Brändström, who had been a volunteer nurse like Florence Farmborough, arrived with her friend Ethel von Heidenstam to organise medical supplies and food parcels. Nicknamed 'the angel of Siberia', she set up a Swedish Aid office in Petrograd, which the Bolsheviks shut down in 1917 – in the same way that they later refused free food shipments for the starving peasants from the American Relief Administration. Undeterred, Brändström managed to return to Siberia in 1919 and 1920, when she was arrested in Omsk and finally expelled from Russia. Lecture tours in America and elsewhere on her experiences and the suffering of the POWs enabled her to raise funds to establish a home for 200 German and Austrian children whose fathers were dead or too traumatised by the war to provide for them.

Some of the Austro-Hungarian POWs were not even in camps, but lodged with Cossack families, like Joseph Bumby, who described the extremely primitive conditions of his accommodation:

The house was a single room, half dug into the ground [for insulation in winter]. The owners kept livestock in the house, so everyone was lousy. The only 'luxury' was the *krasny ugol* or 'beautiful corner', where the icon was kept. The bench and table were never washed, but scraped clean with a knife every Saturday. When the pig had to be killed, we POWs butchered it. Because our hosts did not eat offal, they let us make sausages out of the guts, which we ate with other POWs. One Cossack had taken a Kirghiz wife, which was a sort of custom, so one of our men 'bought a bride' for sixty roubles.[87]

Travelling about the fronts during the Great Retreat of 1915, Knox noted how the common soldiery was exhausted from retreating every night and digging trenches in the morning, only to be shelled in the afternoon by artillery to which the Russian guns could not reply, for lack of ammunition. The 'Official Summary of Operations' on 14 August reported an attack on 76th Division north of the Warsaw-Byalistok railway, where the Russian artillery, owing to a shortage of shells, was unable to develop a sufficiently intense fire to stop the enemy's continuous attacks.

Noting the pathetic mass of fugitives heading east that blocked all the roads as the Russian troops withdrew, he was told that they were not ordered to leave their homes unless their villages were likely to be the scene of fighting. But with all cattle, horses, bacon, tea and sugar already requisitioned or stolen by the retreating soldiers, it was impossible for the peasants to remain. The sheer numbers involved made it difficult for the remaining civilian authorities to make provisions for what amounted to migration on a national scale. There were no trains running in this area. Even if there had been, they would have been of no use to the peasants, who transported as much of their property as they were able to load on long Polish wagons drawn by two horses. The father drove and the mother had to sit on top of the family's belongings with the younger children, while older sons and daughters drove the family's flock of geese or several pigs along the roadside.

Somewhere near a village called Byelsk, Knox noted 20 miles of these wagons, nose to tail. Many families had been on the road for a month and had no idea where they were heading, except that it was away from the fighting. The Russian Red Cross staffed feeding stations at intervals to serve the refugees tea and bread free of charge, and most Russian soldiers treated them kindly enough. Knox noted one Polish peasant driving a cart on which lay the body of his wife, who had died of exposure, with her children lying on the bundles beside her. The father said he would keep going like this until reaching a Catholic cemetery, where he could bury his wife's corpse. Knox concluded:

> It will never be known how many of these poor people died on their pilgrimage along roads studded every few hundred yards with rough crosses to mark the mass graves where cholera victims had been hastily buried.[88]

The refugees had a touching faith that their Russian brothers would at least not let them starve, but this was far from sure. Already in the main cities the first tremors of revolution were being felt and, the longer the war continued, the more powerful these became, with many middle-class members of the State Duma voicing wishes to curb the Tsar's powers radically. There was even a party calling itself the Constitutional Democrats, which wanted to reduce him to the role of a figurehead. Some industrialists resented the government ordering from abroad materiel that they wanted to manufacture, but many whose factories were making munitions put prices up by 100 per cent or more and cheated on the explosives, so that many shells failed to explode and cartridges could not be fired. Some even used the considerable advances paid on contracts for speculative investment instead of purchasing the raw materials and paying the workforce. With the currency plummeting in value, inflation was biting hard, especially in food prices, but wages had not been increased to keep pace and the influx of hundreds of thousands of refugees from the west was placing intolerable strain on the faltering economy.

10

LETTERS FROM HELL

Russia's frontiers were dotted with strategically sited fortress cities, but this was an outdated concept that immobilised artillery which could have been better employed elsewhere. Despite the best efforts of War Minister Vladimir Sukhomlinov, the inertia of senior officers prevented him from freeing much of this artillery from its static role in the fortresses. In 1915 his thinking was proven right, as Warsaw, Przemyśl, Grodno and even Brest-Litovsk either surrendered or were abandoned to the enemy, with the loss of most of their guns and millions of rounds of ammunition of all calibres.[89]

On the Russian northern front, the fortress-city of Kovno[90] was supposed to block any German advance through the Baltic provinces. Its commander, 70-year-old General Vladimir Grigoriev, commanded 90,000 officers and men in a complex of walled citadel and outlying forts with interlocking fields of fire spread out at a radius of eight miles from the city centre. Grigoriev was a prime example of the appointment of Russian officers on grounds of birth and not military competence. On the morning of 15 August 1915 German forces took the south-western outworks. That night, they stormed the forts in this sector, but were driven back. Russian reinforcements began to arrive and were immediately sent into action but, once the outworks were abandoned, the concentrated fire of the enemy's artillery proved too much for the nerves of the half-trained and badly led defenders.

On 16 August the Germans captured the major fort in the south-western sector, and broke through between two other forts, attacking them from their unprotected rear. In the confusion, some of the forts fired on their neighbours under attack, aiding the Germans.[91] At the very beginning of the attack, Grigoriev had created a panic by telling officers who had no intention of running away that the first man to bolt would be shot. Yet, on 17 August, accompanied only by a priest, he left by car for Vilna without telling his chief of staff, so no one knew for some hours that he had gone. By 18 August it was all over, the last defenders literally running or galloping away, to save their lives. A survivor whom Colonel Knox met afterwards informed him that Kovno, although fortified at a cost of millions of dollars in today's money and having many guns and adequate supply of shells, was simply not constructed to resist modern artillery because the only concrete bunker was Grigoriev's personal quarters.

In the headlong flight of the garrison, stores had not been destroyed, permitting the Germans to capture not only 1,300 guns, 53,000 rounds of large shell and 800,000 rounds of light shell, but also millions of cans of preserved meat, which provisioned their operations for the following month. Grigoriev was placed under arrest by Grand Duke Nikolai, court-martialled and sentenced to eight years in prison. Among his many shortcomings was the failure to order the demolition of the railway tunnel east of Kovno, which greatly facilitated General Ludendorff's drive to capture the Baltic ports.[92]

Just when one would think things at the top could not get worse, they did. On 23 August the Tsar sent Grand Duke Nikolai off to command the Caucasus front, appointing himself C-in-C of all the Russian armies. Some said the grand duke had been sacked because the monk Rasputin persuaded the Tsarina, who in turn persuaded her husband to get rid of his uncle. It was a fatal error. Nicholas' idea of raising morale was to visit troops and confine himself to frigidly holding aloft a holy icon, before which the soldiers knelt to receive his blessing, while being asperged with holy water by a priest before advancing to their deaths. The generals at Stavka were appalled because the Tsar was extremely indecisive and ignorant of, and totally uninterested in, all things military. As C-in-C, his 'management style' was to sit in on the planning meetings of Stavka, but leave without saying a word for or against what was being discussed, leaving only confusion in the minds of the generals as to what he wanted or did not want done.

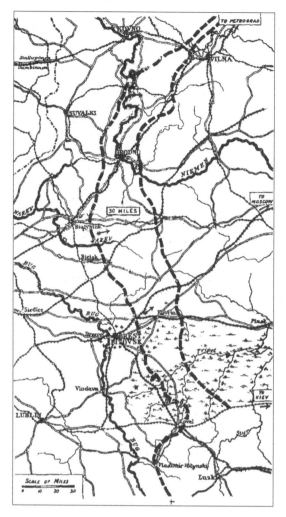

The great retreat after Kovno – a contemporary map with anglicised place names.

By the end of 1915, the Russian lines had been shortened by the loss of the Warsaw salient, making re-supply easier, and the German and Austrian high commands were hesitant to advance too far into the Russian winter, which had been Napoleon's mistake and would be Hitler's. At that point, combat deaths of Russian infantry officers had reduced their number to between 12 and 20 per cent of nominal strength and deaths of other ranks were even higher. Knox calculated that the shortfall in manpower was almost irrelevant because, even had *trained* replacements been available, there were no fresh weapons with which to arm them.

When the Germans on the Western Front began their massive attack on Verdun in February 1916 the French high command requested Stavka to attack again the German positions in East Prussia to prevent troops being moved from there to Verdun. In the area of Lake Narotch[93] the German line was held by General Hermann von Eichhorn's 75,000-strong 10th Army facing two Russian armies totalling 350,000 men commanded by Gen Alexei Kuropatkin. His appalling performance in the war with Japan when, as C-in-C Far East, he had been unable to control Samsonov and von Rennenkampf, had decided Grand Duke Nikolai to refuse him any appointment, but Nicholas II overruled that decision when he replaced his uncle. On 17 March, Kuropatkin's 2nd Army launched its attack to relieve Verdun after two days of ineffective shelling that did little damage on the German side, with the result that the advancing Russian infantry were mown down by well-sited machine guns. The 100,000 Russian casualties included 10,000 men who died of exposure in open trenches. Further south, after one Austrian retreat, Florence Farmborough wrote in her diary:

> One of our transport bosses offered to drive us over to see the deserted Austrian dugouts. One excelled all others in luxury and cosiness. We decided it must have belonged to an artillery officer. It contained tables, chairs, pictures on the armoured walls and books; there was even an English grammar. We toured some of the smaller trenches. These too were amazingly well constructed. I thought of the shallow ditches with which our soldiers had to be content. Even their most comfortable dugouts were but hovels compared with these.[95]

Britain's senior general of the Second World War Sir Bernard Montgomery approved only one Russian general in the tsarist forces. This was Alexei Brusilov, who minimised casualties by making his men dig in properly and undergo specific training for each attack, with full-scale models of the objective. He brought in foreign artillery experts to make his barrages more effective, used cover when available instead of marching men openly across no man's land, where they were mown down in their thousands by machine guns, mortars and artillery. He also employed deception and might have driven his southwestern front forces through the Carpathians all the way to Budapest, had not the army commanders on his flanks refused to support him.[95]

The *gorodskaya duma* – town council – of the Siberian city of Omsk has preserved a fascinating archive of locally conscripted soldiers' letters home from the fronts 2,000 miles away.[96] Many are addressed to the Duma, thanking it for a parcel of what were called in the West 'soldiers' comforts': soap, underpants and vests, tobacco and cigarette paper, needles and thread, writing paper on which the literate could write home. Spoons were another item 'without which one can starve here' as one soldier wrote. Pre-printed cards for the illiterate contained the lines 'I am well/ wounded. I hope you are well. Please send me ...' followed by a long wish list.

The preserved letters also describe the war as seen from the common soldier's viewpoint. On 14 December 1914, machine-gunner S. Gordienko wrote to his family in Omsk: 'Intensive battle. We were sent into action ten times and could not even get a smoke for several days.' Early in 1915 another man asked the Omsk Duma to send to his field postal address: 'a 14-row button accordion because it is spring here and all nature rejoices and we wish to cheer our souls also'. Sentiments were simply, often frigidly, expressed, perhaps because dictated to a literate comrade, like this: 'Hallo, dear wife, receive my Easter greetings. This is to tell you that I received the parcel you sent last December.' On 28 March 1915 rifleman Mikhail Nikiforov wrote: 'Thank you, dear father, mother, brothers and sisters for your valuable gifts. We wish you good health and long life.' Pyotr Dopgayev of 43rd Siberian Infantry Regiment wrote back to the Duma in Omsk during Easter 1915: 'Thank you for the parcel with shirts and cigarettes. We have been at the front for nine months.' A comrade added: 'We are willing to spend our lives for the Motherland and the Tsar but we do not forget you at home.' Viktor Zhanzharov wrote on 29 March 1915: 'Received your gifts. Thank you for not forgetting us. We have now pushed the enemy back [roughly 100 miles].' Literate soldiers wrote at greater length, as in this exchange:

Hallo, dear comrade Fedya!
I write in reply to yours of 14 January. Has Misha been killed? I was in a battle where bullets cut down my comrades, in front, behind, to right and left. The ranks of my friends and comrades are continually thinning, until there comes that second when a bullet or piece of shrapnel ... Samin has been wounded by shrapnel in the leg and is in hospital in Petrograd. I do

not know if he has broken a bone. In battle, bullets punctured my mess-tin and my kit-bag. I had taken cover with kit-bag and mess-tin on my back. My spine is okay but I was wounded in two places. Our old commander was killed at Soldau.[97]

The reply, written on 25 February 1915 from the northern front was:

Hallo, friend of Fedya!
Best wishes for Easter. I wish all of you can spend this holiday in good health, but must inform you that I have been wounded in a battle between Przasnysz and Mlave. In seven battles I was okay, but had to pay the price in the eighth. From 1 February to 18 February we were in action all the time. The big battle was on 2 February, when we lost 90 out of 240 men. On 11 February we attacked a village and gave the Germans hell, but I was wounded by grenade fragments in right side of body – ear, temple, cheek, upper lip, shoulder and bones of middle finger on right hand broken. Small splinters the size of a pinhead got in left eyebrow and right eyelid. If you are writing home at Easter, pass on the news of what has happened to me. I am temporarily in hospital at Vitebsk.[97]

Another soldier wrote to his younger brother at home:

Dear Shura,
I asked you to send tobacco and cigarette papers. It would be nice if you enclosed some Siberian canned goods also. Maybe I am not going to come back alive, but all is in the hands of God. I am living in a tent in the forest with combat all around against Germans and Austrians. Many prisoners. There are no civilians here because the Austrians took them as forced labour. We had an air raid the other day – thirty-two aircraft. Above our heads now is an aerial battle. Our planes are being attacked by five Austrian bandits. The other day one of their planes killed several of our horses and one man. So far I am in good health.[98]

How long Shura's brother stayed healthy, we do not know. A new menace was threatening the Tsar's armies. On one day in June 1915 the Germans introduced a new weapon into the war in the east when 13,000 cylinders of chlorine gas were released against the Russian lines, killing thousands of men whose gas masks were stored hundreds of miles away in Warsaw and never were distributed to combat troops. Perhaps it was fortunate that the common soldiers had no idea that Brusilov's worst problem was not logistics, nor even the enemy forces ranged against him but his fellow commanders, as recorded in his memoirs:

> By noon on 10 June 1916 we had taken [Brusilov lists prisoners, weapons captured and booty]. At this stage I was called to the telephone for a somewhat unpleasant conversation with [Stavka] to the effect that [neighbouring Gen] Evert would not attack on 14 June [as agreed in support of Brusilov's advance] because of bad weather, which made the ground too soft, but would postpone his advance until 18 June. If ordered to attack, he would do so, but without any chance of success. He had requested the Tsar's permission to change the focus of this attack and the Tsar had given his consent.
>
> I told [General Mikhail V.] Alexeyev [the senior general at Stavka] that this was exactly what I had feared. Even an unsuccessful attack on the other fronts would immobilise enemy forces that could be used against me, whereas the failure of [generals] Evert and Kuropatkin to attack at all left the enemy free to move forces from their sectors. I therefore requested that the Tsar review his decision. Alekseyev replied that it was not possible to question a decision of the Tsar, but Stavka would send me two additional army corps as compensation. I said that moving two corps with all their logistics and support on our inadequate railways would give the enemy, on his far more efficient rail system, time to move not two, but ten, corps against me. I knew very well that the Tsar was neither here nor there in this matter, since he understood little of military affairs, but rather that Alekseyev, who had been subordinate to Kuropatkin and Evert in the Russo-Japanese war, knew exactly what was going on, and was covering up for them.
>
> General Alexandr Ragoza, who had been my subordinate in both peacetime and war, told me afterwards that he had personally gone to Evert at this time to inform him that his attack was well prepared, had sufficient resources to succeed, and that delay would affect his men's morale adversely. He requested permission to make a report to this effect for forwarding to the Tsar. Evert at first agreed, then refused to forward the report. Ragoza believed that Evert's motive for repeatedly postponing his

attack was jealousy of the success of my offensive and fear of being shown up by me.[99]

In the Carpathians, combat was complicated by having men from the same ethnicities on both sides. The diary of an unnamed Austrian lieutenant had the following entry for 17 November:

Sergeant Corusa reported some thirty Russians in front of our line, who called out, in German and Hungarian, 'Cease fire!' At this double command, fifty of our men left their shelter behind the trees. The Russians opened rapid fire on our poor simpletons and then bolted. Hardly fifteen men came back untouched. Poor Michaelis, the bookseller, hit in the left shoulder by a bullet which came out the other side, was killed and buried there. A Romanian stretcher-bearer laid him on straw at the bottom of a trench and recited a paternoster over him. Two of the other officers had been seriously wounded, so I was the only one left, out of all those who had left Fagaras [modern Făgăraş in Romania] with the battalion.

In the afternoon I took fifty men to hold a slope covered with juniper trees. The men hastily dug trenches, and I made a shelter of boughs. There was no question of lighting fires, so when it snowed once more, everything was wrapped in a mantle of snow. In the evening, when I went to inspect the men lying in their coffin-shaped scrapes covered with juniper branches, they looked to me as if they had been buried alive. Those poor Romanians![100]

The diary entry for 20 November describes officers and men delousing themselves:

Issued with winter underclothes and defying the cold, the men lost no time in undressing to change their linen. I saw human bodies which were nothing but one great sore from the neck to the waist. They were absolutely eaten up with lice. For the first time I really understood the popular curse, 'May the lice eat you!'

One of the men, when he pulled off his shirt, tore away crusts of dried blood, and the vermin were swarming in filthy layers in the garment. The poor peasant had grown thin on this, with projecting jaw and sunken eyes.[101]

The point of including here the excerpt from the Austrian lieutenant's diary is that conditions were at least as bad for the men in Russian uniform they were trying to kill, or were being killed by. Visibility was so reduced in the Carpathian Mountains by juniper bushes growing thickly everywhere that the lieutenant's detachment had to fire blind through the undergrowth whenever they heard what appeared to be enemy movement. When the lieutenant went to reconnoitre one suspected enemy position, he narrowly missed being shot by a 300-strong battalion of his own infantry. Although the enemy was only thirty paces distant, the undergrowth was so thick that nothing could be seen of them. He wrote:

> Private Torna came to our shelter to announce, 'Sir, the Russians are breaking through our line on the top of the hill!' I asked my friend Lt Fothi to take command in the trenches, pulled on my boots, took my rifle, and ran to the edge of the woods. I could hardly believe my eyes. Along the whole company front, men in Russian uniform and some of our men were threatening each other with fixed bayonets and, in places, firing at each other. In one place, some Russians [sic] and some of our men were wrestling on the ground to get at a supply of bread intended for 12th Company. This struggle of starving animals for food only lasted a few seconds until they stood up, each man having at least a fragment of bread, which he devoured voraciously. This is how bread reconciles men even on the field of battle, when they make peace to get a scrap of bread.[102]

An hour later, a group of men in Russian uniform appeared 200 paces away on the edge of the woods with rifles shouldered, beckoning the lieutenant's men to approach. A squad of twenty men under a sergeant major was ordered to surround the Russians with fixed bayonets and bring them in. The Austrian lieutenant's diary continues:

> I clambered over the body of a man whose brains were sticking out of his head, and signed to them to surrender, but they still called to us without attempting to move. I thereupon gave the order, 'Fire!' and held my own rifle at the ready. At this point my Romanians refused to fire, and, what was more, prevented me from firing also. One of them put his hand on my rifle and said, 'Don't fire, sir. If we fire, they will fire too. And why should

Romanians kill Romanians?' He meant that those men were from Russian Bessarabia [and spoke a dialect of Romanian].

I tried to make my way towards them but two of my men barred my way, exclaiming, 'Don't go and get yourself shot!' It was incredible. Our men were advancing towards the enemy with their arms shouldered, and were shaking their hands. It was a touching sight. I saw one of my Romanians kiss a man in Russian uniform and lead him back to our lines. Their arms were round each other's necks, like brothers. It turned out they had been shepherd boys together in Bessarabia. We took ninety Russians [sic] as prisoners in this way; whilst they took thirty of our men off with them.[102]

That inconclusive day was considered a victory because the company had prevented the Russian troops from outflanking their positions. So men who had distinguished themselves all received the second-class medal for valour. Three officers, including the writer of the diary were also awarded the Signum Laudis bar. After that, they marched through thick forest to divisional HQ at Hocra, the winter conditions making it a different hell. By the time they arrived late at night, company strength had dwindled to a quarter of what it had been at the start of the march. Even some of the veterans dropped out, weeping from exhaustion, and were abandoned en route. It was, as the lieutenant said, by the mercy of God if they survived the freezing night and the wolves in the forest.

The company was dissolved after having been reduced to the strength of a platoon. On 27 November the survivors left Havaj early, but marching was difficult, for the men were worn out and the lieutenant admitted to being 'nothing but a shadow'. During one halt, Austrian bureaucracy caught up with these exhausted men, who were required to make a full return of all missing kit. This was a nonsense for men whose uniforms were in rags, and filthy, with lice swarming all over them. Most of them were fighting in the snow-covered forest without boots, and had wrapped rags around their tattered socks to avoid losing their feet to frostbite.

At midday the lieutenant and his men set off again up a forested hill badly cratered by Russian artillery, with shells of all calibres falling thick and fast and machine gun bullets penetrating the undergrowth from hidden positions. At the top of the hill, the unit came under the orders of a colonel, who ordered several men to take a house about 1,000m behind the Russian front line, saying that they would be shot if they returned, having failed in the mission. They realised that he had gone mad, but the men obeyed and few returned.

Throughout that winter, the senseless killing ground on and on. Men on sentry duty had to be relieved every two hours on account of the bitter cold. By the end of November, of all the officers in the battalion only the sub-lieutenant and the surgeon were left; of the 3,500 men on the original roll call a mere 170 remained. Of the sub-lieutenant's company, which had been 267 strong, only 6 now survived. A bag of bones shaking with fever, he was given permission for convalescent leave, said farewell to his last few men and had to walk for two whole days to reach a town, from where he was driven to the railhead and caught the last train to Budapest. He ends his diary, 'God had willed that I should return alive.'[103]

Even when they did eventually get word, 'news from home' was unlikely to motivate the average Russian conscript. The seeds of rebellion were already germinating as the New Year of 1917 dawned. Lenin was still in Switzerland and Trotsky was held in a POW camp at Amherst in Nova Scotia, where he was making a nuisance of himself with the other prisoners and the personnel, after being forcibly removed from the Norwegian ship *Kristianiafjord* bringing him back to Europe from New York, where he and his family had been living on 164th Street in a walk-up apartment costing $18 per month. He was still in the camp, on the wrong side of the Atlantic, when soldiers sent to restore order in Petrograd joined forces with the rioters in the streets and occupied the Duma building on 26 February 1917. Throughout the vast Russian Empire, just about every commodity was either in short supply or impossible to obtain; even basic food had to be queued for. Hundreds of thousands of homeless refugees from territories captured by the Central Powers added to the strain on the system. Inflation mounted; wages did not. The troops' dissatisfaction with the many obviously incompetent generals led to massive desertion and open mutinies at the front. At home, strikes – particularly in the war industries – became increasingly disruptive.

The Duma warned Nicholas II that society was collapsing and advised him swiftly to form a constitutional government, as was done on paper after the 1905 revolution, but Nicholas had recently discovered dominoes and was currently devoting more time to mastering the intricacies of the various games one can play with them than to the war or affairs of state. The Tsarina Alexandra was in deep mourning for Rasputin, who had been assassinated rather messily in December by a cabal of nobles, determined to rid the court of his defeatist influence on the German-born Tsarina. In between visits to his tomb, constructed at her command in the royal village of Tsarskoye Selo, she blamed the social unrest on the rabble in the streets and the politicians in the Duma, advising her husband by letter that the workers would go obediently back into the factories, if he threatened to send every striker to the front. With desertion from the Russian fronts running at the rate of 30,000-plus every month, or 333,000 men in one year, this was hardly useful advice.

As to the lives of the predominantly peasant population of eastern Poland and the Bukovina, fought over for the second or third time in this war with all the men of military age conscripted by one side or the other, the suffering of the women, children and the elderly defies even imagination. Successful Brusilov's 1916 offensive undoubtedly was in military terms, but with Russian losses in the war so far amounting to 5.2 million dead, wounded and captured, even the long-suffering subjects of Tsar Nicholas II were aghast at the scale of fatalities. Bereaved families from the Baltic Sea to the Pacific Ocean and from the White Sea to the Caucasus mourned the loss of fathers, sons, brothers, uncles and cousins.

Despite all its other concerns, the provisional government allowed the Petrograd Soviet to bully it into protesting to the British government at the detention of Trotsky in Canada because of his many speeches and writings against the war effort, with the result that he was taken out of the camp, reunited with his wife Natalya and their sons – all the family being put aboard the SS *Helig Olaf* to continue the journey to Russia. As the ship pulled out of the port of Halifax, Nova Scotia, Trotsky was seen shaking his fists at British officers on the dockside and cursing England, which he blamed for making him late for the revolution. Having no further trouble while travelling through Sweden and Finland, he eventually arrived on 4 May – one month after Lenin's return – at Petrograd's Finland station, to be given a hero's welcome from revolutionary socialists of several hues, impressed by his history of heading the Petrograd Soviet during the 1905 revolution, his prison sentences, periods of internal exile and his record of relentless writing and speaking during the years of exile in Western Europe. Only the Bolsheviks regarded his return warily, perhaps with the exception of Lev Kamenev, married to Trotsky's sister Olga. A less arrogant personality would have felt his political way cautiously after being away so long but, as historian Robert Service commented, Trotsky was 'thirty-eight years old and brimmed with energy and self-belief. He felt he was coming back to fulfil his destiny.'[104] He also had the advantage of the long absence allowing him to step down from the train at the Finland Station and voice the same ideas he had promoted twelve years before – many of which had meantime become Bolshevik Central Committee policy. While he and Natalya threw themselves into the daily hurly-burly of revolutionary debate, at which Trotsky was a master, their sons Lëva and Sergei were welcomed by Trotsky's first wife Alexandra and her two daughters by their common father and spent the summer at the Finnish seaside resort of Terijoki, just like the sons of any bourgeois family from Petrograd, so their parents were not short of cash.

In the late spring of 1917 Florence Farmbrough's *letuchka* was posted to north-eastern Romania, where the villagers – all of whom kept some chickens – refused to sell them eggs. When they complained of this to a French-speaking Romanian officer, he told them politely enough that his own people had not enough food for themselves. So, the nurses were reduced to living on *kukuruza* – a gruel made from maize usually fed to ducks and chickens. Although Jews would rent them accommodation, the Romanian peasants refused to, on the grounds that Russian soldiers had regularly looted private property at gunpoint and had also broken into official food stores when their own supplies failed to arrive.

Managing to set up a dressing-station nevertheless, the nurses found two Russian female soldiers among their first batch of wounded. They belonged to the Women's Death Batallion, formed and commanded by an amazing woman called Maria Bochkaryova. After leaving two wife-beating husbands, she had been given the Tsar's personal permission to enlist in 25th Tomsk Reserve Battalion, where she defied abuse and harassment by her male comrades, fighting alongside her third husband until he was killed in Galicia. Appalled by the number of soldiers deserting on all the fronts, she had returned to Moscow with her slogan 'If the men will not fight for Russia, we women will'. Her original 2,000 volunteers were whittled down by harassment from their male comrades and also by the ferocious discipline Bochkaryova imposed. Finally, their numbers dwindled to a hard core of less than 300 fighting on the Galician and Romanian fronts. Both the women soldiers being treated for wounds by Letuchka No. 2 were, Florence noted, too shocked to say very much about their experiences in combat, but the driver of their ambulance cart said that the Women's Death Battalion had been 'very cut up' by the enemy. Nor were they the only women in combat in Romania, where some local women were fighting alongside their menfolk in the region of Ilişişti. Their wounded were also treated by the *letuchka* nurses.

The poverty of the Romanian peasants was epitomised when Florence, a keen photographer in her spare time, wanted to take the picture of a woman in traditional dress, who agreed to pose for her providing the family's most precious possessions – her husband's boots – could be prominent in the shot. The nurses' patients were not only adults of both sexes, but also young children, usually the victims of shrapnel bursts. Increasing numbers of unkempt and filthy Turkish prisoners of war were also brought in and cleaned up. Their wounds were dressed and they were given clean shirts and trousers. Even when the wounded being treated at the *letuchka* were deserters with obviously self-inflicted wounds, the nurses caring for them increasingly came in for verbal abuse from Russian mutineers, who were stirring up trouble among the Romanian soldiers. What she described as 'strange-looking men', some in uniform and some in civilian clothes, harangued large numbers of angry soldiers at unofficial meetings, making revolutionary speeches and urging them to desert in order to save their own lives. The revolution had caught up with the war.

At Stavka, Knox was told that the shortage of rifles and compatible ammunition was due to losses of weapons with men who had been taken prisoner, plus those wounded and killed during retreats. Yet, on several occasions he had seen perfectly serviceable rifles lying on battlefields three and four days after the fighting, with no attempt made to recover them. Other shortages included 500,000 missing pairs of boots, sorely needed by men in snow- or water-filled trenches during harsh winter weather. As early as December 1914 there had been instances of men shooting themselves in the leg or foot, who were helped back to the rear by an unnecessarily high number of 'carers'. Knox observed that when an Austrian attack was coming in, the local Polish peasants sat tight, but when the advancing troops were German, they fled eastwards towards Russia. What roads there were, were blocked with long columns of farm carts transporting families with all their moveable possessions. Old people, women and children huddled on top of their pitiful bundles, hungry and shivering in the cold and rain.

II

GOD HELP RUSSIA!

The name of the Russian capital had been changed at the start of the war from the Germanic Sankt Peterborg chosen by Peter the Great to the Russian form Petrograd, likewise meaning 'Peter's town' in honour of its founder. Whichever name was used, in the early months of 1917 discontent was mounting due to the capital's crippling shortages, with only one-third of the minimum supplies of food and fuel reaching the city. The 1916 harvest had been good, but nationwide chaos on the railways due to the armies' requisitioning of locomotives and rolling stock prevented food reaching the towns. In addition, inflation was running at 400 per cent since the summer of 1914. The Duma pleaded with Nicholas to release strategic stockpiles of food in government warehouses, which he refused to do, because the Tsarina informed him that there was nothing to worry about. The State Duma reconvened itself on 14 February under its chairman Mikhail V. Rodzianko. Apart from debating in the Tauride Palace the alarming deterioration of the political situation at home and the appalling news from the fronts, there was little it could do, having been repeatedly undermined by Nicholas and the Tsarina.

The largest employer in the city was the Putilov heavy engineering plant, which held the licence to produce the 150mm Schneider-Creusot howitzers, Austin armoured cars and many other foreign inventions desperately needed at the battlefronts. It should therefore have been running at a handsome profit, although when Duma-appointed administrators checked the books, they found the bank accounts empty, with two of the directors reputed to have fled to the Crimea or abroad after stealing a million roubles from the company. Thus, when on 18 February 1917 the 20,000 employees at the Putilov works demanded a wage rise in keeping with the inflation of food prices, the management's reply was a lockout, which in turn sparked strikes all over the city. By 22 February more than 100,000 workers were protesting in the streets of Petrograd. The next day was International Women's Day – 8 March according to the Gregorian calendar – and women from many other factories, whose conscripted husbands were at the front or among the 6 million casualties already suffered in the war, joined the strikers.

This spontaneous rebellion, known as the February Revolution, needed no coordinating committees or political prompting. A total of 500,000 protesters marched through the streets with poorly written, homemade banners demanding the backpay owing to soldiers at the fronts, increases in their wages and food for the children of these 'defenders of the motherland' fighting in Poland and Galicia. The rationing of bread inspired other banners demanding simply *Khleb i Mir* – bread and peace! It was a political snowball, with some groups of women actually demanding the same pay as men doing the same work.

General Sergei S. Khabalov, commander of the Petrograd Military District, was ordered by northern front commander Nikolai V. Ruszki to restore order by commanding garrison troops to shoot *into* the crowds of protestors. However, the 170,000 troops under his nominal command in the city were not the prestigious regiments whose names they bore, but in many cases only reserve companies made up of callow recruits without much training, commanded by wounded or sick officers, whom the Tsar actually referred to as 'the heap of invalids'. The first-rate troops already lay in their graves, far to the west. It was no surprise that, on the following day, these men refused to obey orders and instead joined the protestors as a sign of their own discontent. The morning of 27 February saw an open mutiny in 4th Company of the Pavlovsky Regiment, with men refusing to go on parade and shooting two of their officers. The mutiny spread to other regiments. Soldiers arrested or shot policemen. The guards at the Peter and Paul fortress surrendered to the rebels, who distributed thousands of rifles and ammunition from the arsenal to the demonstrators. By the end of the day, Gen Khabalov and other loyalist officers realised they had completely lost control of the city, with armed demonstrators and the political and criminal prisoners released from jail shooting down any loyal troops, police and private citizens in the streets who dared oppose them. Government buildings, including the headquarters of the Okhrana, had been set on fire and there was widespread looting of bakeries and other food shops and the nearly empty grain stores. Clashes broke out between police and loyal forces on the one side and armed students and mutinous soldiers on the other, who rounded up at gunpoint in the streets the Okhrana agents sent to arrest them, or shot them on the spot. This was open revolution, a state of anarchy that would claim more than 1,300 lives in the following few days.

Nicholas returned from the Alexander Palace in Tsarskoye Selo – the 'royal village' outside Petrograd – to Stavka at Mogilev, 500 miles to the south, more concerned about his children's measles and his own chest cold than what was happening in the capital. In a telegram to the Tsarina, he complained about having to forego his usual bedtime game of patience and told her that the foreign generals at dinner in headquarters with him had been so sorry to hear about the children's measles. In answer to her advice that he should be strong, he betrayed a catastophic failure to grasp the reality of the situation:

That is quite right. Be assured that I do not forget; but it is not necessary to snap at people right and left every minute. A quiet, caustic remark or answer is often quite sufficient to show a person his place.[106]

And that was written by the man who had appointed himself the supreme warlord of the Russian armies! In another letter dated 24 February, Nicholas wrote:

My brain is resting here. No Ministers, no troublesome questions demanding thought. I consider that this is good for me, but only for my brain. My heart is suffering from separation [from you]. I hate this separation, especially at such a time. I shall not be away long, [but] direct things as best I can here, and then my duty will be fulfilled.[107]

In the early hours of 25 February, he wrote:

Before going for a walk [in the morning] I shall go to the monastery and pray to the Holy Virgin for you and the children [with measles]. The last snowstorms, which ended yesterday, have put the armies in a critical position all along our southwestern railway lines. If the movement of trains is not restored at once, real famine will break out among the troops in 3-4 days. It is terrible. Good-bye, my love, my dear little wifey. May God bless you and the children!

Ever your most loving little husband, Nicky.

Any excuse Nicholas had for his ostrich posture vanished when he was advised of the seriousness of the political crisis in Petrograd by a telegram on 26 February from Duma Chairman Rodzianko – despised by Nicholas as 'that fat Rodzianko'. It included the words:

General discontent is growing. There must be a new government under someone trusted by the country. Any procrastination is tantamount to death.[108]

Deluded, Nicholas preferred to believe the Tsarina's totally erroneous advice that the Duma was overreacting, and therefore did not bother to reply to Rodzianko. With more and more previously uncommitted citizens sympathising with the demonstrations, most of the garrison, including the squadrons of mounted Cossacks formerly used to brutally suppress any civil disorder with whips and sabres, also mutinied. On the Nevsky Prospekt, Petrograd's main throughfare, tens of thousands of protestors paraded, packed shoulder to shoulder. Among the banners claiming bread and peace was always one reading simply '*Gazeta Pravda*' to advertise the Bolshevik newspaper. People were hacking tsarist symbols off buildings and tearing down national flags. Nicholas' telegram to the Tsarina that day read:

Yesterday I visited the ikon of the Holy Virgin and prayed fervently for you, my love, for the dear children, for our country, and also for Anna [Vyborova, the lady-in-waiting who was the Tsarina's closest friend]. Tell her that I have seen her brooch, pinned to the ikon, and touched it with my nose when kissing the image. This morning, during the service, I felt an excruciating pain in the chest, which lasted for a quarter of an hour. I could hardly last the service out, and my forehead was covered with drops of perspiration. I cannot understand what it could have been, because I had no palpitation of the heart; but later it disappeared, vanishing suddenly when I knelt before the image of the Holy Virgin.

I hope Khabalov will be able to stop these street disorders. Protopopov must give him clear and definite instructions.[109]

Alexander D. Protopopov was the syphilitic Interior Minister who, like the Tsarina, consulted the dead Rasputin in spiritualist séances for medical advice. During the prorogation of the Duma, and the Tsar's repeated absences when he was at Stavka, Protopopov had governed Russia as an unusual troika with the Tsarina and her intimate Anna Vyrobova – both women being acolytes of Rasputin until his murder in December.[110]

Khabalov had no chance of executing the Tsar's orders. On 25 February 1917 he had posters printed and displayed everywhere in Petrograd, warning people to keep off the streets on pain of death, but that Sunday crowds of demonstrators ventured forth, suffering 200 casualties, despite some soldiers deliberately firing over their heads. With demonstrators being gunned down in the streets of Petrograd, the Tsarina devoted one entire letter to her husband to her visit to Rasputin's grave in Tsarskoye Selo, writing, 'It seems to me that everything will be all right. The sun is shining so brightly and I feel such peace and comfort at his dear grave. He died to save us.'[111]

Men of the Pavlovsky Life Guards shot the officer who commanded them to open fire on the demonstrators. Nicholas ordered General Ruszki to move front-line troops back from the northern front to sort out the rioting in Petrograd, and decided to head back to the royal family in the well-guarded Alexander Palace at Tsarskoye Selo. In Petrograd, Prime Minister Prince Golytsin used a piece of blank paper already signed by Nicholas to fabricate an ordinance suspending the Duma, but it was a case of too little too late, with regiment after regiment already siding with the insurgents.

Rodzianko, chairing a meeting at the Tauride Palace of deputies who refused to go home, telephoned the Tsar's brother Grand Duke Mikhail begging him to come to Petrograd. There, he conferred with the provisional committee. Although everyone present had good intentions, this was the blind leading the blind. Foreign observers recorded what daily life was like in Petrograd. Meriel Buchanan, daughter of the current British

Ambassador, returning from a trip to Finland, found the streets of the capital blocked by overturned cars and trams.

Also in Petrograd there was a number of British servicemen. In addition to Colonel Knox, who reappeared at the embassy from time to time with reports for forwarding to the British government in London via the diplomatic bag, several other British officers were staying at the capital's Astoria Hotel, where foreign observers had been quartered with Russian officers and their wives. Outside this precarious haven, conditions in the streets were unpredictable, with bursts of machine-gun fire and snipers shooting from rooftops. On one occasion a mob including mutinous sailors from the Kronstadt naval base broke into the Astoria, shot a woman in the neck and killed a Russian general before seizing all the tsarist officers' swords and side arms. Unable to accept this humiliation, some officers committed suicide. The mutineers placed armed guards in the hotel, preventing entry by anyone who did not have a room key.[112] A young Royal Navy Able Seaman recorded his impressions on arrival at Petrograd:

It was snowing fairly heavily. We made some tea while waiting for our baggage, and had to go underneath [sic] the station to get the water. What a sight! Everything was smashed up, evidently there had been a large food store there. All the shops were closed, except the bakers, outside of which people were formed in long queues. Occasional shots were still being fired. Just before our train left, some excitement was caused by several machine guns opening fire outside the station. It appears a police spy was seen on the roof of a house and they meant to make sure of him. The belt of one of the machine guns jammed and there was not one soldier there who knew what was the matter. One of our Petty Officers set it going again.[113]

The smoke of black powder in the streets blew away the incense-perfumed mystical-religious bond between the last Romanov autocrat and his long-suffering people. The Duma was the best thing to come out of the 1905 revolution, but Nicholas' successive dissolutions of it had angered even moderate elements of the population. Already, peasants were illegally seizing land and the empire's ethnic minorities were clamouring for self-determination. Also on 28 February Nicholas entrained to return to Tsarskoye Selo in the belief that his presence near the capital would have some effect. From Vyazma en route, he telegraphed the Tsarina:

Left this morning at 5 o'clock. In thought I am always with you. Wonderful weather. I hope that you are feeling well and are calm. Many troops have been sent from the front [to put down the rioting]. Heartiest greetings, Nicky.[114]

Later, from Likhoslavl, he sent another telegram:

Thanks for news. Am glad that all is well with you. Hope to be home to-morrow morning. Embrace you and the children. God guard you![115]

It was not to be. The imperial train was halted at Malaya Vishera, 100 miles short of the capital, by railway personnel acting on instructions from Petrograd, and forced to divert to Pskov, the northern front HQ. A telegram from Nicholas to Rodzianko offering to 'make concessions' elicited the terse response that it was too late for that. General Ruszki consulted all the other front commanders by telegraph, the consensus of their replies being that the only useful thing Nicholas could do, was abdicate. Informed of this by General Ruszki, Nicholas listened with no visible emotion, but sent him a signed act of abdication at 3 p.m., in his characteristically muddled way naming his 14-year-old son Alexei as successor. It was a pathetic idea, since the Tsarevich suffered from haemophilia and the slightest accident, or even a minor fall, was liable to cause him to bleed to death. When doctors pointed it out that, since his parents would be exiled, Alexei would be unlikely to live long, Nicholas named the boy's youngest uncle, Grand Duke Mikhail, instead:

We transmit the succession to Our brother, the Grand Duke Mikhail Alexandrovich, and give Him Our blessing to mount the Throne of the Russian Empire. We direct Our brother to conduct the affairs of state in full and inviolable union with the representatives of the people in the legislative bodies on those principles which will be established by them, and on which He will take an inviolable oath. In the name of Our dearly beloved homeland, We call on Our faithful sons of the fatherland to fulfill their sacred duty to the fatherland, to obey the Tsar in the heavy moment of national trials, and to help Him, together with the representatives of the people, to guide the Russian Empire on the road to victory, welfare, and glory. May the Lord God help Russia!

On the same evening, two delegates from the Duma arrived at Pskov and were conducted to the imperial train, where the Tsar handed them the abdication document, after which they set off back to Petrograd with it. On 2 March Russia was therefore without a Tsar, the Romanov dynasty having ended to the sound of shouting in the streets by thousands of its former citizens. Nicholas noted in his diary that night, 'All around me is treachery, deceit and cowardice.'[116] Yet, twelve members of the dissolved Duma had the courage on 3 March to form a provisional government to restore law and order under the popular liberal Prince Georgi E. Lvov, known for never getting excited, in uneasy collaboration with the newly formed Petrograd Soviet of Workers' and Soldiers' Deputies consisting of 2,500 delegates claiming to represent the workforce and military units in the Petrograd area.

Britain's King George V had sent a telegram to his cousin Nicholas, offering asylum in Britain. Arrangements were made through the neutral Swedish government for a Royal Navy cruiser not to be attacked by the Kaiserliche Kriegsmarine while conveying the former Russian royal family to Britain, but the Soviet committee minuted:

> It has been decided to inform the Provisional Government at once that it is the determination of the Executive Committee not to permit the departure of Nicholas Romanov for England, and to arrest him. It has been decided to confine Nicholas Romanov in the Trubestkoy Bastion of the Peter and Paul Fortress, changing its commanding personnel for this purpose. The arrest of Nicholas Romanov is to be made at all costs, even at the risk of a severance of relations with the Provisional Government.[117]

Izvestiya of 4 March published the Grand Duke's renunciation of the succession on the previous day, which included the words:

> Animated by the thought that the good of the State is above other considerations, I have decided to accept the supreme power, only if that be the desire of our great people, expressed at a general election for their representatives to the Constituent Assembly, which should determine the form of government [whether monarchy or replublic] and lay down the fundamental laws of the Russian Empire.

With a prayer to God for His blessings, I beseech all citizens of the Empire to subject themselves to the Provisional Government, which is created by and invested with full power by the State Duma, until the summoning, at the earliest possible moment, of a Constituent Assembly, selected by universal, direct, equal, and secret ballot, which shall establish a government in accordance with the will of the people.[118]

The Petrograd Soviet recognised the provisional government after it had pledged itself to proclaim:

an immediate amnesty for all political prisoners and exiles in Siberia;

freedom of speech, the press and freedom of assembly;

the abolition of capital punishment;

the abolition of all class, group and religious restrictions;

the election by secret ballot of a constituent assembly, to draw up a new constitution for Russia;

the replacement of the police by a people's militia;

democratic elections of officials throughout Russia;

retention of their arms by the military units that had taken part in the rebellion;

the extension of civil rights to soldiers subject to military discipline.[119]

After the February Revolution the dead were hailed as martyrs and their coffins carried by a throng of thousands to a common grave on Mars Field under banners promising eternal honour to the fallen. British ambassador Charles Buchanan wrote to London that nothing comparable to these crowds had ever previously been seen in Europe. Among the first exiles to return from Siberia were Stalin, Muranov, Kamenev and Sverdlov. They found Molotov and Shlyapnikov writing editorials in *Pravda* attacking the provisional government and immediately replaced them, with Stalin turning the editorial attitude 180 degrees to one of cautious support for it. In the edition of 28 March, he wrote:

The mere slogan 'Down with the war' is absolutely impractical. As long as the German Army obeys the orders of the Kaiser, the Russian soldier must stand firmly at his post, answering bullet with bullet and shell with shell. ... Our slogan is pressure on the Provisional Government with the aim of compelling it to ... attempt to induce all the warring countries to open immediate negotiations ... Until then every man remains at his fighting post.[120]

The moderate tone gained support for the three 'reasonable Bolsheviks' in the provisional government, but more extreme comrades considered they should be expelled from the party. Lenin, desperate to grab control of the situation, began immediately to undermine the provisional government and attack Stalin's group with a series of *Letters from Afar*, although he and his ideas had little support, even among Bolsheviks. Significantly, at the first meeting of the Petrograd Soviet in the State Duma building, among the banners displayed was a large one reading '*Doloi Lenina!*' – 'Down with Lenin!'[121]

A 35-year-old socialist revolutionary lawyer named Alexander Kerensky – a former neighbour of Lenin's in Simbirsk and the only clean-shaven member of the State Duma among a forest of moustaches and beards, worn to demonstrate mature masculine power – managed to have himself elected Minister of Justice in the provisional government as well as vice chairman of the Petrograd Soviet. After it passed a resolution banning committee members from serving in the provisional government, he made a brilliant speech that won him the right to be the sole exception to that rule. It seemed briefly that Russia had found a leader acceptable to both liberals and revolutionaries. On 28 March he arrived in Tsarskoye Selo, to advise Nicholas how to behave. Nicholas' diary note reads:

After mass Kerenski [sic] arrived and requested that we confine our meetings to mealtimes, and that we sit apart from the children. This, he claimed, was necessary in order to placate the Soviet of Workers' and Soldiers' Deputies. I had to submit so as to avoid the possibility of violence.[122]

Viktor Chernov, political leader of a million peasants, supported Kerensky, who, for the time being, styled himself 'minister president' and was so popular that he was pelted with flowers thrown by leisured ladies from their balconies as he drove past in his open car. Although other Bolsheviks returning from exile in Switzerland, including Georgi Plekhanov, also supported Kerensky and the war effort, Lenin labelled them 'social-chauvinists' and declared, 'Kerensky is a tool of the landlords and capitalists'. He fired off a broadside of catchy but meaningless slogans such as 'Peace, bread and land'; 'End the war without annexations or indemnities'; 'All power to the Soviet'; and 'All land to those who work it. Russia belongs to the workers and peasants.'

On 9 March Nicholas was allowed to return to the Alexander Palace in Tsarskoye Selo, where the palace guards refused to parade and the sentries would not present arms, addressing him to his face as 'Nikolai Romanov'. Although the provisional government stated that the former royal family was being guarded for its own protection, Nicholas, Alexandra and their children were effectively prisoners.

Nicholas wrote in his diary:

Arrived safely at Tsarskoe Selo at 11:30. But, God, what a difference! On the street, around the palace, inside the park, wherever you turn there are sentries. Went upstairs and saw dear Alix [Tsarina] and the precious children. She looked cheerful and well. The children were lying in a darkened room, but were in good spirits except Maria, who recently came down with the measles. We lunched and dined in the playroom with Alexei. Walked with Valia Dolgoruki and worked with him in the little garden, as we may not go further. After tea I played a game of Solitaire. In the evening we visited all the occupants of the other wing and found them in their places.[123]

The diary records 'a good night's sleep' and another outing into the garden on the following day, during which the guards were 'more agreeable', although still 'slovenly'. Apparently kept in ignorance of the Soviet's refusal to let him depart for Britain, Nicholas wrote about burning some papers and sorting out things he was intending to take into exile.

On 1 May – chosen as International Workers' Day by the 2nd Congress of the Socialist International in Paris 1891 – Lenin addressed a large crowd, arguing that the country needed a second revolution to honour the February martyrs. On 7 May a dictatorship of the *soviety* was declared in Petrograd at the same time as a crisis inside the provisional government over whether or not the war should be continued led to Kerensky becoming Minister for War and setting out a few days later to tour the battle fronts, exhorting mass meetings of soldiers to 'do their duty', no matter what was happening on the home front. Having served a term in prison as a revolutionary himself, he abolished the death sentence for military offences and undermined the authority of officers by replacing them with *soviety soldatov* – soldiers' committees. Nevertheless, General Brusilov did manage to assemble thirty-one divisions on the sector he thought most likely to crack and open the way to Lemberg and the Drohobych oil fields, the capture of which might have strengthened the provisional government's fragile power base.

Back in Tsarskoye Selo, on 9 June Nicholas noted, 'Exactly three months since I came from Mogilev and here we are confined like prisoners.' A month later, he heard that shooting had broken out again in Petrograd after many soldiers and sailors arrived from Kronstadt to oppose Kerensky's provisional government. 'Absolute chaos,' Nicholas wrote. 'Where are those people who could take this movement in hand and put a stop to strife and bloodshed? The seed of all this evil is in Petrograd and not everywhere in Russia.' He was still deluding himself that because the mass of 'good Russians' were on his side, the troubles would soon pass. In fact, for the Tsar and his family to become overnight impotent prisoners left the devout but illiterate peasants who made up the majority of the Russian people and of the conscripts at the battle fronts confused and all the more easily influenced by the educated revolutionaries from the cities who talked so convincingly of a new age dawning, where everyone would be equal – as promised so long ago by Catherine the Great.

To forestall any possibility of a conservative counter-coup in favour of the Tsar, the dual power ordered the royal family to be transported by train into Siberia 'for its own protection'. Nicholas, Alexandra, their five children and a retinue of forty-five servants were transported by train nearly 1,500 miles eastward to Tobolsk in Western Siberia, where they were placed under house arrest in the governor's mansion to await their unhappy fate. By this time, Meriel Buchanan was working as a volunteer nurse in a Red Cross hospital in Petrograd for wounded soldiers – until they too were infected by the political fever of the times and refused to obey the instructions of the doctors and nurses, forcing the closure of the hospital, after which there was no medical care for the injured. She wrote in her memoirs how 'ruffians with unshaven faces took control of the streets'.[124]

12

WHITE NIGHTS, RED DAYS

For several months Lenin and the other expatriate revolutionaries in Switzerland had been following from afar the chaos on the battlefields and in the streets of Russia while negotiating with German Foreign Office officials for a safe and acceptable way of getting back there. One method seriously considered was to transport them clandestinely to the German front lines and arrange a truce, during which they could walk through the Russian lines, but this was discarded as making them too obviously German agents. Finally, a plan was agreed, in the hope that their return would result in more strikes on the home front and even more mutinies throughout the Russian armies, forcing the provisional government to sue for peace and enabling the Central Powers to switch as many as a million men to the slogging match on the Western Front. On 25 March, the German Foreign Ministry undertook to make available clandestine transport facilities to take expatriates to the Baltic coast and then via neutral Sweden and Finland to Russia. The only snag in this route was that British agents in Finland might be able to prevent them crossing the Finno-Russian border.[125] Proving that there is nothing new about deniable clandestine operations, the mission had been approved by German Chancellor Theobald von Bethmann-Hollweg, conducting negotiations with Lenin through a chain of intermediaries, but the Kaiser was not initially informed of this ungentlemanly ploy.[126]

Paranoia being a characteristic of revolutionaries, Lenin and Grigori Zinoviev – his closest collaborator at the time, born Hirsch Apfelbaum aka Ovsey-Gershon Radomylsky – feared that staying any longer in

Switzerland might see them sidelined by the socialist-revolutionary members of the provisional government and their fellow Bolsheviks in the Petrograd Soviet. Against that, returning to Petrograd at this juncture could see them accused of being German agents – which they effectively were. To feed the pretence that they were acting on their own unassisted initiative, it was agreed that they would pay third-class fares to travel on a special train granted extraterritorial rights while crossing Germany. Lenin was particularly nervous at this time because he was almost unknown to the great Russian public, owing his pre-eminence in émigré circles partly to covert support from the Okhrana's European agents, who subsidised him because he was unable to work with anyone for long before precipitating yet another schism in the socialist revolutionary ranks.[127]

To the great relief of the small circle privy to the plan in the German High Command and Foreign Ministry, on 4 April the expat Russians indicated their readiness for a group of 'twenty to thirty' to leave for Russia.[128] On 16 April 1917 the group of thirty-plus revolutionaries, including Lenin's wife Krupskaya and her friend Inessa Armand, currently Lenin's mistress, boarded what became known as 'the sealed train' in Berne.

Neglected by historians for years because her relationship was yet another state secret – revealing that Lenin had a human side to him, and also because the Stalinist USSR was misogynistic and ignored the part women had played in the revolution – Inessa Armand was much more than 'just a bit on the side'. Born Elisabeth-Inès Stéphane d'Herbenville, the daughter of a French opera singer and his half-English music teacher wife, after her father died when she was only 5, she was brought up by a French aunt and grandmother working as teachers in Russia. Because Russian is an inflected language, she changed her name from Inès to Inessa, which can be declined like a Russian name. At the age of 18 she married Alexander Armand, one of the sons of a wealthy family who owned textile factories in the town of Pushkino. Enthused by radical political philosophy, he accepted an open marriage, in which she bore him four children before having another by his brother, Boris. He, like Inessa, was a socialist who attempted to organise the workers in the Armand family factories; her philanthropic activities included founding a school for poor children. In 1903 she joined the Social Democratic Labour Party and left her husband the following year, travelling to Sweden, where she was active in feminist politics.

Returning to Russia, she spent a brief spell in prison until freed in accordance with Nicholas II's 1905 Manifesto. Re-arrested on 9 April 1907 for distributing Bolshevik propaganda, she was sentenced this time to two years' exile in the Far North, but escaped and returned to Paris, where she met Lenin, Zinoviev and other Bolsheviks. In 1911, because she spoke five languages fluently, Lenin made her secretary general of the Committee of Foreign Organisations established to liaise with, and bring under his control, all pro-Bolshevik émigrés in Western Europe. Krupskaya recorded everyone's appreciation of Inessa's culture, ability to play the piano professionally and her joie de vivre. Yet the outspoken Russian-Jewish-Italian activist Anzhelika Balabanova criticised the newcomer to their inner circle for dressing to please Lenin and relaying slavishly his every word in whatever language she was talking.

Returning to Russia in 1912, to work for the election of Bolshevik candidates to the Duma, Inessa was arrested in September and imprisoned for six months. Travelling after her release to Kraków, where Lenin was then living, she rented a room in Kamenev's house nearby and, according to Krupskaya, brought some life and gaiety into the grim, revolution-obsessed Bolshevik circle. Her ten-year affair with Lenin was common knowledge and, according to Kollontai and Balabanova, Inessa had a sixth child by him, as well as joining Kollontai and Krupskaya as joint editors of the news-sheet *Rabotnitsa*, or *The Working Woman*. Despite her intimacy with Lenin, he criticised her writing mercilessly, treating her as a lackey, like any other comrade. During the First World War, when Inessa lived with Lenin and Krupskaya in Switzerland, she believed that Russia should continue fighting until victory; he at the time wanted Russia to end its war, the more chaos, the better. None of his other close associates would have dared to disagree with him on this, or any other, issue. So, when he ordered her to accept his ruling, Inessa gave way.

The so-called 'sealed train' was actually a single carriage of eight second- and third-class compartments, single men roughing it in third while families travelled in second, with one second-class compartment reserved for Lenin, Krupskaya and Inessa. From here Lenin emerged once to yell at everyone to be quiet because he was working and, on another occasion, to solve the problem of the queue for the toilet by obliging everyone waiting to take a numbered piece of paper and wait their turn.

What was supposed to be a clandestine journey started in an unusual manner. Swiss counter-intelligence had been closely watching all the Russian conspirators since the start of the war. This is the official police report of the departure of Lenin's group:

> At 3.20 p.m. the express train was about to depart [with] one carriage full of Russian revolutionaries. I also saw the Russian named Lenin, who was obviously travelling as the leader of the group. It seems that the departure should have taken place in secret, but present at the station were approximately another 100 Russians of both sexes, who saw off those who were leaving with mixed feelings. Those in favour of pursuing war against Germany to the very end were cursing like cabmen, shouting that those who were travelling were German spies and provocateurs, or that 'You will all be hanged, Jewish instigators that you are!' Other cries were, 'Provocateurs, scoundrels, pigs,' etc. When the train started to move off, the travellers and many of their friends who had remained began to sing the Internationale, while the others began again to yell at them, 'Provocateurs! Spies!' etc.[129]

All the doors of the carriage were kept locked throughout the journey, with the exception of one in the compartment of the two German escorting officers on board. The only hitch in the plan came when the sealed carriage missed its connection with a northbound train somewhere in Germany because, for security reasons, the railway system had not been informed of its existence. This obliged the two escorting officers to accommodate the party of revolutionaries locked up incommunicado for the night in a small provincial hotel. The much reproduced iconic Soviet painting 'Lenin at the Finland Station' showed him heroically clinging onto the outside of Finnish locomotive No. 293 as it pulled into the Finlyandski Vokzal at the other end of the journey, waving a footplate man's cap at the cheering crowd. Like most Communist icons, it was a fantasy. Arriving in Petrograd on 3 April (new calendar) he stepped out of his compartment and was hustled by a group of Bolshevik workers to what had been the Tsar's waiting room, now renamed the 'People's Room'. Totally ignoring the welcome speech of Chkheidze, the chairman of the Soviet, he greeted the throng in the name of the February Revolution, as though he had been a prime mover, ignoring all those who had actually taken part.

Escorted from the station to the Kshesinskaya Palace, where the Bolsheviks had their headquarters, he again showed his contempt for the Soviet and the provisional government and just about everyone else. But sailors of the 2nd Baltic Fleet openly condemned him for accepting German money and assistance, students demonstrated against him outside the palace and a delegation of wounded soldiers and sailors arrived with banners inviting 'Lenin and company' to return to Germany, where they belonged.[130] In the Duma building, on the day after his return, another returned exile who had been a member of the Bolshevik Central Committee declared, after hearing him speak, that Lenin was no longer a Marxist, but an anarchist. It was the consensus of opinion that he had shot himself in the foot. Kerensky said, 'This man will destroy the Revolution!'[131]

As all clandestine operations officers know, revolutions cost money – with which the Bolsheviks were richly provided through the chain of bankers moving funds covertly from Germany through special accounts. Cut-outs and front companies were used so that the money was not traceable back to the German government. Director Olof Aschberg of the Swedish Nya Banken admitted to being the Bolsheviks' banker, with as much as 60 million gold marks passing through his hands – the equivalent of 3 million pounds sterling, or in today's values £180 million. One bagman alone, N.M. Weinberg, Petrograd agent for Berlin bankers Mendelssohn & Co., paid out 12 million roubles direct to the Bolsheviks in Russia, cash in hand 'against signature acknowledging receipt'.

After the revolution, the Soviet regime did everything in its power to obscure the money trail, which disproved the myth of the spontaneous Bolshevik 'revolution of workers and peasants'. On 20 December 1917 Felix Dzerzhinsky was appointed head of the Bolshevik secret police designated *chrezvechainaya komissiya* – the extraordinary commission,[132] whose acronym *che-ka* became 'Cheka', the first in the line of Soviet secret police organisations. Dzerzhinsky, an ascetic, round-shouldered man of normally mild appearance who saw himself as the saint of the revolution, was a dysfunctional sociopath so devoid of normal emotion that he forced his wife to have their son adopted into a working-class family, to ensure that he grew up 'socially correct'. Ordered by Lenin to recover the incriminating Mendelssohn company receipts, he arrested Weinberg, who was stripped and tortured in the Butyrka prison. The receipts having been already forwarded to Mendelssohn & Co.'s accounts department in Berlin as a matter of course, Weinberg could not save himself, and was shot – as he probably would have been anyway.[133]

The amount of German money handed over to a group of dissidents who *might* stage a coup d'état was colossal for the time but, given the escalating costs of the war, this clandestine financing seemed a worthwhile gamble in Berlin. As so often fixation on the short-term target completely blinded the planners to the long-term danger of their plan. After the war, the Kaiser's normally perceptive Eastern Front commander, General Max Hoffmann, admitted, 'We neither knew nor foresaw the danger to humanity from the consequences of this journey of the Bolsheviks to Russia.'[134] Even Ludendorff admitted in his memoirs:

> Our government, in sending Lenin to Russia, took upon itself a tremendous responsibility. From a military point of view, his journey was justified, for it was imperative that [tsarist] Russia should fall.[135]

The transparent device of Lenin's group paying a third-class fare for a journey impossible at that time without the active help of the German government did nothing to protect the Bolsheviks from more accusations by their revolutionary rivals and by the provisional government that they were paid enemy agents. Russian Social Democratic revolutionary David Shub was personally acquainted with Lenin and the other Bolshevik leaders, having shared their exile in Western Europe after escaping from internal exile in Siberia, to which he was sentenced for his role in the 1905 revolution. In 1948 his book titled *Lenin: A Biography* was published in the USA and immediately attacked by hard-line Stalinists as a fiction. So vituperative were these attacks that Shub wrote a detailed defence that was published in the 1950 March–April issue of *New International* magazine. His first paragraph included the words:

> I am sufficiently familiar with the tradition of Bolshevik polemics not to be surprised by the abusive and defamatory character of Mr Schachtman's review [of the book].

Among the numerous points on which Shub took issue with Schachtman is the matter of the German subsidies:

> If the reader turns to pp. 211–16 of my book, he will … learn of financial transactions between Berlin, Stockholm and Petrograd revealed through the interception of 29 telegrams exchanged between the Bolshevik intermediaries who handled the transfer of funds for the Party. We find that 800,000 roubles were withdrawn from the Siberian Bank in Petrograd within two months by a confessed Bolshevik go-between. We find an admission by the same individual (who handled funds which reached the Siberian Bank from the Disconto Gesellschaft in Berlin via the Nea [sic] Bank of Stockholm) that she had instuctions 'to give Koslovsky, then a Bolshevik member of the Soviet Executive Committee, any sum of money he demanded; some of these payments amounted to 100,000 roubles.[137]

Shub also quotes Tomáš Masaryk, first president of Czechoslovakia, the French military attaché in Petrograd and a French Socialist Minister, who provided corroboration of the German subsidies to the Bolsheviks.[137] It has also been suggested that an important reason for Stalin's murder of Trotsky was to prevent him from ever validating accusations that the October Revolution was financed by Berlin.

Trotsky arrived back in Russia via the US and Canada in spite of British attempts to prevent him doing so, which ceased when HM Ambassador in St Petersburg Sir George Buchanan advised the Foreign Office that this might provoke pro-Trotsky socialist revolutionaries to attack British businesses in Russia. Lenin was playing his favourite game of undermining all other claimants to power and confusing the uncommitted with his talk of 'traitors to Socialism', 'the deception of the masses by the bourgoisie' and 'placing power in the hands of the proletariat and the poorest strata of the peasantry'.[138] In April, he issued a series of 'Theses', proclaiming 'revolutionary defeatism' without attracting many followers. *Pravda*'s reaction was:

> As for Lenin's general scheme, it seems to us unacceptable in that it starts from the assumption that the bourgeois revolution is ended, and counts on an immediate transforming of this revolution into a Socialist revolution.[139]

Meanwhile at the several Russian fronts, the killing continued. By mid-June the anti-war *soviety* in major towns and the armed forces were sufficiently organised to assemble at the First All-Russian Congress of Soviets, where Socialist Revolutionaries were in the majority, followed by the Mensheviks and Bolsheviks, in that order. Lenin addressed the congress on 17 June, arguing that the Soviet was the counterpart of the French Revolutionary Convention of 1792 and should immediately seize all power from the provisional government. Kerensky rose to protest that this would lead to dictatorship – which was Lenin's purpose. While he was greeted with applause and cheers from the mutinous soldiers and sailors, Kerensky's moderate voice was not. Without waiting for the term spin-doctor to be invented, Lenin took the small-circulation news-sheet *Pravda,* which had been the party's mouthpiece since 1912, and used the laundered German subsidies to unleash a huge PR campaign, an important element in which was a daily printing of 300,000 copies of the paper under his personal editorial control.

The stress of daily confrontation since his return, after the relative calm of life in Switzerland, had worn him down. Prematurely, a Bolshevik coup was planned but fizzled out. He left on 29 June, to stay out of danger with friends across the Finnish border in the small village of Neivola, only two hours by rail from Petrograd.[140] There he had what sounds like another nervous breakdown, not even reading the newspapers to know what was happening in the Russian capital. On 4 July Maximilian Savelov, a member of the *Pravda* editorial staff, arrived to warn him that things were getting out of control in Petrograd. They caught the next train back there. On the following day, the newspaper *Zhivoye Slovo* denounced the Bolsheviks for being German agents. Worse was to come. On 6 July warrants were issued for the arrest of Lenin, Zinoviev and Kamenev as German spies after evidence was released by the provisional government that the Bolsheviks were financed by Berlin with Alexander Parvus as a go-between.[141] Lenin went underground, hiding in friends' apartments. However, scooped up in the search net, Krupskaya was arrested with another comrade mistaken for Lenin, but to whom he bore no physical resemblance. As historian Robert Service remarks, this was yet another proof that Lenin was virtually unknown to the general population and even to the Okhrana agents searching for him.[142]

The quasi-rebellion that had begun in Petrograd and Moscow spread rapidly to every city in European Russia and more slowly beyond the Urals to the shores of the Pacific. While the moderate liberals and socialists in the Duma continued to support the war effort, mutinies at the fronts rapidly grew too widespread for firing squads to execute all the ringleaders. The soldiers' editions of *Pravda* which circulated at the fronts carried the message 'Lay down your arms and go home!'[143]

Against this, Kerensky, as Minister for War, called on all ranks to strike at the enemy on the south-western front. General Brusilov's attack, known as the Kerensky Offensive, was an insufficiently strong attack launched by Russian 7th, 8th and 11th armies south of Tarnopol on 1 July. Brusilov was using the same logic that had won success the previous year: attacks and diversions to wrong-foot the enemy along a 100-mile front, of which the main axis was on a front of 30 miles, heavily supported by artillery. Unwisely seeking to share the glory of a victory he wrongly anticipated, Kerensky toured the first line units in military uniform, haranguing them to fight for '*Mat' Rossiya i Svoboda*'– 'Mother Russia and their own freedom' – with no mention of the Tsar. The Brusilov/Kerensky Offensive was crippled by increasing desertion and open mutinies in many of the Russian units involved and refusal to obey orders among Ukrainian soldiery, who hoped to force the Russian provisional government to grant autonomy to their nation.

Because he feared nationalist feelings among the ethnic minorities of his own empire, the Tsar had refused pleas from Czech and Slovak POWs to be allowed to fight against their overlords in the dual monarchy. Now, in an attempt to counteract the mutinies, volunteer POWs were armed and allowed to play their part in brigades formed from comrades who preferred to take their chance on the field of battle, rather than waste away in Siberian camps for the rest of the war. Brusilov placed the Czech Legion in the line opposite two Czech regiments in Austro-Hungarian uniform. Refusing to fire on their own countrymen in Russian uniform, 3,000 of these men walked across no man's land to surrender, some changing uniform there and then to turn their weapons on yesterday's comrades in the opposing trenches.

In the first week of July, it did seem that Brusilov's luck of the previous year was holding: a 20-mile-wide breach was forced in the enemy front; the most significant advance was achieved on the left, or southern, flank of the offensive by Cossack General Lavr Kornilov, whose 8th Army pushed back the enemy 20 miles. OHL rushed German reinforcements from the Western Front and on 19 July its Südarmee counter-attacked with two German and nine Austro-Hungarian divisions. With its supply lines overextended, the right flank of Brusilov's advance crumpled. Tens of thousands of soldiers deserting turned this retreat into a rout characterised by sabotage of military equipment and mutinies which made it plain that, although some units would still defend their lines if attacked, hardly any were prepared to accept again the rate of casualties inevitable in an offensive. Sick and exhausted, Brusilov attempted to control this uncontrollable situation, while Kornilov argued that attack was all that mattered. Kerensky sacked Brusilov and attempted to restore discipline by reintroducing the death penalty, which General Kornilov imposed rigorously for mutiny or desertion, causing an even further drop in morale.

In April 1917 the Bolsheviks had formed a 'military organisation' to enlist mutinous soldiers and sailors into their ranks. The Bolshevik Military Organisation (BMO) attracted 30,000 active members from 500 military units to an all-Russian conference in June. Discontent with the war saw a new rebellion break out in July. Between 3 and 5 July, on the old calendar, thousands of armed workers and soldiers demonstrated against the provisional government in the streets of Petrograd. Lenin, as always refusing to accept anyone else's lead, at first forbade 'his' Bolsheviks from taking part, but Trotsky was still not a member of Lenin's party. He showed physical courage when the leader of the SR Party Viktor Chernov was arrested at the Tauride Palace by militant demonstrators and rescued by Trotsky fighting his way through the angry throng to pull Chernov out of the car, in which they intended driving him away to an unknown fate. In the night of 4 July loyal troops moved in and secured the centre of Petrograd by midday on 5 July. A second official investigation by the provisional government into the Bolsheviks' suspicious finances revealed legal proof that Lenin's faction was funded by German money and resulted in a public accusation of treason by the Minister of Justice. It was left to the provisional government to issue arrest warrants against all the returnees accused of being German agents.

At a meeting on 15 July organised by anarchists, mutinous soldiers of the 1st Machine Gun Regiment were persuaded to join the strikers. Under the aegis of the Bolshevik Military Organisation, itself under pressure from rank-and-file soldiers but without the sanction of the Central Committee, the machine gunners enlisted soldiers from other regiments in Petrograd and Moscow to support the strikers and obey, not their officers but their own soldiers' committees.

On 15 July anarchist groups summoned soldiers of the mutinous 1st Machine Gun Regiment, which had refused several times to move to the front, to demonstrate on the following day in Petrograd, Moscow and other industrial cities. This attracted followers from the disaffected garrison troops and striking workers, who marched with them under the slogan '*Vsya vlast sovetam*' – 'All power to the soviets'. Paradoxically, the socialist-revolutionaries, Mensheviks and Bolsheviks all refused for different reasons to join them, prompting Lenin to give it his blessing in an endeavour to grab control. Back in Petrograd, on 16 July 1917,[144] the first provisional government met its inevitable end amid the widespread disorder of what were called 'the July Days', lasting from 16 to 20 July, during which period Lenin made some speeches urging restraint but was clearly out of his depth as things were developing too fast for him to control.

If this sounds confusing, it was. Pavel Milyukov, the leader of the 'Kadets', or Constitutional Democratic Party, described the situation as 'chaos in the army, chaos in foreign policy, chaos in industry and chaos in the nationalist questions'. The 'nationalist questions' covered the independence movements in the Baltics, the Caucasus and Ukraine, where an armed uprising in Kiev was suppressed by Russian force of arms. One would think that Lenin would leap into the breach to exploit all this indecision and take control, but on the afternoon of 16 July it was the trio of Kamenev, Trotsky and Zinoviev who tried to stem the wellspring of discontent in the streets, against the wishes of leading members of the Bolshevik Party while the BMO mobilised reinforcements from the front lines and dispatched several armoured cars to capture key posts in Petrograd including the Peter and Paul Fortress.

An enormous demonstration of more than 500,000 strikers, soldiers and sailors in Petrograd on 17 July went off at half-cock – the demonstrators suffering 600–700 casualties from loyal troops. The socialist-revolutionaries and Mensheviks took against the Bolsheviks and supported soldiers loyal to the provisional government who were disarming the demonstrators and arresting the ringleaders. Despite Trotsky, Kamenev and Zinoviev trying to control the developing situation, in the confusion the Bolsheviks' offices were torched as were the offices of *Pravda*. There could have been no clearer statement of the gap that now separated the Bolsheviks from all the other revolutionary parties. Considering how many hundreds of thousands of words have been devoted to the history of Soviet Communism, it is interesting that there is no reliable published record of the internal discussions of the Bolshevik leadership at this time, with some members urging an intensification of activity and others, including Lenin, undecided what to do next. In the middle of the night on 18 July after the provisional government brought a number of loyal troops from the front to the streets of Petrograd and won over some previously neutral garrison troops, the Bolshevik Central Committee decided to call off the street demonstrations. Whether this was before or just after Kerensky ordered the arrest of Lenin and the other leading Bolsheviks, accused of inciting rebellion 'with German financial backing', is hard to untangle.

On 19 July the provisional government ordered the arrests of Lenin, Zinoviev, Kamenev as well as Lunacharsky, Raskolnikov and Alexandra Kollontai – the pioneer feminist and prolific writer on social questions. Although she rejected political feminism as a bourgeois irrelevance in the perfect socialist state, the USSR turned out not to be that state, with only two women ever making it onto the Politburo. Kollontai wrote: 'The separation of kitchen chores from marriage would be as great a reform as the separation of Church and State.'[145]

The government charged them with incitement to armed insurrection with the financial support of the German government – in other words, treason. Prince Lvov resigned on 21 July and was replaced as prime minister by Kerensky on the following day. Lenin warned Trotsky that they would all be shot. He afterward said that the only thing which saved them was the chronic indecisiveness of the provisional government, afraid to move too decisively against the Bolsheviks in case this upset the other socialist parties. Indecisiveness on both sides, then, during the 'July Days', which spluttered to a halt with Trotsky, Chkheidze and others telling the Kronstadt sailors, mutinous soldiers and workers from the Putilov factory to go back to work as the time was not yet right for a full-blooded revolution. Trotsky, Kamenev and Lunacharsky were arrested on 25 July.[146] Lenin, as he had done before, slipped away to hide with Zinoviev in the suburban home of a Bolshevik railway worker named Sergei Alliluyev, whose daughter Nadezhda would become world famous as Stalin's second wife, committing suicide in 1932. From there, Lenin fled in disguise – a wig to cover his bald pate – to safety in Helsingfors. It is difficult to untangle the power struggle between Lenin's faction, the BMO and the Petrograd Soviet for and against the spontaneous street demonstrations because no records were kept, but even Lenin could not make up his mind on the best course to follow.

Initial support for Kerensky's provisional government faded away when it became clear that his policies were unlikely to produce peace in the near future. He designated Boris Savinkov as Deputy Minister of War and appointed General Lavr Kornilov C-in-C of all Russian forces. Gen Brusilov, who knew him well, categorised Kornilov as having 'the heart of a lion and the brains of a lamb'.[147] For the business community and the Kadet Party, he was seen as the salvation of all Russia's woes, but his recipe proved disastrous. On 19 August Kornilov posted one Russian and one Cossack cavalry corps to the region of Petrograd, plus the *Dikaya Diviziya* or Savage Division of Muslim Caucasian cavalry, with the aim of taking over the capital and executing all the alleged German agents there, particularly the Bolsheviks, and every member of the Petrograd Soviet. In the army generally, officers blamed the recent reverses on the battlefield on the mutinies and desertions, and praised the reintroduction of the death penalty at the front and the abolition of the various soldiers' *soviety* that had been perverting normal military discipline since February. Yet, when Kornilov's soldiers attempted a military coup, it was aborted by revolutionary railwaymen, who refused to transport them to Petrograd, forcing them to continue on foot until their route was blocked by 20,000 Red Guards – deserters and mutineers who had been armed by the Petrograd Soviet – facing them in defence of the capital. Included among them were a number of Caucasian Muslims, present at a conference in Petrograd, who persuaded the Savage Division – all strapping soldiers from the Caucasus – that the mission with which they had been tasked was treasonous.

News of all this unrest prompted Gen Ludendorff to exploit his enemy's crippling internal problems by a bold drive towards Petrograd itself. By capturing Russian-controlled ports along the Baltic littoral, he could bring in supplies to his advancing troops by sea, avoiding the problems of extended terrestrial supply lines. Continuing the offensive in Estonia, on

3 September 1917 Ludendorff's cousin General Oskar von Hutier crossed the Daugava or Western Dvina river, making liberal use of the artillery by firing 20,000 gas shells on the first day of the attack and followed up with special storm troops, who used flame throwers, light mortars and light machine guns to make a rapid advance, bypassing Russian strongpoints, which they left for the slower heavy troops to reduce with artillery.

Construction by the engineers of pontoon bridges over the Dvina – the modern border between Latvia and Belarus – allowed nine German divisions to cross in forty-eight hours. After offering feeble resistance, the defenders withdrew after hanging deserters on the spot, and left behind 250 artillery pieces, with the Germans in complete control of the important seaport of Riga by the end of the fourth day. From Riga to Petrograd as the crow files is less than 300 miles, and the news of this defeat shattered any public confidence in Kerensky's provisional government. As head of government, his problems were insurmountable: the heavy losses on the battle fronts; mutinous soldiers deserting in ever larger numbers; other politicians doing their best to undermine him. There was zero enthusiasm to continue the war, even by those who had supported it; and there were shortages of food and supplies, impossible to remedy in wartime conditions.

By autumn 1917 it was estimated that 2 million men had deserted from the Russian armies. At the end of August, Kerensky fell out with Gen Kornilov and the provisional government was so apprehensive about the nearness of the German forces in Riga that it decided the prudent thing was to transfer the administration to Moscow, the old medieval capital. On 6 October a decree was issued announcing the transfer of several departments of state to Moscow, starting on 12 October. Kornilov was punished by cashiering from the army and incarcerated in the Bykhov Fortress with thirty of his officers, but would later escape in the confusion of the full-blown revolution and raise an anti-Bolskevik army in the civil war, being killed while fighting the Reds in the town of Ekaterinodar in April 1918. Ironically, the Bolsheviks were the ones who benefitted from Kornilov's attempted coup, because among the political prisoners freed was Trotsky. Many workers had been given weapons by the provisional government to defend Petrograd, which they kept and used later in the autumn. The worst damage suffered by Kerensky was that his imprisonment of Kornilov and his increasingly favourable overtures to the revolutionary socialists alienated virtually all of the officers in the armed forces, so that when he appealed for their support in October, few responded. In the immediate future, however, public anger over Kornilov's perceived mutiny resulted in officers being shot, hanged and drowned by their men.

Declaring a Russian Republic under his leadership, Kerensky clung to a semblance of power a little longer. His father had been Lenin's headmaster, and the two families knew each other well, which may be why he was allowed to escape in disguise after the revolution. He died in New York in 1970 and was buried in Putney Vale cemetery, just a few miles from the Communist pilgrimage site of Karl Marx's tomb in Highgate.

Thanks largely to Lenin's huge German-financed PR campaign, both the Moscow and Petrograd *soviety* came under Bolshevik control, the latter arresting the members of the Duma on 25 October. News of this reached even Letuchka No. 2 in Romania when newspapers arrived with reports of rioting in Moscow and people starving in Kiev, where there was an outbreak of cholera. Soldiers were also falling ill with *chornaya ospa* (black smallpox), which was always fatal. A nurse returning from leave in the Caucasus told Florence Farmborough that food was scarce even in that traditional land of plenty, with tea and sugar already rationed. The only good news was that the nurses' salaries were raised from 50 roubles to 75 roubles a month – roughly £7.50 – but this was a time when a pair of boots, soon worn out in the damp and the mud, cost 100 roubles. Given permission to take some leave in Moscow, Farmborough had to literally fight her way onto trains, insulted because of her nurse's uniform by mobs of mutineers deserting en masse. Having elbowed her way to a seat, she dared not leave it even to go to the toilet on the long and tedious journeys, lest a deserter immediately take it and refuse to give it up on her return.

Satisfied that Petrograd was safely under Bolshevik control, Lenin decided to return from Finland towards the end of October. But his recent hectoring letters to the Bolsheviks in Petrograd ordering them to take action immediately, which included a totally unfounded allegation that Britain and Germany were about to conclude a separate peace,[148] reached the point where his letters were torn up, his return was temporarily forbidden and Trotsky was elected chairman of the Petrograd Soviet, replacing Chkheidze. Lenin returned nevertheless and harangued

the Bolshevik Central Committee at a secret meeting on 23 October
on the necessity of an immediate armed uprising against the provisional
government, finally wearing down almost all the opposition until the vote
was taken, with ten for and only two votes against. On Trotsky's initiative,
a Military Revolutionary Committee was set up.

At the first All-Russian Congress of Soviets in June, only 105 of the
749 delegates had been Bolsheviks. Before the second congress was
due to commence – on 25 October according to the Julian calendar or
6 November under the modern European calendar – with 390 Bolsheviks
out of 649 delegates, Lenin was insistent with Stalin and Trotsky that the
uprising against the provisional government must be a fait accompli. So
it was that the Military Revolutionary Committee burst into the Winter
Palace, which was already under threat from the mutinous Kronstadt
sailors manning the big guns of the cruiser *Aurora* and by the cannon of
the Peter and Paul Fortress. They placed the members of the provisional
government under arrest, marching them through the streets, suffering
the jeers of onlookers, and locked them up in the Fortress. Hearing the
news, Lenin discarded his disguise and announced to the All-Russian
Congress that *the* revolution had begun. Some hundred delegates walked
out in protest at the Bolsheviks' unilateral uprising, increasing his majority
even further.

The congress argued its way through the night inside the Smolny
Institute, a former school for daughters of the nobility, breaking up at
dawn – when armed revolutionaries stormed the Winter Palace. Or did
they? Actually, this is another myth. Because Lenin considered that the
newly invented cinema film was the most important of the arts for propaganda purposes, a heroic reconstruction, to be shown around the world,
was filmed with soldiers firing volleys of blanks and brave workers lying in
the snow, acting dead. In the event, the Winter Palace garrison had dwindled, partly by the defection of mutineers and partly due to lack of rations,
from its normal complement of 2,000 to three squadrons of Cossacks,
some cadets and 137 women of 1st Battalion of the Petrograd Women's
Brigade, who had recently paraded in front of Sylvia Pankhurst, taking the
salute. Lacking sandbags, they had stacked logs against the external walls
to absorb artillery shells. This inadequate garrison was swiftly overcome
and locked up by the Military Revolutionary Committee. Taking his life
in his hands, General Knox secured the release of the female soldiers from

the Winter Palace by threatening their captors that he would otherwise tell the world how the Bolsheviks were treating women.

By the morning of 26 October – or 8 November on the modern calendar – the palace and virtually all places of strategic importance in Petrograd, like the main telegraph office, government ministries and power stations, were occupied by the Bolshevik activists. It was far from a bloodless coup. Conservatively estimated at 7,000, those killed included many innocent bystanders.[149] Appearing that afternoon at the Congress the Bolshevik leaders were reportedly greeted with thunderous applause. Having decided to eschew bourgois titles and call themselves people's commissars, united in the Soviet Narodnikh Kommissarov or Soviet of People's Commissars, abbreviated to Sovnarkom, they proclaimed a 'temporary' administration headed by Lenin as Chairman, with Trotsky as Commissar of Foreign Affairs and Stalin as Commissar of Nationality Affairs, which seemed appropriate since he was such an obvious foreigner.

Trotsky issued an order to the armies, ordering the soldiers to arrest all their officers, but without lynching any, because he wanted them kept for the humiliation of show trials. Then, the men at the front were to elect representatives to contact the enemy. His edict ended, 'The keys of peace are in your hands!' It was what the nation had been waiting to hear. On 22 November Lenin and Stalin used the direct telephone line to Mogilev to order General Dukhonin, who had replaced Kornilov as C-in-C, to cease hostilities and open negotiations for an armistice. When he refused, People's Commissar Krylenko was despatched to Mogilev with a group of Red Guards and Kronstadt sailors to replace Dukhonin and agree to any terms for an armistice. Dukhonin refused to yield and was killed by the Red Guards.

13

PEACE?

A number of foreigners travelled to Russia for various reasons to witness the extraordinary events happening there. They ranged from ardent sympathisers with the Bolsheviks like American journalists Louise Bryant and her lover John Silas Reed to serious writers like Hugh Walpole and Somerset Maugham. Bryant had been raised by her engine-driver stepfather, but Reed came from a prosperous middle-class family and had attended Harvard University before taking up journalism, writing for far-Left newspapers. Bryant was an anarchist and feminist, Reed a Communist, but both wrote up the October Revolution in glowing terms for their US publications. The romance, their writings and the tragedy of Reed's death from typhus in 1922 made *Reds*, the 1981 film about them – starring Diane Keaton and Warren Beatty, with Jack Nicolson playing playwright Eugene O'Neill, the third member of their ménage – a box office success in many countries.

The Bolsheviks needed friends like that. Another was the future successful children's author Arthur Ransome, reporting the revolution favourably in Russia for the *Daily News* and *Manchester Guardian*, during which he fell in love with Trotsky's secretary, Evgenia P. Shelepina, who became his second wife. The anti-war vicar of St Margaret's church, Altrincham, Hewlett Johnson, later to be famous as 'the Red Dean' of Canterbury, was placed under MI5 surveillance for praising the revolution in public.[150] Bruce Lockhart, who was neither historian nor economist, but who was in Petrograd and Moscow at the time as an accredited diplomat, wrote with the benefit of hindsight in 1931:

The revolution took place because the patience of the Russian people broke down under a system of unparalleled inefficiency and corruption. No other nation would have stood the privations which Russia stood [sic], for anything like the same length of time. As instances of the inefficiency, I give the disgraceful mishandling of food supplies, the complete breakdown of transport, and the senseless mobilisation of millions of unwanted and unemployable troops. As an example of the corruption, I quote the shameless profiteering of nearly everyone engaged in the giving and taking of war contracts. Obviously, the Emperor himself, as a supreme autocrat, must bear the responsibility for a system which failed mainly because of the men he appointed to control it. There was only one way to save Russia from going Bolshevik. That was to allow her to make peace. It was because Kerensky would not allow her to make peace that he went under. It was solely because he *promised* to stop the war that Lenin came to the top.[151]

By the end of the second day at the Smolny Institute, the Congress of Soviets had elected a council of people's commissars to serve as an interim government, with Bolsheviks naturally holding the majority of posts. The council in turn formed a Central Committee, itself subordinated to an elite policy office, or Politburo, consisting of just seven members, of whom three held the power. Strangely in such a xenophobic country, they were the Tatar Lenin, the Jew Trotsky and the Georgian Stalin, recently emerged from the shadows. Future commissar for Foreign Trade Leonid Krassin wrote to his wife in Sweden:

The Bolsheviks, after smashing Kerensky and occupying Moscow, have failed to reach an agreement with other [socialist] parties and they go on issuing new decrees on their own responsibility daily. All work is coming to an end. It means the ruin of [industrial] production and transport; meanwhile the armies at the front are dying of hunger. All the leading Bolsheviks [named] have come round, excepting Lenin and Trotsky, who remain as uncompromising as ever and cannot be persuaded to alter their attitude. I am afraid the outlook is black indeed.[152]

On 9 November R. Kühlmann, State Secretary at the Foreign Ministry in Berlin requested a further 15 million marks from the 'extraordinary [or secret] budget' for the Bolsheviks and indicated future need for further sums.[153] With the party's financial stability thus assured, the Bolsheviks urgently needed to halt hostilities against the Central Powers, so that they could use their armed supporters, known as the Red Guards, to eliminate all forces in Russia still loyal to the Tsar and impose their rule on all the other revolutionary groups.

On 10 November the Bolsheviks issued a decree abolishing the freedom of the press 'temporarily' until the new regime had taken firm root. The Liberal press was the first to go, followed by the Socialist Revolutionary and Menshevik parties, Lenin, on 17 November declaring:

> 'The state is an institution built up to exercise violence... now we want to exercise violence in the interests of the people.'

Bolshevik censors also imposed fines for 'unfavourable' news published, Maxim Gorky's *Novaya Zhizn* being punished with a fine of 35,000 roubles.

Taking up his duties as Commissar for Foreign Affairs, Trotsky moved his family in with other top people living on the upper floors of the Smolny Institute, in which were the Bolsheviks' offices. He took advantage of this to have a daily siesta upstairs in his somewhat spartan accommodation, often interrupted by a visit from his two daughters by Alexandra. Among the foreign correspondents also welcomed there was Louise Bryant, who described the living conditions:

> Trotsky and his pretty little [second] wife, who hardly spoke anything but French, lived in one room on the top floor [of the Smolny Institute]. The room was partitioned off like a poor artist's attic studio. In one end were two cots and a cheap little dresser and in the other a desk and two or three cheap chairs. There were no pictures, no comfort anywhere.[154]

Gradually, Trotsky the maverick took more responsibility for the administration: drawing up procedures for the revolutionary tribunals to try those accused of counter-revolutionary tendencies, including former tsarist officers; putting in hand the change from the Julian calendar to the Gregorian, to march in step with the rest of Europe, if only on deciding the date; hobnobbing with foreign representatives; bringing Lettish riflemen to Petrograd as bodyguards; demanding crackdowns on what remained of the bourgeois newspapers and giving press conferences, at which he became the voice of Sovnarkom. He also never tired of pointing out to the other commissars those duties in which they were, to his mind, insufficiently zealous. It was not a character trait that won him supporters, whatever the public thought about his rousing speeches, and was to leave him almost friendless when his star was no longer in the ascendant and Stalin was intent on killing him. Even what looked to outsiders as Trotsky's close collaboration with Lenin was deceptive: the two men hated each other, neither being able to play second fiddle to anyone for long. In Trotsky's case, losing a game of chess with a friend was enough to end the friendship.

One of Lenin's most repeated promises from his return in April to November after the revolution was that the Bolsheviks, once in power, would swiftly summon an elected Constituent Assembly. Against this, his *Theses on the Constituent Assembly* published in *Pravda* argued that class conflicts, conflicts with Ukraine, and the Kadet-Kaledin uprising had made formal democracy impossible, so the Constituent Assembly must unconditionally accept sovereignty of the Soviet government or it would be dealt with by revolutionary means. After the Bolsheviks had done everything possible to delay the election, when it happened the result was a shattering rejection of them, their candidates receiving only 9 million out of 36 million votes, netting 175 seats out of 707 against the Socialist Revolutionaries' 370, which gave them a clear majority. However, at the first session of the assembly the Bolshevik minority caused such uproar and confusion that any pretence of democracy was abandoned and the session ended after less than twenty-four hours. A foretaste of Bolshevik tactics came on 30 December when many Socialist Revolutionaries were arrested for counter-revolutionary conspiracy. In March 1918 the SR members of the Assembly still at liberty walked out and did not return.

The Central Powers wanted urgently to end with war with Russia, so that they could transfer troops to the Western Front. After the ceasefire was agreed by the Bolsheviks on 15 December 1917, OHL immediately began moving troops out and AOK in Vienna began moving Austro-Hungarian units to reinforce its forces fighting on the Isonzo front in Italy. The Soviet delegation to the peace talks at Brest-Litovsk was headed by Adolf Yoffe, and included Anastasia Bizenko, the first woman diplomat, whose credentials included assassinating a tsarist official in November 1905. Lev Kamenev left a record of the initial contact at Brest-Litovsk, the border city where, in peacetime, the bogies of passenger trains were changed from European standard to Russian gauge and freight in both directions had to be re-loaded on wagons of the different gauge. He wrote:

> We crossed the line, led by a bugler carrying a white flag. Three hundred metres from the German wire, we were met by German officers. At 5 o'clock, blindfolded, we were taken to the battalion staff, to present our credentials to two officers of the German General Staff, who had come for that purpose. Negotiations were conducted in French. Our proposal to negotiate an armistice on all the Russian fronts preparatory to concluding peace, was transmitted direct by telegraph to the commander of all German forces on the Russian fronts and to the German General Staff.
>
> At 6.20 pm we were driven to meet General von Hofmeister, who informed us that a reply would probably be received within twenty-four hours. Yet, just over an hour later a preliminary answer from the General Staff gave agreement to our proposals. By midnight, General von Hofmeister had given us a written reply. Since our communication had been in Russian, this was in German.

It read:

> The German commander of the Ostfront is authorised by the German High Command to enter into negotiations with the Russian High Command, which is requested to appoint a commission with written authority to be sent to the commander of the German Ostfront, who will likewise name a commission with special authorisation.
>
> The day and time of the meeting are to be fixed by the Russian High Command and communicated to the German command in time to prepare a special train for the purpose. Notice must be given of where it is to cross the front.[155]

After the crossing point had been agreed, and the time stipulated as noon on 22 December under the new calendar, the Russian negotiators were blindfolded anew and conducted back to their own lines.

On the following day, OHL sent to German Eastern Command a list of ten points to be included in the eventual peace agreement. Until then the German and Austro-Hungarian diplomats had been in favour of mild terms that could swiftly be agreed so that the mass of troops on the Eastern Front could be released for service in the West and the dual monarchy in Budapest allowed to recover from the economic and political stresses of the war that seemed increasingly liable to fragment its prewar empire. Indeed, Austrian Foreign Minister Ottokar von Czernin was a strong advocate of 'peace now', having convinced his emperor that the regime could not survive another winter of war. However, Hindenburg and Ludendorff took a strictly military view and were intent on a punitive peace treaty that would annex more than 500,000 square miles of formerly Russian territory. Such was the power of the military in Germany that their view prevailed over the wishes of the Foreign Office in Berlin, leaving Vienna no choice but to go along with this.

On 22 December 1917 at Brest-Litovsk the Bolshevik delegates led by Kamenev and Trotsky met representatives of Germany, Austria–Hungary, Bulgaria and Turkey to discuss the German peace terms. Point 5 on the agenda was the 'Recognition of the right of peoples to self-determination. Russian evacuation of Finland, Estonia, Livonia, the Moldava, Eastern Galicia and Armenia.'[156] Although the 'right of peoples to self-determination' was originally included in Lenin's own programme, Trotsky refused to give up an inch of the Russian Empire. Nevertheless, to speed things along because Ludendorff wanted to transfer more troops from the Russian fronts as soon as it was safe to do so, on the night of 28–29 December sixty German and Austrian diplomats arrived in Petrograd. They were accommodated in the Grand and Angleterre hotels, forcing Allied officers staying there to pretend they did not see them.[157]

Back at Brest-Litovsk, negotiations dragged on into January because both Trotsky and Lenin, brainwashed by their own propaganda, had convinced themselves that Germany was about to suffer its own revolution since Karl Marx had prophesied that *the* Communist revolution would happen there. True, there were strikes in Berlin and other German cities. In Austria, beset by food shortages and aghast at the scale of casualties at the fronts, strikes also flared up. Trotsky's command of German, gained during his years in Germany, Austria and Switzerland, enabled him to ignore the other side's demands at the negotiating table and hit them with his own. It was said he asked Gen Ludendorf why Germany wanted to detach the Baltic States from Russia, to which Ludendorf retorted, 'To protect my left flank when the next war happens'. In his autobiographical *Moya Zhizn*, Trotsky wrote:

> As Chairman of the Soviet delegation, I decided to put an abrupt halt to the familiarity in relations that had developed imperceptibly during the first negotations … and made it plain that I had no intention of being presented to the Prince of Bavaria. I demanded separately served lunches and dinners on the grounds that [the Soviet negotiating team] had to consult with each other during the intervals. This too was silently accepted.[158]

His blatant stalling tactics were based on an obsession that the strikes in Germany and Austria would rapidly spark nationwide revolutions and bring down both governments, rendering the Brest-Litovsk negotiations pointless. In the event, the anti-war strikes in the Central Powers were broken by executions of the ringleaders. Trotsky amazed the Central Powers representatives negotiating with him by haranguing them like a mob in the street, calling for 'a democratic peace without annexations, reparations, respecting the right to national self-determination'. He was to them an enigma: a Jew who spoke their language fluently, although with a strong Russian accent, but was well-groomed and impeccably dressed – therefore most unlike the image they had of unkempt revolutionaries with uncouth habits and dirty nails. Running out of patience, German Foreign Minister Baron Richard von Kuhlman upped the pressure for a treaty to be signed. Leading the Central Powers' delegation, General Max Hoffmann then brushed aside all the rhetoric, and told Trotsky that, if the Soviet government really wanted peace, it would have to renounce all claims to the formerly Russian-occupied areas of Poland, plus the Baltic states and Ukraine.

PART 3

14

THE STRUGGLE FOR POWER

After travelling back to Russia in the sealed coach, Inessa, as a member of the Moscow Soviet, was an outspoken critic of the Brest-Litovsk treaty, as was Alexandra Kollontai, who threatened to resign her post as Commissar for Social Welfare in protest. It was perhaps to get her persistently independent voice out of Russia for a while that she was sent in 1918 with a delegation to Sweden, England and France, to raise support for the new government. Upon her return, she continued arguing against ratification of the Treaty of Brest-Litovsk and resigned from the government on principle. Her political activities for the rest of that year included organising the First All-Russian Congress of Working and Peasant Women in November 1918.

Given the urgent need to resolve the internal chaos in Russia and Stalin's proclamation at the Third Congress of Soviets that same month of the right of 'all peoples to self-determination through to complete secession from Russia',[159] one might think that Trotsky would agree to any terms which left Russia itself intact. After all, the workers that he professed to represent had marched under the slogan 'peace at any price'. Instead, since many meaningless slogans were being chanted in the streets of Russian cities, he invented a new one on his return to Moscow: 'Neither war nor peace' – i.e. a cease-fire without a formal treaty. Perhaps the saddest slogan of those times was 'All land to those who work it' – a blatant lie, since Lenin already planned to seize, not just the great estates but all the peasants' land too, and collectivise it in a centralised programme directed by party bureaucrats. The slogan was simply a great lie aimed at winning over the confused peasantry, who took the words at face value.

At the time, superficially it seemed that the other socialist revolutionary parties were working in tandem with the Bolsheviks. Yet, on the day scheduled for the opening of the Constituent Assembly, demonstrators supporting the assembly were met with rifle and machine-gun fire from BMO squads, who caused a hundred or more casualties among the unarmed demonstrators. Inside and outside the Tauride Palace, heavily armed Red Guards and soldiers and sailors from Kronstadt with armoured cars and water-cooled machine guns challenged deputies. Members of the public could not gain admission to the galleries, which were monopolised by Bolshevik supporters. Lenin was present, sitting out of the limelight on some steps immersed in his work, as Socialist Revolutionary speakers were menaced with loaded weapons, despite which the deputies continued debating through the night, proclaiming Russia a federated republic with autonomy for all non-Russian constituent ethnic groups. After a brief recess, the deputies found their return to the hall blocked by BMO squads armed with rifles, machine guns and two field guns. On 19 January 1918 a decree of Sovnarkom had abolished the Constituent Assembly and all newspapers reporting the previous day's events were seized and destroyed. As the German minister and future ambassador Count Wilhelm von Mirbach reported to Berlin on 24 January:

> … of all the newspapers in Russia only the Bolsheviks' *Pravda* and *Izvestiya* remain free of a draconian censorship and politicians, [elected] deputies, editors and other such members of the opposition live under continual threat to their liberty, if not worse.[160]

The Finnish government declared independence on 6 December 1917, from which date the country that had been under foreign occupation since 1809, with its eastern frontier only twenty miles from Petrograd, was at last to be governed by its own people. The Ukrainian provisional government likewise proclaimed its independence on 22 January 1918 and agreed a separate peace treaty with the Central Powers on 9 February.

Thinking ahead, Lenin was rightly afraid that evidence of the German financing of the Bolsheviks might surface in future and destroy the myth of the revolution being a spontaneous uprising of Russia's workers and peasants. Early in 1918 Edgar Sisson, a former employee of the US Committee on Public Information, was contacted by Colonel Raymond Robins, an American Red Cross administrator working in Russia, and by other non-Russian Communist sympathisers. They offered Sisson between fifty-three and sixty-eight documents apparently proving that huge injections of German money both before and after the October Revolution had made possible the Bolshevik takeover, and that Lenin's quid pro quo had been forcing through the signature of the second Brest-Litovsk treaty against the wishes of the other revolutionary socialists, who suspected what had gone on but had no proof. After Sisson's return to Washington, the documents were carefully examined and some declared doubtful and others outright forgeries. They were nonetheless published that autumn amid a furore of disagreement over their authenticity. Nearly forty years later, when the documents were closely scrutinised by George Kennan in 1956, they were nearly all pronounced forgeries on the grounds of spelling and other gross errors that were childishly obvious to anyone who could read German and Russian. And yet, German Foreign Office files discovered in the immediate aftermath of the Allied victory in 1945 confirm the story of the Sisson papers.

The explanation is not hard to find. Dzerzhinsky's secret police, the Cheka, had inherited the forgers who previously had worked for the Okhrana, which published the infamous 1903 hoax, *The Protocol of the Learned Elders of Zion*. What better way was there for the Bolsheviks to disprove any allegations of taking German bribes than by having Sisson publish the 'proof' of those accusations in the form of documents that could easily be proven to be forgeries?

Lenin's other embarrassment at the time was that his party could no longer be called Marxist because the manner in which it came to power in the October Revolution contradicted Marxist teaching. So, he reinvented the Bolshevik Party by claiming that its historical justification was a new political philosophy called Marxism-Leninism – a contradiction in terms that stretched his followers' gullet of credibility so wide that all the subsequent contradictions were swallowed whole. Throughout the existence of the Soviet Union, in the resultant jargon-infested ideological confusion, there was only one determinant of orthodoxy: the party itself, which became the sole arbiter of truth, while truth in Russia became whatever the party decreed it to be, with millions of alleged dissenters purging their heresies, if they lived long enough, by sentences to forced labour in the Siberian Gulag.[161] It was intentionally made difficult for foreigners – and indeed Russians – to unravel all this. George Kennan put it well in a despatch of 1944:

> A daring tour de force which the American mind must make, if it is to try to find Russian life comprehensible, [is] to understand that for Russia, at any rate, there are no objective criteria of right and wrong. There are not even any objective criteria of reality and unreality. What do we mean by this? We mean that right and wrong, reality and unreality, are determined in Russia not by any God, not by any innate nature of things, but simply by men themselves. Here men determine what is true and what is false. The reader should not smile. This is a serious fact.[162]

Lenin was already drawing up in private lists of former and current public figures who would have to be eliminated in order to prevent them competing for power with him or simply revealing his various uncertainties. Strangest of all was his list of socialist and other intellectuals who could not be imprisoned or killed because they were too well known and respected outside Russia. These were to be forcibly exiled in late 1922 – literally shipped abroad after arrest by the Cheka, re-named GPU – Gosudarstvennoye Politicheskoye Upravlenie,[163] just before the Soviet Union was declared.[164]

Despite Lenin's talk of national self-determination and Stalin's embarrassing reiteration of that promise, and although still in a state of unresolved hostilities with the Central Powers, the Bolsheviks invaded Ukraine to re-impose Russian rule, obliging OHL to keep a half-million men there, to the great relief of the Western Allies. To force Trotsky back to the conference table German Ostfront commander Max Hoffmann gave the Bolsheviks five days to conclude a peace treaty. Lenin realised that the Bolsheviks' fragile control of government could be shattered by public anger throughout Russia if the war continued, and threatened to resign if Trotsky did not agree terms with the Germans.

Fed up with the Bolsheviks' behaviour in Brest-Litovsk, General Hoffmann sent an ultimatum to the Soviet government, informing them of an impending renewal of his offensive in Ukraine. Debating this on the following day, the Central Committee registered five votes, including

Lenin and Stalin, in favour of accepting the German terms and six against, including Trotsky, on the grounds that no formerly Russian Imperial territory should be given up. As far as Lenin was concerned, the only important thing was to preserve the still fragile Bolshevik control of government. The consensus was that the German troops would refuse to fight in sympathy with the Russian revolutionaries. On 18 February, the Germans attacked and Lenin threatened to resign from the Central Committee and the government if the armistice was not signed, whatever the terms. Under this blackmail, the Central Committee approved the signature of a peace treaty.

On February 26 at a meeting of Sovnarkom, Lenin drew up the decree evacuating the government to Moscow:

1. Moscow chosen as the seat of government;
2. Every department must evacuate a minimum number of leaders of the central administration, 20-30 people maximum (with families);
3. Immediately evacuate the State bank, gold reserves and state papers.

The real plans of leaving were known only by the selected few. The preparation for the departure and phases of departure were kept strictly secret because the government feared not only acts of terror but also the disturbances that could begin if people learned about the move in advance. *Pravda* only announced the moves after the members of the all-Russian Central Executive Committee and the Soviet of People's Commissars had already left Petrograd.

On 3 March, after Trotsky gave way to Lenin's unremitting pressure, the deal was done in Brest-Litovsk and the Soviet delegates signed the 5-language armistice agreement on behalf of the Russian state. In the document, written in German, Russian, Bulgarian, Hungarian and Ottoman Turkish,[165] Russia accepted the loss of Ukraine, Poland, Finland and Belarus, as well as the three Baltic states, which were intended to become German protectorates. Lenin called it 'an obscene peace'[166] despite all his fine talk of national determination, but most of the Russian population heaved a sigh of relief in the belief that their surviving menfolk could at last return home. OHL and AOK took a deep breath of relief that the negotiations had finally resulted in a treaty. Train after train rumbled westwards transporting CP forces and vast numbers of rifles, artillery and ammunition of all calibres to the Western Front in Flanders and the Isonzo, where fighting was to continue for another eight months. Other trains also headed west into Austro-Hungary with cargoes of reparations: grain, sugar, eggs, horses and pigs for slaughter.

The confusingly titled 7th Extraordinary Congress of the SDLP was held in the Tauride Palace in Petrograd between 6 and 8 March 1918 and attended by forty-seven full and fifty-nine consultative delegates. Many delegates could not arrive on such short notice, due to the general disruption of transport and the German occupation of swathes of formerly Russian territory. It was during this congress that the Bolsheviks formalised changing the name of the party to include the word 'Communist' with the following resolution, in Lenin's characteristically confusing style:

The Congress resolves that our Party be named henceforth the Russian Communist Party, with the word 'Bolsheviks' added in brackets.

The Congress resolves to change the Programme of our Party, re-editing the theoretical part or adding to it a definition of imperialism and the era of the international socialist revolution that has begun.

Following this, the change in the political part of our Programme must consist in the most accurate and comprehensive definition possible of the new type of state, the Soviet Republic, as a form of the dictatorship of the proletariat and as a continuation of those achievements of the world working-class revolution which the Paris Commune began. The Programme must show that our Party does not reject the use even of bourgeois parliamentarism, should the course of the struggle push us back, for a time, to this historical stage which our revolution has now passed. But in any case and under all circumstances the Party will strive for a Soviet Republic as the highest, from the standpoint of democracy, type of state, as a form of the dictatorship of the proletariat, of abolition of the exploiters' yoke and of suppression of their resistance.

The economic, including agrarian, and educational and other parts of our Programme must be recast in the same spirit and direction. The centre of gravity must be a precise definition of the economic and other reforms begun by our Soviet power, with a definite statement of the immediate definite tasks which Soviet power has set itself, and which

proceed from the practical steps we have already taken towards expro-
priating the expropriators.

But all was not sweetness and light, whatever the name of the party.
Lenin's resolution approving the terms of the Brest-Litovsk agreement
was historically the most important item on the agenda:

> The Congress recognises the necessity to confirm the extremely harsh,
> humiliating peace treaty with Germany that has been concluded by Soviet
> power in view of our lack of an army, in view of the most unhealthy state
> of the demoralised army at the front, in view of the need to take advantage
> of even the slightest possibility of obtaining a respite before imperialism
> launches its offensive against the Soviet Socialist Republic.
>
> In the present era of the socialist revolution, numerous military attacks
> on Soviet Russia by the imperialist powers (both from the West and from
> the East) are historically inevitable. The historical inevitability of such
> attacks at a time when both internal, class relations and international rela-
> tions are extremely tense, can at any moment, even within the next few
> days, lead to fresh imperialist aggressive wars against the socialist movement
> in general and against the Russian Socialist Soviet Republic in particular.
>
> The Congress therefore declares that it recognises the fundamental task
> of our Party, of the entire vanguard of the class-conscious proletariat and of
> Soviet power, to be the adoption of measures to improve the self-discipline
> and discipline of the workers and peasants of Russia, to explain the
> inevitability of Russia's historic advance towards a socialist, patriotic war
> of liberation, to create everywhere soundly co-ordinated mass organisations
> *held together by a single iron will*, organisations that are capable of concerted
> action in their day-to-day efforts and especially at critical moments in the
> life of the people, and, lastly, to train systematically and comprehensively
> in military matters and military operations the entire adult population of
> both sexes.
>
> The Congress considers the only reliable guarantee of consolidation of
> the socialist revolution in Russia to be its *conversion into a world working-class
> revolution*. [Author's italics]
>
> The Congress is confident that the step taken by Soviet power in view of
> the present alignment of forces in the world arena was, from the standpoint
> of the interests of the world revolution, inevitable and necessary.

Confident that the working-class revolution is maturing persistently in all belligerent countries and is preparing the full and inevitable defeat of imperialism, the Congress declares that the socialist proletariat of Russia will support the fraternal revolutionary movement of the proletariat of all countries with all its strength and with every means at its disposal.[167]

The resolution was adamantly opposed by the left wing led by Nikolai Bukharin, who refused to associate themselves with the Central Committee and demanded that the war be continued. Even among those delegates who supported the treaty, there were substantial disagreements and Lenin's Resolution on War and Peace was only approved on the last day of the congress by thirty votes for, twelve against and four abstentions. Lenin's riposte to Bukharin's supporters was another resolution:

The Congress is of the opinion that a refusal to enter the Central Committee in the situation at present obtaining in the Party is particularly undesirable, since such a refusal is in general impermissible in principle to those who desire the unity of the Party, and would today be a double threat to unity. The Congress declares that everyone can and should deny his responsibility for any step taken by the Central Committee, if he does not agree with it, by means of a declaration to that effect but not by leaving the Central Committee. The Congress is firm in the hope that the comrades will, after a consultation with the mass organisations, withdraw their resignation; the Congress will, therefore, carry through elections without taking the statement of resignation into consideration.

The Brest-Litovsk peace agreement was subsequently ratified by the Extraordinary 4th All-Russian Congress of Soviets held between 14 and 16 March, on the last day of which it endorsed Lenin's decision to move the seat of government 400 miles to the east, with this explanation:

In the state of the current crisis of the Russian revolution the position of Petrograd as the capital has dramatically changed. Thus the Congress resolves to transfer for the time being the capital of the Russian Socialist Federative Soviet Republic from Petrograd to Moscow until the above-mentioned conditions change.

Trotsky's attitude that the 'obscene peace' was unnecessary was totally unrealistic. Although still a magnetic speaker, he had been badly upstaged by Lenin's relentless pursuit of closure to the war Russia had been fighting for almost four years. Historian Robert Service put it succinctly:

> Trotsky was a bad listener. Indeed his ears were deaf to the case made by others. In any private discussion, he wanted to do all the talking. His changes of mind tended to be abrupt – and he did not care to alert his comrades in advance. He was willing, time and time again, to turn the Party upside down rather than concede to his opponents.[168]

Faced down by Lenin, he was now reduced to blustering and sulking. On one issue, however, he remained intractable: a refusal to go back to Brest-Litovsk and sign the deal. He preferred to resign as People's Commissar for Foreign Affairs, to avoid that humiliating duty. Nor would Lenin, despite having engineered its ratification by the 4th Congress of Soviets, perform that task. The unpleasant task was allotted to Grigori Sokolnikov, while Lenin agreed to Adolf Joffe's suggestion that Trotsky's talents must not be lost to the party and could best be used by making him Commissar for Military Affairs – which proved to be a brilliant decision. Trotsky, however, was unsure whether his Jewish origins did not disqualify him for this office, but Lenin won and Trotsky was back in Sovnarkom wearing his new headgear, a peaked military cap.

15

ENEMIES AT THE GATES

In his resolution on the peace of Brest-Litovsk, Lenin foresaw the Western Allies seeking revenge for the Bolsheviks' taking Russia out of the war because the first overt Allied intervention had been launched from British-occupied Mesopotamia towards the end of 1917, when it was obvious that Russia's change of regime was inevitably going to produce an armistice. Dubbed 'Dunsterforce' after its commander Colonel Lionel Dunster, the mixed column of British and Empire troops had a rather vague brief until it was tasked with occupying the important Caspian oilfields before the Turks could do so and make available their output to the Central Powers' war effort. In the confusion of Central Asian politics and local Leftish revolutionary socialists declaring the Central Transcaspian Dictatorship, in opposition to the Bolsheviks under Lenin, Dunsterforce's mission eventually failed.[169] Similarly, in August 1918 an Anglo-Indian force under General Malleson in Tashkent, sent in support of Transcaspasian forces, found itself enmeshed in Central Asian feuding, as Dunsterforce had been. Having achieved nothing useful, Malleson's little army was eventually withdrawn in January 1919.

After the signature of the Brest-Litovsk treaty in March 1918, with the capital of the Russian state now once again Moscow, this extract from Report No 9 by Count Wilhelm von Mirbach, the German Minister in Moscow, to his chancellor in Berlin, gives a chilling picture of life in the city at this confusing time:

Anyone who knew [Moscow] in the days of its glory would hardly be able to recognise it now. In every part of the city, and especially in the central commercial quarter, countless bullet-holes in walls and windows are evidence of the bitter battles that were fought for its possession.

The fighting referred to in von Mirbach's report was due to a Left SR army of about 1,800 armed men bombarding the Kremlin with field artillery and seizing the main telephone exchange and telegraph office, which they held for two days. Von Mirbach's report continued:[170]

Even the Kremlin has suffered terribly. Various of its gates are badly damaged; the Iberian Gate has been partly destroyed and is now only boarded up. Hardly any better-dressed people are to be seen. [It is] as if the whole of the previously governing class and the bourgeoisie had disappeared off the face of the earth. Hardly anything can be bought in the shops except dusty remnants of past splendour, and these only at fantastic prices. It is unwise to go out towards evening, as at that time of day one often hears rifle fire and more or less serious skirmishes seem to take place continually. The factories are at a standstill and the land is still, to all intents and purposes, not being cultivated.[171]

Dzherzhinsky's first major action for Lenin was to execute all 1,500 political prisoners in Petrograd for the crime of counter-revolutionary activity before he left for Moscow, where he selected the offices of the All-Russian Insurance Company – an imposing building at No. 22, Lubyanka Street – as the headquarters of the Cheka. The address was to be a synonym for terror through the next seven decades.

The collapse of the Russian fronts and the loss of the immense resources in manpower of tsarist Russia were sources of concern for the Western Allies not only because the Central Powers were now able to transfer thousands of men and all their equipment, including artillery, to the Western Front, but also because large dumps of materiel previously shipped to Russia for use against the Central Powers were still lying in various ports, principally Murmansk and Archangel in the Far North and Vladivostok in the Far East. These might now be handed over to the Germans, who were known to have asked for them. With the Baltic countries now in the German sphere and Estonia fighting off a Bolshevik army with the help of White Finnish volunteers, a division of the Kaiser's troops had landed in Finland in April 1918, to assist a nationalist army under General Mannerheim to stamp out the pro-Communist Red Finns. Captured Reds were sent to concentration camps, as they were also in Estonia. The German landing in Finland gave rise to speculation in Petrograd that their presence was a preliminary to a German invasion of Russia from the northwest to capture Murmansk and Archangel, and simply commandeer all the British supplies there.

In the same month the Cheka initiated an undeclared war against the anarchists in Petrograd and Moscow, forcing those who escaped to go underground, which was becoming more and more difficult, since their sympathisers feared suffering the same fate. In Rostov, Briansk and Ekaterinburg anarchists broke into the prisons where their comrades were detained and liberated all the prisoners, calling for a general revolt against the Bolshevik regime.

On May Day of 1918 Lenin watched the parades in Red Square. He was living in the Kremlin with Krupskaya, his sister Maria and their maid, but although they ate off Tsar Nicholas' silver and fine porcelain, their fare was frugal. Visitors complained that the heating was inadequate and there were never enough teaspoons because the guests stole them. On 10 May the first requisitions of cereals and meat were decreed. Dismayed, the peasants, who had thought they would be masters of their own land in fulfillment of the Bolshevik slogan 'All land to those who work it!' slaughtered animals illicitly and refused to sow seed for the next harvest. Dzerzhinsky's remedy was to unleash on them armed units of Cheka soldiery, which hardened the peasant's refusal to be milked of their produce. Educated town dwellers talked of the 'Carthaginian peace' of Brest-Litovsk and surviving Rightists made secret overtures to the Germans in the hope that they would renew offensives to drive out Lenin and his Bolsheviks, but OKH gave all its priority to the war in the West.

The anti-Bolshevik revolutionary socialist Nikolai V. Tchaikovsky was president of the Administrative Board, or regional government, of the North Region based in Archangel. It was he who invited British forces to intervene, followed a request of the Murmansk *soviet* that had been approved by the government in Moscow. In a speech on 14 May 1918, Lenin justified this by saying that British and French forces had landed to defend the northern seaboard because German and White Finnish forces were threatening it across the Karelian frontier. The governments in Paris and London had agreed to mount a military intervention to land troops at the two ports of Archangel and Murmansk to safeguard the materiel, with the possibility of somehow making it available to the several anti-Bolshevik armies in Russia and helping them to overcome the new regime in Moscow, leading to a possible resurrection of the Russian fronts.[172] The last possibility was a pipe dream, but that was not understood in the West. French and British forces already being fully stretched on the Western Front, an appeal was made to Washington, where President Wilson agreed to allocate 5,000 officers and men, designated the American North Russia Expedition Force, but usually referred to as 'the Polar Bears', to share the burden of this intervention in the Far North.

A second force of 8,000 men, designated the American Expeditionary Force Siberia, was also despatched to Vladivostok,[173] to safeguard the Allied supply dumps there and along the Trans-Siberian. This force had uneasily to cohabit with a 70,000-strong Japanese contingent in and around Vladivostok, Tokyo being an ally of the Western Allies at the time. The Japanese would be the last to leave the Asian mainland – in 1922 – and finally withdrew from Northern Sakhalin under American pressure in 1925. Although not intended as an interventionist force, the Czech Legion of 42,000-plus prisoners released from tsarist POW camps was a force to be reckoned with. Their release had been agreed by the Kerensky regime, authorising them to form an army to resume the fight *in France*. To delay their appearance there, German pressure at Brest-Litovsk required them to be repatriated via the longest route through Vladivostok, from where Allied vessels would transport them around the globe to Western Europe.

While they were still en route across Siberia, Trotsky issued an ultimatum that they must now join the Red Army – whose full title was *Raboche-Krestyanskaya Krasnaya Armiya* or Workers' and Peasants' Red Army – or be sent back to POW/concentration camps. Having already tasted Russian hospitality, the Czechs decided instead to stay where they were. The Trans-Siberian was genuinely over-loaded with westbound trainloads of Central Powers POWs who had been released from the camps in Siberia and were prepared to don uniforms and fight again for their old masters. Under the Treaty of Brest-Litovsk the

Soviets were required to repatriate them speedily, so the eastbound Czechs had a low priority on the line. Their progress stopped entirely at Chelyabinsk on 14 May 1918, when a released POW being repatriated westwards threw a stone that killed a legionnaire. Tensions between the eastbound Czechs and their westbound compatriots, whom they regarded as traitors, were high. Hauling the stone-thrower off his train, the legionnaires lynched him on the spot. After local Bolskeviks arrested several Czechs for this, other legionnaires occupied the whole city with some bloodshed and released their comrades from jail, proceeding to take over Petropavlovsk, Kurgan, Novonikolayevsk and several other towns along the railway until in August 1918 they were masters of the Trans-Siberian from the Pacific coast as far as Kazan, where they effected a purge of Red sympathisers.

Some sources, however, disagree as to exactly why and how the Czechs became masters of the strategic railway line. As so often, after Brest-Litovsk, when Russian history was completely rewritten in accordance with the party line and even Allied accounts conflict, confusion rules. Some historians believe that the takeover of thousands of miles of track across hostile territory could not have been accomplished spontaneously, which would indicate that British and/or French money was made available to a body calling itself the Czech National Council, which financed the extended coordination called for by such an exercise. There may be truth in that; but more to the point was the flood of Cossacks, Socialist Revolutionaries and other non-Bolsheviks who allied themselves with the Czechs to occupy the vast extent of land between Kazan and the Pacific. Suffering some casualties, the Czech Legion and its allies kicked the Bolsheviks out of Vladivostok after fifty-eight days of skirmishes, and then demanded stores and arms from the Allied dumps at the port so they could travel back along the railway to rescue the large number of their comrades far in the rear, who had taken control of the major Siberian city of Irkutsk after fighting with the Bolsheviks there. It says something about their esprit de corps that the slogan painted on the cattle wagons in which they lived on the railway was 'Each of us is a brick, together we are a rock'. With the free Czechs taking control of a critical stretch of the Trans-Siberian, armoured trains belonging to both sides thundered eastwards and westwards through the regions they controlled, laying waste towns and villages suspected of harbouring the enemy. It was, in fact, a

Czech column nearing Ekaterinburg that triggered the murders of the Romanovs.

As Commissar for War, Trotsky was showing something like genius for a man with no military experience. Although he claimed to have learned much in Serbia during the Second Balkan War, he had never risked going anywhere near the front, writing his articles for the Ukrainian newspaper *Kievskaya Mysl* at a safe distance from the fighting. His management technique in the civil war was to turn the Red Guards into the Red Army under the command of former tsarist officers and NCOs closely supervised by political commissars to form a disciplined force capable of confronting some 200,000 men in the several foreign interventionist armies on Russian soil and the various White groups. The Reds had the advantage of being able easily to move forces from one front to another along internal lines of communication, whereas the interventionists and the Whites were handicapped by the vast distances separating them, which precluded any coordinated moves, even had their leaders a common strategy. Also, their men were war-weary after four years of fighting and wanted only to go home, where their families were clamouring for their return after the Armistice and the German surrender in November 1918. The Red conscripts had no possibility of early release. Indeed, Trotsky's methods caused far higher casualties in the Red Army than those suffered by the Whites.

To kick the Czech Legion and other White forces out of Kazan, Trotsky's Order of the Day tasked the Fifth Red Army ...

> ... to wrest Kazan from [the enemy's] grasp, to throw back the Czech mercenaries and the officer-thugs, drown them in the Volga, and crush their criminal mutiny against the workers' revolution. In this conflict we are using not only rifles, cannon and machine guns, but also newspapers. For the newspaper is also a weapon. The newspaper binds together all units of the Fifth Army in one thought, one aspiration, one will. Forward to Kazan![174]

At the beginning of the operation, the Reds' disposition was as follows: To the west of Kazan was the Fifth Army of the Eastern Front and the Red Volga Flotilla; to the east of Kazan was part of the Second Army. On 7 September the Reds started shelling the city and took some outlying villages. On 9 September a beachhead was established against the western part of the city. On 10 September the city was taken by storm, most of the White defenders managing to get away down the Volga. Those who literally 'missed the boat' were executed by the victorious Reds.

For most of this time, Stalin had been absent from Moscow, travelling from one front to the other. Even when ordered to return to his duties with Sovnarkom, he headed to the Urals three months later with Dzherzhinsky. Even Lenin found him impossible to control. At the slightest contretemps, Stalin's trump card was to threaten to resign. Although fighting on the same political side since Trotsky had rejoined the Bolsheviks, Lenin never relaxed with him and Stalin sided with Lenin, having hated Trotsky since they first met in Vienna in 1913 – this with a hatred that would end only with the murder in Mexico. At one point, Stalin wrote to Lenin:

> Trotsky, generally, cannot refrain from histrionic gestures. At Brest-Litovsk he harmed our cause with his incredibly 'leftish' speeches. Regarding the Czechs, he similarly harmed the common cause with his [pompous] announcements in the month of May. Now he's on about discipline, yet all this Trotskyist discipline [in the Red Army] actually consists of having the most prominent people active at the front watching the behinds of military specialists from the non-Party camp of counter-revolutionaries. Trotsky can't sing without falsetto. Therefore, I ask now, before it is too late, to have Trotsky removed, put in his place and given limits, for I fear that his unhinged commands will create discord between the army and the command staff and destroy the front.
>
> I'm not a lover of tittle-tattle and scandal, but feel that if we don't immediately restrain Trotsky, he'll ruin the whole Red army with his 'leftist' and Red discipline, which will alienate even the most disciplined comrades.[175]

On Stalin's visits to the fronts where the Red Army confronted White or interventionist forces, punishing officers and others by public executions, he was also building a bureaucratic power base. He was on the Central Committee; he was still Commissar for Nationalities; he chaired the drafting of the constitution of the RSFSR; he was also chairman of the Revolutionary Military Council of the southern front; he was involved in planning Soviet governments for the Baltic states; very importantly, he was in the Politburo and Orgburo. Although not in supreme command, he was involved in the 1920 war between Poland and the RSFSR where British Foreign Secretary Henry Curzon drew a line on the map to separate Polish-speakers to the west from Ukrainian- and Belarussian-speakers to the east – a solution that Stalin fought. This accretion of power passed largely unnoticed by the general public because Stalin did little public speaking like Trotsky and had scant time for publishing papers like Lenin. When Lenin later proposed at the Eleventh Party Congress in March and April 1922 that Stalin should replace Vyacheslav Molotov as General Secretary of the Russian Communist Party, he was so firmly ensconced in power that no one could dislodge him, despite many people saying that no one person could satisfactorily fulfil the duties that went with so many posts simultaneously.

In the summer of 1918 Lenin's only non-Bolshevik supporters – the Left Social Revolutionaries – demanded an end to the grain requisitions, the dissolution of the Red Army and the Cheka and cessation of combat with the Czech Legion. Lenin refused outright, ordering the arrest of the LSR leaders. Surviving members of the LSR executive committee ordered Jakov G. Blumkin, a Chekist officer despite his political affiliation, to assassinate German ambassador Count von Mirbach on 6 July, in the hope that this would provoke renewed German attacks, forcing the Russian armies to renew the fight. With Blumkin on the run, Lenin ordered the execution of twenty or so LSR hostages to placate German anger at the breach of diplomatic status.

Something of the political atmosphere across Russia can be gleaned from Lenin's telegraphed instructions of 9 August 1918 to the Nizhny Novgorod Soviet's president, who was ordered to suppress the peasants' protests against grain requisitioning by establishing a dictatorial troika of himself and two other Bolsheviks to effect a mass terror, in which 'the hundreds of prostitutes' who were causing the Red soldiers to get drunk must be shot or deported. Lenin ordered massive reprisals with summary execution for anyone caught in possession of a firearm, as well as deportations of Mensheviks and other 'unreliable' elements. Yet his philosophy regarding the peasantry was confused. On the one hand, he constantly harped on the need to win all the peasants to the side of the Reds by preaching class warfare; on the other, he set up committees of the most disadvantaged peasants, which alienated many others and used armed force to compel the peasants to hand over their grain. The Penza Soviet was ordered to crush without pity the *kulaki* [peasants resisting grain requisitions]:

> Comrades! The kulak uprising in your five districts must be crushed without pity. The interests of the whole revolution demand such actions, for the final struggle with the kulaks has now begun. You must make an example of these people. (1) Hang (I mean hang publicly, so that people see it) at least 100 kulaks, rich bastards, and known bloodsuckers. (2) Publish their names. (3) Seize all their grain. (4) Single out the hostages per my instructions in yesterday's telegram. Do all this so that for miles around people see it all, understand it, tremble, and tell themselves that we are killing the bloodthirsty kulaks and that we will continue to do so. Reply saying you have received and carried out these instructions. Yours, Lenin.[176]

Stalin used open brutality to enforce the requisitions and came down on any resistance by burning down entire villages. His behaviour too was frequently contradictory; while wooing the non-Russian minorities in the Caucasus, he ordered punitive measures against Cossacks and Caucasian peoples who defied the Moscow regime. On the southern front, he also committed Red forces to unequal battles where they were bound to suffer higher losses than the Whites. This brought criticism from Lenin, who did not directly accuse Stalin, but supported Trotsky's management of the Red Army, including his policy of using former tsarist officers under the control of political commissars. Stalin instead sacked many officers and confined them aboard a barge on the Volga, which he intended to sink with them battened down below decks.

Former officers, peasants ... Stalin's paranoia saw enemies and deliberate sabotage everywhere. When supplies of ammunition failed to arrive at the siege of Tsaritsyn, he accused the Red Army's logistical officers of '*formennoye predatelstvo*' – 'betrayal by those in uniform'. This became Soviet policy, with hundreds of thousands of innocent people accused of sabotage and counter-revolutionary activities to account for the shortcomings of the system itself. Trotsky too was happy to order both officers and their political commissars executed after prudent retreats, which he had not ordered.

Caught in the middle of all the violence, the peasants suffered. The *Manchester Guardian* Moscow correspondent Malcolm Muggeridge wrote of meeting some of the unfortunate kulaks targeted by Lenin, Stalin, Trotsky and Dzerzhinsky at the railway station of Rostov-on-Don in the Caucasus:

> A group of peasants were standing in military formation, five soldiers armed with rifles guarding them. There were men and women, each carrying a bundle. Somehow, lining them up in military formation made the thing grotesque – wretched looking peasants, half-starved, tattered clothes, frightened faces, standing to attention. These may be kulaks, I thought, but if so they have made a mighty poor thing of exploiting their fellows. I hung about, looking on curiously, wanting to ask where they were to be sent—to the north to cut timber [or] somewhere else to dig canals – until one of the guards told me sharply to take myself off.[177]

That evening, he witnessed a crowded street where some people 'holding fragments of food':

> inconsiderable fragments that in the ordinary way a housewife would throw away or give to the cat. Others were examining these fragments of food. Every now and then an exchange took place. Often, what was bought was at once consumed. There is not 5 per cent of the population [here] whose standard of life is equal to, or nearly equal to, that of the unemployed in England on the lowest scale of relief.[178]

Of another meeting with arrested kulaks, Muggeridge wrote:

> At a railway station early one morning, I saw a line of people with their hands tied behind them, being herded into cattle trucks at gunpoint – all so silent and mysterious and horrible in the half light, like some macabre ballet.[179]

Muggeridge's later dispatches were not used and he was sacked by the *Manchester Guardian*, which was editorially in sympathy with 'the great Soviet experiment', as it was called.

Inside Russia, there were still many people who were not pro-Red. The Left Socialist Revolutionary Party (LSR) had split off from the Socialist Revolutionary Party in September 1917 and refused to support Lenin's autocratic rule or accept the Treaty of Brest-Litovsk. Lenin's reaction was to banish members of the party from any government role, although some members continued to participate in other soviet organisations, including the Cheka. Denouncing the Bolsheviks' alleged abandonment of the principles of international socialism, the LSR leaders decided on a series of anti-Bolshevik actions in July. Following Blumkin's assassination of German ambassador von Mirbach on 6 July in the hope that this would cause the Germans to tear up the Treaty, on 30 July LSR member Boris M. Donskoi assassinated the German governor of Ukraine, General Hermann Eichhorn. After Lenin banned the LSR as a political party and shut down its publications, arresting and executing the leadership, the Bolsheviks were at last the only effective political party in Russia, with the Mensheviks hanging on uneasily until banned in their turn in 1921.

Proving that no one was safe from an assassin's bullet in Russia, in January 1918 a shot was fired at Lenin in his car, but missed. On 30 August 1918, after Lenin had spoken at a meeting in a Moscow munitions factory and was walking back to his car, a 28-year-old Left Socialist Revolutionary member named Faiga Chaimovna Roytblat, aka Fanya Kaplan, called out that he had 'betrayed the revolution'. She had already served eleven years' hard labour in Siberia for attempted assassination of a tsarist functionary before being released in the amnesty after the February Revolution. When Lenin turned to answer her accusation, Kaplan fired three shots from her revolver at point-blank range, only two bullets hitting him – probably because she had suffered damage to one eye as a result of severe beatings during her time in tsarist prisons. Wounded in the neck and arm, Lenin collapsed and was driven to his apartment inside the Kremlin, not to a hospital for removal of the bullets because he was terrified other assassins might be waiting there, to finish the job. Several conspiracy theories were based in the alleged poor eyesight of Kaplan and her refusal to say who had given her the revolver, but conveniently, she was executed three days later before she could be put on public trial, remaining a heroine of the LSR party. On the same day Kaplan shot Lenin, another LSR member shot and killed Mosei Uritsky, the head of the Petrograd Cheka, before being gunned down in his turn.

Other LSR members meanwhile arrested Dzherzhinsky, seized important buildings in Moscow and used the telegraph network to issue a call for revolt against the Bolsheviks. Lenin still controlled the telephone

Nineteenth-century industrial unrest sparked the Chartist movement in Britain. Thousands of workers at their meetings (below) believed social conditions could be improved within the existing social framework. Two prosperous German philosophers, Karl Marx (left) and Friedrich Engels (right) argued that Communist revolution was the only way to change society.

After horrific casualties in Russia's 1904 war with Japan, unarmed workers and peasants tried to present a petition to Tsar Nicholas II (above in contemporary engraving and below in Soviet artist's impression). Hundreds were killed by soldiers shooting into the crowd of men, women and children on Bloody Sunday, 22 January 1905.

Strikes and sabotage spread across Russia to Vladivostok and south to the Caucasus (below). Included in the thousands of political prisoners exiled to Siberia were three revolutionaries, shown in their Okhrana mugshots: Lenin (left), Trotsky (centre) and Stalin (right).

After all three escaped abroad, Lenin (above, left) and Trotsky (above, right) fell out for fifteen years. Lenin, the cold theorist, thought the chaos of war would offer the best chance of success for the next revolution. Stalin (Okhrana ID sheet below) became a Georgian bandit organising protection rackets and bank robberies, not always for the cause of revolution.

On 28 June 1914 Archduke Franz Ferdinand, heir to the Austro-Hungarian throne, made a state visit to Sarajevo in Bosnia-Herzegovina with his wife, Countess Sophie (above). Shot by a Serbian terrorist, both died. Although the assassin was immediately arrested (below), this event would eventually trigger the First World War.

... Serbien
muss sterbien!

The newspaper cartoon (above) shows the strong fist of Austria squashing the ugly little Serbian assassin. But treaties between Austria and Germany and between Britain, France and Russia set the whole continent at war. Below, Russian soldiers march into East Prussia.

Refusing to speak to each other, or allow their staffs to do so, Russian generals Samsonov (left) and von Renenkamf (right) repeated there the same mistakes that killed thousands unnecessarily in the 1904 war. Russian losses mounted into the millions buried in unrecorded shallow mass graves.

The Russian C-in-C Grand Duke Nikolai (left) was unable to control the incompetent generals. British observer Colonel Alfred Knox (right) reported to London how Russian soldiers often had the wrong bullets for their rifles and could not return enemy fire, causing casualties, desertion and mutinies.

Unable even to read a map, the Tsar (above, left with Gen Alexeyev) sacked the Grand Duke and appointed himself C-in-C. He was up against the German warlords Hindenburg and Ludendorff (right). More dangerous was Israil Gelfand (below, left), who persuaded German chancellor Bethmann-Hollweg (below, right) to transport Lenin's revolutionaries from Switzerland to Russia with enormous subsidies from Berlin, to finance a revolution taking Russia out of the war.

Tsar Nicholas (above, right with royal family) was dominated by the German-born Tsarina, who was under the influence of the monk Grigori Rasputin (above, left). Prince Georgi Lvov (below, left) tried to make a constitutional monarchy but was replaced as prime minister by Alexander Kerensky (below, right); but even he could not stem the tide.

Armed revolutionaries took over the streets (above) and the first committee or *soviet* of soldiers' representatives occupied the parliament building (below).

Совѣтъ Солдатскихъ Депутатовъ въ Государственной Думѣ.

25

Bolsheviks arriving at Brest-Litovsk (above) negotiated a peace treaty with the Central Powers, which enabled Lenin and Trotsky to conscript mutinous soldiers and workers (below) into the Red Army, to fight their internal enemies.

In the civil war phase of the revolution, atrocities were committed by both sides. Above, released Czech POWs hang Bolshevik prisoners. Below, Red soldiers survey their victims in Vladivostok.

Millions of men fought each other across the vast expanse of Russia. Admiral Kolchak (above, right) was styled Supreme Ruler of the White anti-Bolshevik armies, but several Russian generals like Anton Denikin (below with officers, men and a British Mk V tank) conducted their own campaigns.

Considered internal enemies by the Bolsheviks, the Romanovs were arrested. Nicholas II was reduced to chopping firewood at Tsarskoye Selo (above). Under house arrest in this fortified villa at Ekaterinburg (below, left), the whole family was murdered by Commissar Yakov Yurovsky (below, right).

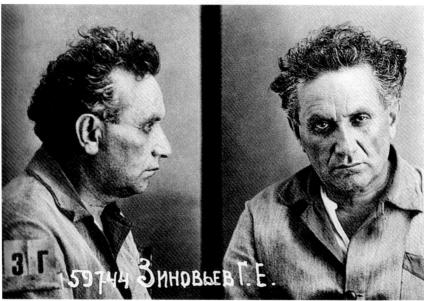

Stalin murdered all the Old Bolsheviks because they knew too much about him. Lenin's close associate Grigori Zinoviev (top, in 1918) was reduced in 1936 to NKVD prisoner 59744 (mugshot above) and shot. In 1940 Stalin had Trotsky murdered in Mexico. Below is one of the last photographs of him (in centre of group) with his wife and friends shortly before he died with Mercader's ice pick buried in his brain.

network and used it to summon his Lettish mercenaries and groups of Bolshevik workers to restore order in the capital, releasing Dzherzhinsky unharmed, to the greater misery of millions. Shortly after that, sailors in Kronstadt executed some 500 hostages held on the island. Deserters from the Red Army received short shrift. A typical report to Moscow from a provincial Cheka office in June 1919 recorded the arrest of families belonging to deserters from the Red Army. From each family, one member was shot until the deserters came out of the forests and surrendered. Thirty four of them were shot too.

In the Far North, Canada undertook to post troops to Murmansk and also to Vladivostok on the Pacific coast. A Royal Navy squadron of cruisers and destroyers in the Baltic under Rear-Admiral Edwyn Alexander-Sinclair also visited Estonian and Latvian ports, landing supplies and assuring the governments there that the cruisers' heavy guns would target any Bolshevik land forces coming within range. The Navy also had a flotilla of submersibles[180] based in Reval – modern Tallinn – which Commander Francis Cromie re-located with its Russian depot ship to Helsingfors to avoid confronting mutinous Russian sailors on the rampage in Estonia. When White-Red combat in Helsingfors made that haven equally unhealthy for British crews, the redoubtable Cdr Cromie scuttled his vessels at sea and most of his men made their way home via Murmansk. Another larger-than-life character, Commander Oliver Locker-Lampson commanded the Armoured Car Division of the Royal Naval Air Service, which had at one time before the Armistice held 25 miles in the Russian front lines for ten whole days after mutinous troops downed arms and walked away from their trenches. Where the armoured car division obtained supplies of motor fuel and oil, is a mystery, but they had allegedly supported Kornilov's rebellion while dressed in Russian uniforms, ranging afield as far as Kursk, 1,000 miles south of Murmansk.[181] The failure of the northern adventure starting in May 1918 was, according to Bruce Lockhart, due to the fact that…

We [the British] had committed the unbelievable folly of landing at Archangel with fewer than twelve hundred men. It was a blunder comparable with the worst mistakes of the Crimean War. The weakness of our landing force in the North resulted in the loss of the Volga line and in the temporary collapse of the anti-Bolshevik movement in European

Russia. In the absence of a strong lead from the Allies, the various counter-revolutionary groups began to quarrel and bicker among themselves. The accuracy of my dictum that the support we would receive from the Russians would be in direct proportion to the number of troops we sent, was speedily proved. The broad masses of the Russian people remained completely unmoved.

The consequences of this ill-considered venture were to be disastrous both to our prestige and to the fortunes of those Russians who supported us. It raised hopes which could not be fulfilled. It intensified the civil war and sent thousands of Russians to their deaths.[182]

One month after the surrender of the Central Powers, on 18 December 1918 a French interventionist force sent by President Clemenceau and commanded by General Henri Berthelot integrated Polish, Greek and Romanian elements to land on the Black Sea coast of what is now Ukraine, much of which was occupied by German and Austrian troops. Further east, the White generals Alexeyev and Kornilov gathered an army of 3,000 men in the Don region, which was swiftly overcome by 10,000 men sent against them by Trotsky. With Kornilov killed in action at Ekaterinodar, his chief-of-staff, Lieutenant-General Anton I. Denikin, took command of the White Volunteer Army, which was the most important anti-Bolshevik force, with whom Berthelot could ally himself. Denikin was preparing to march on Moscow until forced to retreat southwards to the Donbas region in terrible weather conditions. Regrouping, he led what looked like being a successful drive on Moscow in summer 1919, but was foiled by Trotsky forming a temporary alliance with Nestor Makhno's Ukrainian Black Army of anarchists.

One of the key battles of what was called 'the civil war' phase of the revolution took place at Tsaritsyn, where Major Ewen Cameron Bruce MC of the British Tank Corps, who had lost an arm by an act of hero-ism in Flanders, commanded a squadron of Mark V tanks. He and his men were under orders to give instruction in the use of tanks to suitable men of General Pyotr N. Wrangel's White Army, but not get involved in combat. Having twice being driven back by Red forces occupying Tsaritsyn, Wrangel decided to await reinforcements. Bruce volunteered instead to lead another advance with his tanks. His preparation included effecting a reconnaissance in an RAF fighter of 47 squadron on 28 June

1919, during which he shot down a Red observation balloon before the observer could inform the forces in the city of the presence of tanks with Wrangel's men. On the following day, several of the two-man Mk Vs led an advance through the wire that caused the Reds to flee in panic before the tanks' thirsty six-cylinder engines ran out of petrol. On 30 June enough petrol was siphoned from here and there to fill up one tank, which Bruce drove right into Tsaritsyn under heavy fire, taking 40,000 prisoners and capturing the city for Wrangel. Bruce was awarded the DSO and a given a couple of medals by Wrangel.

In the end, his bravery counted for little. In January 1920 the city was retaken by Red forces commanded by future Soviet marshal Kliment E. Voroshilov. Because Stalin was also present, Voroshilov prudently let him take all the credit for this victory. The city was re-named Stalingrad in 1925, as which it was the site of one of the most significant battles in the Second World War. With Stalin falling posthumously into disgrace, it has been called Volgograd since 1961.

So-called anarchist battle groups, whose weapons included firearms, explosives and agricultural tools, attacked anyone they came across, the biggest terrorist attack coming on 25 September 1919, when one of these groups blew up the Moscow headquarters of the city's Communist Party, killing a dozen members inside and wounding fifty others. Predictably, the Cheka responded with increased arrests, violence and executions by firing squad, until the last battle group blew themselves up while besieged by Cheka 'anti-terrorist' troops.

Makhno defeated Denikin at Orel, 400 miles south of Moscow, in October 1919. Having weakened the Ukrainians, Trotsky's Red Army attacked and defeated the rump of Makhno's force before driving Denikin's Whites further south, where they enforced a White Terror, summarily shooting and hanging suspected pro-Bolsheviks and unleashing pogroms against Jews because so many activists in the Bolshevik movement were Jewish. Although responsible for killing far fewer supposed enemies, there were also other White terrors in the civil war. Berthelot's army left Russian soil in April 1919 after briefly occupying Odessa, disillusioned with the senseless bloodletting by Red, White and Ukrainian armies during early 1919, with little to choose between them as allies. With their departure, Denikin's Volunteer Army was left to its unhappy fate.

In the west, Ukrainian guerrilla bands continued for years to harass Bolshevik occupation forces. After the Turkish surrender to the Entente in 1918, the three Caucasian republics of Azerbaijan, Armenia and Georgia enjoyed temporary freedom – until Trotsky sent in the Red Army, subjugating Azerbaijan in April 1920. In December, the former Russian Imperial province of Armenia was incorporated into Soviet Russia.

During February to April 1921 the Red Army invaded and reconquered Georgia, Stalin's homeland. In Central Asia, the October Revolution had prompted Uzbekistani Muslim nationalists to declare autonomy, terminated by the Red Army in February 1918. This sparked a prolonged anti-Russian resistance movement, despite which the Emir of Bukhara and the Khan of Khiva were bloodily deposed in 1920, so that by the end of 1921 Communist puppets controlled the region under Moscow's iron control. Neighbouring Turkmenistan was laid waste by war between invading Bolshevik troops and those of the Social Revolutionary Trans-Caspian Provincial Government. In April 1919, Soviet rule was imposed by force. In Kazakhstan, the Red Army drove out White forces and easily overcame a weak provisional government established after the demise of the tsarist regime. Here also, a Communist puppet government was imposed in August 1920 – after which, as in the other Central Asian republics, a state-controlled influx of Russian settlers changed the demography permanently.

Also in 1919, after years of denigrating feminism as a bourgeois irrelevance in the perfect Soviet society, Inessa Armand, together with Krupskaya and Alexandra Kollontai, set up *Zhenskii Otdel*, or the women's department of the party, abbreviated to *Zhenotdel*. Its purpose was to improve the status of women in Soviet society, fight illiteracy, promote education, open day care centres and endow women with the right to divorce or to have an abortion. This significant monument to their lives was abolished under Stalin in 1930 because he ruled that 'the women's question' had been resolved – as indeed it had, but not in the way Inessa and Kollontai had hoped. Both women had, in fact, destroyed their health by self-neglect in pursuit of their political beliefs.

16

BLOODY MURDER

Given the Bolshevik government's more pressing other problems, it is not surprising that it failed to allot great priority to what to do with the Romanovs. The conditions of their detention grew stricter, and Nicholas must have heard that it was intended to give him a show trial in Moscow. Petty restrictions increased: he was forbidden to wear epaulettes on his uniform and the princesses were the constant target of insults from the guards. On 1 March 1918, the whole family was placed on military rations, excluding butter and coffee, and were deprived of most of their household servants. In April 1918 the government in Moscow moved Nicholas, Alexandra and their daughter Princess Maria westwards back to Ekaterinburg, but Alexei was too ill to travel with them and remained in Tobolsk with the other three princesses until May, when the family was reunited in a villa at Ekaterinburg belonging to an industrialist named Ipatyev, which had been requisitioned that April by the Ural Soviet and designated with deliberate ambiguity 'Dom osobovo naznacheniya' – the house of a special purpose. The building was fortified with several machine-gun posts and surrounded by a palisade to prevent anyone outside seeing what was happening in the house or garden, or even who was there. Armed sentries patrolled both inside and outside the fence.

It was perversely the success of the anti-Bolshevik Czech Legion advancing westwards along the Trans-Siberian to capture Ekaterinburg for its armaments factories and as an important rail junction that terminated this situation. In June 1918 the Czech force was reported to be only 30 miles away with every likelihood of reaching the town in the near future. So far as is known, its mission was not to rescue the royal family, but to secure that stretch of the Trans-Siberian and exploit the arms factories and the mineral deposits of the Urals. So unstable was the military situation generally in the region that the Ural Soviet's commissar Yakov M. Yurovsky, who was in command of the prison house, decided on 29 June 1918 to send a representative to Moscow for instructions what to do with the royal family. By then, after moving the Romanovs several times during their house arrest of sixteen months, any original idea there may have been of letting the Western Allies ransom them, for money or in some kind of prisoner exchange, had palled.

When the matter was discussed by the Central Committee in Moscow there were just seven members present, three of them being Lenin, Dzherzhinsky and Sverdlov. Alarmed at the news of the Czechs' approach, they ordered Yurovsky to organise and arm a dozen comrades to help kill the Tsar and his family after arrangements had been made for the disposal of the bodies, so that the Romanovs' remains could not become objects of veneration for any revanchist group. Their remaining servants were also to be killed, so that no witnesses were left.

On 12 July Yurovsky's representative reported back to Ekaterinburg. It is not necessary to reconstruct what must have happened at the Ipatyev villa because, to clear his name against accusations of personal benefit in stealing any of the royal family's valuables, in 1934 Yurovsky wrote a full account of his actions, taking the trouble to point out anything of which he was not certain. The report makes clear what a messy and disorganised way this was, in which to kill a dozen very important hostages:

At about 11 o'clock at night on 16 July I assembled the men again, handed out the revolvers and announced that soon we had to begin liquidating the prisoners. I told Pavel Medvedev he had to check the guard outside and inside [the villa Ipatyev] thoroughly. He and the guard commander had to keep constant watch over the area around the house and in the house and to maintain communications with me. I also told him that at the last moment, when everything was ready for the execution, he had tell the guards and the others in the detachment not to worry about any shots they might hear from the house, and not to leave the premises. If there were any unusual amount of unrest [in the town], he was to notify me through the established line of communication.

The truck [which should have arrived at 11 p.m.] did not arrive until half past one. The extra wait caused some anxiety. Only when the truck had arrived – or after telephone calls that it was on the way – did I go up to waken the prisoners. [The Tsar's doctor] Botkin slept in the room nearest to the [stairs]. He came out and asked me what the matter was. I told him to wake everybody, because there was unrest in the town and it was dangerous for them to remain on the top floor of the villa. I said I would move them to another place. Gathering everybody consumed a lot of time, about 40 minutes. When the family had dressed, I led them [and Dr Botkin, Alouzy Tropp, the Tsar's valet, and Ivan Kharitonov, the cook] to the room in the basement that had been designated earlier. It must be said here that when Comrade Nikulin and I thought up our plan, we did not consider beforehand that (1) the windows would let out noise; (2) the victims would be standing next to a brick wall [with the risk of ricochets]; and finally, (3) it was impossible to foresee that the shooting would occur in an uncoordinated way. That should not have happened. Each man had one person to shoot and so everything should have been all right. The causes of the disorganized firing became clear later. Although I told [the victims] through Botkin that they did not have to bring anything with them they collected various small things – pillows, bags and so on and, I think, a small dog.

I ordered them to stand along the wall. Obviously, at that moment they did not imagine what awaited them. Alexandra Feodorovna [the Tsarina] said 'There are not even chairs here.' Nicholas was carrying [Crown Prince] Alexei. He stood in the room with him in his arms. Then I ordered a couple of chairs to be brought. On one of them, to the right of the entrance, almost in the corner, Alexandra Feodorovna [the Tsarina] sat down. The daughters and [Anna S.] Demidova [the Tsarina's personal maid] stood next to her, to the left of the entrance. Beside them Alexei was seated in the armchair. Behind him Dr. Botkin, the cook and the others stood. Nicholas stood opposite Alexei. At the same time I ordered the men to go down and to be ready in their places when the command was given. Nicholas had put Alexei on the chair and stood in such a way, that he shielded him. Alexei sat in the left corner from the entrance, and so far as I can remember, I said to Nicholas approximately this, [that] his royal and close relatives inside the country and abroad were trying to save him, but the Soviet of Workers' Deputies had decided to shoot them. He asked 'What?' and turned toward

Alexei. At that moment I shot him and killed him outright. He did not get time to face us to get an answer. At that moment disorganized, not orderly, firing began. The room was small, but everybody could come in and carry out the shooting according to the set order. But many shot through the doorway. Bullets began to ricochet because the wall was brick. Moreover, the firing intensified when the victims' shouts rang out. I managed to stop the firing but with great difficulty.

A bullet, fired by somebody in the back, hummed near my head and grazed either the palm or finger – I do not remember which – of somebody. When the firing stopped, it turned out that the daughters, [the Tsarina] Alexandra Feodorovna and, it seems, Demidova and Alexei too, were alive. I think they had fallen from fear or maybe intentionally, and so they were alive. Then we proceeded to finish the shooting. Previously I had suggested shooting at the heart to avoid a lot of blood. Alexei remained sitting petrified. I killed him. They shot the daughters but did not kill them. Then Yermakov resorted to a bayonet, but that did not work either. Finally they killed them by shooting them in the head. Only in the forest did I finally discover the reason why it had been so hard to kill the daughters and Alexandra Feodorovna.

After the shooting it was necessary to carry away the corpses, but it was a comparatively long way [to the truck]. How could we do it? Somebody came up with an idea: stretchers. We did not think about it earlier. We took shafts from the sledges and, I think, put sheets on them. Having confirmed they were dead, we began to carry them out, when it was discovered that traces of blood would be everywhere. I said to get some smooth woollen military cloth immediately and put some of it onto the stretchers and then line the truck with it. I directed Mikhail Medvedev to take the corpses. He was a Cheka man then and currently works in the GPU. He and Pyotr Zakharovich Yermakov had to take the bodies away. When they had removed the first corpse, somebody – I do not remember exactly who – said that someone had taken some valuables. Then I understood that evidently there had been valuables in the things that [the Romanovs] had brought with them. I stopped the removal immediately, assembled the men and demanded the valuables be returned. After some denial, two men returned the valuables they had taken.

After I threatened the looters with shooting, I got rid of those two and ordered Comrade Nikulin – as far as I remember – to escort the bodies, having warned him about valuables. I first collected everything – the things they had taken and other things as well – and I sent all of it to the commandant's office. Comrade Filipp Goloshchyokin, apparently sparing me [because] my health was not very good, told me not to go to the 'funeral' but I worried very much about disposing of the corpses properly. So I decided to go personally, and it turned out I did the right thing. Otherwise, all the corpses would have wound up in the hands of the White Guards [or the Czechs]. It is easy to imagine how they would have exploited the situation.

After instructions were given to wash and clean everything, at about three o'clock or even a little later, we left. I took several men from the indoor guards [at the villa]. I did not know where the corpses were supposed to be buried. As I have said, Filipp Goloshchyokin had assigned that to Comrade Yermakov. Yermakov drove us somewhere at the Verkh-Isetsky Works. I was never at that place and did not know it. At about two-three versts, or maybe more [say, a couple of miles] from the Verkh-Isetsky Works, a whole escort of people on horseback or in carriages met us. I asked Yermakov who these people were, why they were there. He answered that he had assembled those people. I still do not know why there were so many. I heard only shouts 'We thought they would come here alive, but it turns out they are dead.' Also, it seems about three-four versts farther our truck got stuck between two trees. There where we stopped, several of Yermakov's people were stretching out girls' blouses. We discovered again that there were valuables and they were taking them. I ordered that men be posted to keep anyone from coming near the truck.

The truck was stuck and could not move. I asked Yermakov, 'Is it still far to the chosen place?' He said 'Not far, beyond the railroad embankment.' And there behind the trees was a marsh. Bogs were everywhere. I wondered 'Why had he herded in so many people and horses? If only there had been carts instead of carriages.' But there was nothing we could do. We had to unload to lighten the truck, but that did not help. Then I ordered them to load the carriages, because it was already light and we did not have time to wait any longer. Only at daybreak did we come to the famous gully. Several steps from the mine where the burial had been planned, peasants were sitting around the fire, apparently having spent the night at the hayfield. On the way we met several people. It became impossible to carry on our work in sight of them. It must be said, the situation had become difficult.

Everything might come to nothing. At that moment I still did not know that the mine would not meet our needs at all. And those damned valuables!

Just then I did not know that there was so much of them or that the people Yermakov had recruited were unsuitable for the project. Yes, it was too much! I had to disperse the people. I found out we had gone about 15-16 versts [about 10 miles] from the city and had driven to the village of Koptyaki, two or three versts from there. We had to cordon the place off at some distance, and we did it. Besides that, I sent an order to the village to keep everybody out, explaining that the Czech Legion was not far away, that our units had assembled here and that it was dangerous to be here. I ordered the men to send everybody back to the village and to shoot any stubborn, disobedient persons, if that did not work. Another group of men was sent to the town because they were not needed. Having done all of this, I ordered [the men] to load the corpses and to take off the clothes for burning, that is, to destroy absolutely everything they had, to remove any additional incriminating evidence if the corpses were somehow discovered. I ordered bonfires [to be lit].

When we began to undress the bodies, we discovered something on the daughters and on Alexandra Feodorovna. I do not remember exactly what she had on, the same as on the daughters or simply things that had been sewed on. But the daughters had on bodices [into which had been sewn] diamonds and [other] precious stones. Those were not only places for valuables but protective armour at the same time. That is why neither bullets nor bayonets got results. By the way, only they were responsible for their dying agony [because the jewels prevented them being killed by the first shots]. The valuables turned out to weigh about one-half pud [8 or 9 kilos]. Greed was so great that on Alexandra Feodorovna, by the way, there was simply an enormous piece of round gold wire, turned out as a sheer bracelet and weighing about one pound. All the valuables were ripped out immediately, so that it would not be necessary to carry the bloody rags around with us.

Valuables discovered by the White Guards later had undoubtedly been sewn into other clothes, after burning which, they remained in the ashes. Several diamonds were handed over to me the next day by comrades who had found them there. How did they overlook the other valuables? They had enough time for it. Most likely they simply did not figure it out. By the way, one has to suppose that some valuables will be returned to us through Torgsin[183] because they were probably picked up by the peasants of the Koptyaki village after our departure. The valuables had been collected, the [clothes and other] things had been burned and the completely naked corpses had been thrown into the mine. From that very moment new problems began. The water [in the shaft] just barely covered the bodies. What should we do? We had the idea of blowing up the mines with bombs to cover them, but nothing came of it. I saw that the funeral had achieved nothing and that it was impossible to leave things that way.

It was necessary to begin all over again. But what should we do? Where should we put the corpses? About at 2 p.m. I decided to go to the town, because it was clear that we had to extract the corpses from the mine and to carry them to another place. Even the blind could discover them. Besides, the place was exposed. People had seen something was going on there. I set up posts, guards in place, and took the valuables and left. I went to the regional executive committee and reported to the authorities how bad things were. Comrade Safarov and somebody else, I do not remember who, listened but said nothing. Then I found Filipp Goloshchyokin and explained to him we had to transfer the corpses to another place. When he agreed I proposed to send people to raise the corpses. At the same time I ordered him to take bread and food because the men were hungry and exhausted, not having slept for about 24 hours. They had to wait for me there. It turned out to be difficult to get to the corpses and lift them out. The men got very exhausted doing it. Apparently they were at it all night because they went there late.

I went to the town executive committee, to Sergei Yergerovich Chutskayev, who was its chairman at the time, to ask for advice. Maybe he knew of a place. He proposed a very deep abandoned mine on the Moscow high road. I got a car, took someone from the regional Cheka with me – Polushin, I think – and someone else and we left. But one and a half versts away from the appointed place the car broke down. The driver was left to repair it, and we continued on foot. We looked over the place and decided it was good. The only problem was to avoid onlookers. Some people lived near the place and we decided to take them away to the town and after the project allow them to come back. That was our decision. We came back to the car but it had to be towed. I decided to wait for a passing car. A while later some people rode up on two horses. I stopped them. The fellows seemed to know me. They were hurrying to the plant. With great reluctance they gave us the horses.

While we rode, another plan took shape: burn the corpses. But nobody knew how to do it. The plan came to me of burying them in groups in different places. The road leading to Koptyaki is clay near that gully. If we buried them there without onlookers, not even the devil would find them. To bury them and to drive over them several times with the string of carts would result in a mishmash and that would be that. So there were three plans. There was nothing to drive, there was no car. I went to the head of the military transportation garage to find out if there were any cars. There was a car, but it was the chief's. I forgot his surname; it turned out he was a scoundrel and, it seems, he was executed in Perm. Comrade Pavel Petrovich Gorbunov, who is now deputy chairman of the state bank, was the manager of the garage or deputy chairman of military transportation. I do not remember which. I told him I needed a car urgently. He said 'I know what for.' He gave me the chairman's car. I drove to Voikov, head of supply in the Urals, to get petrol or kerosene, sulphuric acid too (to disfigure the faces) and, besides that, spades. I commandeered ten carts without drivers from the prison. Everything was loaded on and we drove off. The truck was sent there. I stayed to wait for Polushin, the main 'specialist' in burning, who had disappeared somewhere. I waited for him at Voikov's. I waited for him in vain until 11 p.m. Then I heard he had ridden off on horseback to come to me but he fell off the horse, hurt his foot, and he could not ride. Since we could not afford to get stuck with the car again, I rode off on horseback about midnight with a comrade – I don't remember who – to the place the corpses were. But I also had bad luck. The horse hesitated, dropped to its knees and somehow fell on its side and came down on my foot. I lay there an hour or more until I could get on the horse again. We arrived late at night. The work extracting [the corpses] was going on. I decided to bury some corpses on the road. We began to dig a pit. At dawn it was almost ready, but a comrade came to me and said that despite the order not to let anybody come near, a man acquainted with Yermakov had appeared from somewhere and had been allowed to stay at a distance. From there it was possible to see some kind of digging because there were heaps of clay everywhere. Though Yermakov guaranteed that he could not see anything, another comrade began to demonstrate that from where he had stood it was impossible not to see.

So that plan was ruined too. We decided to fill in the pit. Waiting for evening, we piled into the cart. The truck waited for us in a place where it seemed impossible to get stuck. We headed for the Siberian high road. Having crossed the railway line, we transferred two corpses to the truck, but it soon got stuck again. We struggled for about two hours. It was almost midnight. Then I decided that we should do the burying somewhere around there, because at that late hour nobody actually could see us. Only the watchman of the passing track saw several men, because I sent for railway sleepers to cover the place where the corpses would be put. The explanation for needing these was that the sleepers had to be laid for a truck to pass over. I forgot to say that we got stuck twice that evening or, to be precise, that night. It is necessary to say that all our men were so tired. They did not want to dig a new grave.

But as it always happens in such cases, two or three men started working, then the others began. A fire was made and while the graves were being prepared we burned two corpses: Alexei and Demidova. The pit was dug near the fire. The bones were buried, the land was leveled. A big fire was made again and all the traces were covered with ashes. Before putting the other corpses into the pit we poured sulphuric acid over them. The pit was filled up and covered with the railway sleepers. The empty truck drove over the sleepers several times and rolled them flat. At 5 or 6 o'clock in the morning, I assembled everybody and stated the importance of the work completed. I warned everybody to forget the things they had seen and never speak about them with anybody. Then we went back to the town. Having lost us, the fellows from the regional Cheka, such as Comrades Isay Rodzinsky, Gorin and somebody else arrived when we had already finished everything.

In the evening of the 19th I went to Moscow with my report.[184]

On 19 July 1918 *Izvestiya* announced the death of the Tsar, but reported that the 'wife and son of Nicholas Romanov' had been sent to 'a safe place'. Even in the widespread bloodshed of the civil war, Lenin shied away from admitting the murders of the entire family although, as Trotsky remarked, leaving any of Nicholas' children alive would have created a pretender to the throne of all the Russias, so it was important that the Romanov line be completely extinguished. Grand Duke Nikolai Mikhailovich had been shot in Perm and, in the week following the massacre in the Villa Ipatyev, seven other members of the Romanov family were executed by firing squads in the Urals region. The killing of the doctor and household servants simply because they were witnesses, would have caused no comments in Russia at the time, after all the deaths in combat or, after arrest, by Cheka firing squads.

There were many conspiracy theories. One was that the villa had been built on the site of a church – which was true – with a secret tunnel linking it with the building used as the British consulate; that a clandestine team of British agents used the tunnel to rescue one of the princesses, injuring her arm in the process. Another was that all the family were rescued in this way and that the Tsar had been recognised much later disguised as a priest or monk, and so on. The most famous 'survival story' was of Anna Anderson, whose claim to be the Grand Duchess or Princess Anastasia was supported by several relatives and intimates of the royal family, and who had a comprehensive knowledge of family matters that survived many traps set for her, in which she corrected false information for several decades after first surfacing.[185]

Less than a week after the murders, the Czech Legion column closed in on Ekaterinburg, which they occupied on 25 July, still believing that some of the Romanovs were alive. The reluctance of the Soviet government to admit to the killings continued until July 1977, when Mikhail A. Suslov, a Politburo member with a record of organising genocidal deportations, ordered that the villa be razed to the ground, to remove any possibility that forensic work might reveal traces of the murders. The work was allegedly supervised by Boris Yeltsin, who was then first secretary of the regional party machine. In 1990 the site was returned to the Orthodox church, which built a new church there, consecrated in 2003.

With Yuritsky's report being a state secret, like so many other things in the Soviet Union, it was to be more than five decades before the graves of the Romanovs were discovered by amateur archeologists in 1976, in a birch forest six miles north of Ekaerinburg. Two of the bodies, however, were missing until July 2007, when 46-year-old builder and amateur historian Sergei Plotnikov was exploring an overgrown hollow near the excavated graves of the rest of the family. After his metal prod hit something hard under the ground, he and a friend started to dig, unearthing several bones and a fragment of a child's cranium. They called in a team of archeologists, who continued the excavation of human remains which had been attacked by acid and burned in a fire.

A few weeks later the remains were identified by a forensic pathologist as being from a young teenage boy and a woman in her early twenties. Dr Pogorelov, deputy director of the Sverdlovsk archeological institute, revealed at a press conference that a total of forty-four bone fragments, ranging from a few millimetres to several centimetres, had been recovered, plus seven teeth, three bullets of various calibres, a piece of dress material and other artifacts. In the circumstances, it seemed probable that these were the remains of Prince Alexei and Grand Duchess Maria. A local journalist working for *Komsomolskaya Pravda* questioned how Plotnikov had succeeded where professional archeologists had dug extensively in 1991. It appeared that they had run out of money and left an 8-metre square plot unexplored – which included the awkward hollow where Mr Plotnikov, made the new find. He, a man of as few words as Vladimir Putin, said simply, 'We got lucky.'[186]

Subsequent DNA tests on the remains of the Romanov bodies confirmed the identities by comparison with those of surviving relatives, including the Duke of Edinburgh. Fragments of the Tsar's neck vertebra and lower jaw were also matched to bloodstains on a shirt he had been wearing when a police bodyguard attacked him with a sabre during a state visit to Japan while he was still Crown Prince in March 1894. The mitochondrial DNA of the adult female remains matched the blood of female descendants of the Tsarina's grandmother Queen Victoria. Bones belonging to Nicholas, Alexandra and three of the princesses were reburied in July 1998 in the Cathedral within St Petersburg's Peter and Paul fortress, which had featured in the 1917 revolutions. The burial in a specially dug crypt in a side chapel of the cathedral, in the presence of members of the Romanov family, was ironically also supervised by Boris Yeltsin, at the time the bottom-pinching President of the Russian Federation. The ceremonial ended with a nineteen-gun salute – two short of the traditional imperial salute because Nicholas had abdicated before his murder. After DNA analysis of the remains discovered by Plotnikov confirmed that they came from Alexei and Maria, they were also laid to rest in the crypt.

17

THE ENEMIES WITHIN

Under the tsarist regime it had been necessary to have an internal passport in order to leave one's village. Even today, Russians must have an international passport to travel abroad, like citizens of most other countries, and also an internal passport, called *vnutrenny pasport* or *propiska* to travel within the Russian Federation. In destroying the infrastructure of the Imperial regime, the October Revolution produced a brief interlude of personal freedom such as the Russian people had never known. Aristocrats and the richer bourgeois citizens had been able to travel abroad before, but during this period more than 3 million educated Russians, more or less fluent in second languages, took the chance to flee abroad with their families, abandoning their homes, property and businesses. The more provident refugees headed for wherever their money had been stashed away; poorer ones ended up in Shanghai, Singapore, India, Latin America, Australia – wherever local regulations and low cost of living permitted them to settle, however precariously, and live on a pittance. Because the majority had fluent French, in Paris and Marseille it was common to see princes, dukes and generals driving taxis, waiting on tables and carrying bags; their wives cleaned floors and took in washing and ironing. That they were right to leave their homeland, was proven when thousands of their friends and relatives were imprisoned, sent to labour camps – at one time 5 million were locked away in the Gulag – or executed for 'counter-revolutionary activities', a catch-all offence used throughout the seventy years of Communist rule.

Within Russia there was a widening rift between the Bolsheviks and the other revolutionary socialists who opposed Lenin's autocratic dissolution of the Duma and many of his other actions, when he rebranded his party as the All-Russian Communist Party[187] to mark its opposition not only to capitalism and any surviving supporters of the tsarist regime lurking in the woodwork, but also the foreign socialist parties, whether or not they had supported their national governments during the war, *and* all the other Russian socialist parties. These former allies were henceforth to be treated as dangerous enemies.

Conventionally the long periods of fighting between various White and interventionist forces and the Reds is referred to as 'the civil war', but it is more logical to regard it as the consolidation of Bolshevik power against considerable resistance, largely overcome with brute force by Trotsky. In June 1918, Lenin created a new economic programme labelled *voyenny kommunism*, or 'war communism'. It covered the nationalisation of all banks, shipping companies, international trade, agriculture and grain supplies, mining companies, the oil business and all commercial concerns employing more than ten people. In addition, the railway system and all its employees were placed under military discipline. To the horror of the peasants, who had believed that the October Revolution, in which so many had died, would give them the land they farmed, all land was now decreed to be state property, to be farmed industrially under commissars following directives from Moscow, drawn up by party functionaries who knew nothing about growing crops or raising animals. Agricultural land was arbitrarily grouped into *kolkhozy* – collective farms run by committees. Even the *kolkhozy* had no heavy equipment. As late as the 1950s machines like tractors, reapers and binders were held in regional *motor-traktorniye stantsii*, or tractor stations, to be allocated to each *kolkhoz* on a rota system for a limited number of days, with the responsibility for maintenance forever squabbled over by the users and the station personnel.

The Russian Empire was replaced by four socialist republics: the Russian and Transcaucasian Soviet federated socialist republics and the Belorussian and Ukrainian soviet socialist republics. In Ukraine, despite the installation of a soviet regime that ousted a nationalist provisional government after the break-up of the Tsarist Empire, there was no wish to be 'south Russia' any longer. Ukrainians looked to Austro-Hungary for protection, which was forthcoming because of the importance to Vienna and Budapest of Ukraine's fertile black soil *chernozem* grain-growing area – which the Red Army had twice invaded in attempts to re-impose Russian rule.

Coming on top of the corruption under the tsarist regime and the depredations of the war, Lenin's policy of war communism finally shattered the economy. Many factories had to close for lack of raw materials, laying-off workers and leaving their families to starve. Lenin's insistence on central planning by theoreticians, with scant hands-on experience of anything useful, was compounded by the exodus of the middle classes, including most people with managerial or business experience.

Lenin's constant paranoia seemed, to him at least, justified after Kaplan's assassination attempt. At the beginning of September, he unleashed a Red Terror, with Dzerzhinsky's enthusiastic support, using the Cheka rank-and-file to arrest and summarily execute *anyone* who could remotely be suspected of anti-Bolshevik feelings, or against whom they had personal grudges. The victims, many killed after torture, ran into uncounted thousands. To be condemned, it was not necessary to be guilty of anything; the problem for the innocent was to prove their innocence. How does one do that? A joke of the time tells of a kangaroo arriving at the Polish frontier and asking for asylum on the grounds that they are killing all the rabbits in Russia. 'But you're not a rabbit,' says the frontier guard. 'How do I prove that?' retorts the kangaroo.

There were also tens of thousands of armed anti-Bolsheviks within Russia, who suffered, as had the interventionists, from their geographical separation while Trotsky could move his rigidly controlled Red forces from front to front far more easily. Anti-Bolshevik militias formed spontaneously in mid-1918 and became knows as 'the Whites' to distinguish them from Trotsky's Reds. Although white had been the symbolic colour of the Romanovs, not all these anti-Bolsheviks wanted to restore the Tsar. Nor were they all volunteers, several White generals imposing conscription on men of military age in the areas they controlled.

In the Kuban General Bogayevsky was raising a cavalry army of Cossacks. On the Volga, Viktor M. Chernov, who had been Kerensky's Minister of Agriculture and head of the Constituent Assembly, was attempting to revive the peasant rebellions of the past, now that it was obvious the peasants could expect nothing good from the Bolsheviks. In the Caucasus and elsewhere it was sometimes hard to say whether an anti-Bolshevik rebellion was political or nationalist, as when a longtime Marxist named Noe Zhordania proclaimed the Democratic Republic of Georgia and permitted Britain and other powers to ship weapons through

Map of White and Red forces with anglicised place names.

the country to the White forces. Ossetian and Abkhazian civilians suffered attacks, as did Armenians and Azeris.

In addition to open rebellions throughout the former tsarist empire, the Cheka and Red Army units were tasked with suppressing strikes caused by Bolshevik policies, particularly food shortages, when rations fell far below those issued to Red troops. Not far from Georgia, in Astrakhan between 2,000 and 4,000 strikers had their wrists tied behind them and were weighted down with heavy stones before being drowned in the Volga in March 1919, their corpses carried downriver into the Caspian Sea. Nor were the strikers the only victims. Under the cover of suppressing that strike, as many as 1,000 civilians accused of being bourgeois were similarly executed. Even in the former capital Petrograd Cheka special forces stormed the Putilov Works in March 1919, arresting 900 strikers, at least 200 of whom were summarily shot without trial.

In November 1918 the coalition government of Siberia formed by the Socialist Revolutionaries and Mensheviks was overthrown in a military coup d'état whose leading officers asked the famous Arctic explorer Alexander Kolchak to take command. He refused at first but was declared *Verkhovny Privatel* or Supreme Ruler and promoted himself to the rank of admiral for the sake of appearances during a power contest between the military and the Socialist Revolutionaries. After local Cossacks had arrested many politicians, the others voted dictatorial powers to Kolchak, who did allow hostile politicians to emigrate, mostly to France. Some SR factions called for his assassination, but when Viktor Chernov attempted to organise a revolt against him in Omsk, it was put down in a bloody repression by Cossacks with hundreds of deaths. Kolchak's forces were for a time trained by British and American military advisers and publicly approved by President Clemenceau, Prime Minister Lloyd George, US President Wilson and Italian Prime Minister Orlando who presumably closed their eyes to the thousands of murders of Bolshevik and Revolutionary Socialists taken prisoner; this was shrugged off by Kolchak, quoting as precedent what he alleged to have been English practice during the Wars of the Roses. Seeing which way the wind was blowing, local tribal leaders submitted to him with the traditional gifts of live geese, bread and salt, which the embarrassed admiral awkwardly handed over to his aides.

In March 1919 Kolchak's army began a westward push into Bolshevik-held territory, advancing as far as Kazan and Samara on a 200-mile wide front before being halted and pushed back by the Reds after a twenty-five-day struggle with Trotsky personally taking command at Kazan and setting up a defensive line between that city and the Ural Mountains. Given the paranoia with which the main movers of the revolution regarded each other, it says something about the unsatisfactory state of the Red forces in Kazan that Trotsky asked Lenin to send Stalin and Dzerzhinsky there to purge the regional commissars responsible for the low morale and their poor military showing against the Whites. Dzerzhinsky, as always, devoted himself to bloody repression, while Stalin, as always, played the political game. Hardly had he arrived than he was trying to push Trotsky into sacking the former tsarist officers and place the Red Army political commissars in command, something Trotsky had no intention of doing. In yet another Red Terror, even the dead were made to serve the revolution, being buried under banners bearing the slogan '*Smert vragam trudavavo naroda*' – death to the enemies of the working people.

Lenin and Trotsky had shared the assumption that the success of their revolution would light a powder train, igniting fires of rebellion against capitalist governments worldwide. At first, it seemed they might be right. On the night of 7–8 November 1918 King Ludwig III of Bavaria was deposed by a Red coup, of which the leader, Kurt Eisner, was himself assassinated three months later. In revenge, the Bavarian revolutionary committees carried out a Red Terror, murdering thousands of perceived enemies to impose a short-lived soviet republic. This was repressed by federal German troops in May 1919, after which a backlash White Terror was unleashed against the defeated Communists.

Just five days after Eisner's Bavarian coup, an uneasy coalition of nationalists and socialists proclaimed Hungary's independence from Austria as the Hungarian Democratic Republic. After months of dissension, the regime was overturned by more extreme revolutionary socialists led by Béla Kun, a Hungarian POW captured in 1916 who had stayed in Russia after the revolution to become an agent of the Cheka. He declared war on the newly created state of Czechoslovakia, but when Russian reinforcements promised by Lenin failed to arrive, was forced to retreat. Serbian, Czech and Romanian troops occupied two-thirds of the country and withdrew in March 1919, when Kun declared his country the Hungarian Soviet Republic. Together with his sadistic mistress Razalia Zemlyachka – likewise a Cheka officer and already guilty of several mass murders – Kun conducted a Red Terror[188] and used his Red Army to reconquer much of the territory that had been lost to the foreign invaders. He then followed Lenin's recipe for disaster, alienating the peasantry by confiscating private estates for the state instead of distributing the land to those who lived and worked on them. Driving the economy to a standstill, with even food distribution impossible, he lost any vestige of popular support and fled to Vienna on

2 August, subsequently leading other unsuccessful coups in Germany and Austria during the 1920s until eliminated in Stalin's purges, accused of that other catch-all crime, Trotskyist deviation.

In north-western Russia, General Nikolai Yudenich was a long-service veteran in the Tsar's service, who had been commanding operations against the Turks in the Caucasus before the revolution. Retired by Kerensky, he went underground, reappearing in late 1918 to assume control of anti-Bolshevik forces along the Baltic coast and forming a White army with one officer to every eight men. With support in materiel, but not boots on the ground, from Britain, Yudenich launched an attack in the direction of Petrograd on 17 October 1919 when the bulk of the Red Army was committed to fighting in Siberia and southern Russia. The Red resistance collapsing before them, they reached Tsarskoye Selo in sixteen days and dug in only twenty miles from Petrograd. Lenin wanted to abandon Petrograd to Yudenich, but, according to Alexander Naglovsky, then transport commissar of the Northern Commune, which included Petrograd, Trotsky demanded and received from Lenin approval to take 'all necessary measures' in the former capital, including a bloodbath of Bolshevik officials who had, in his view, failed in their duty.

He then again exploited the Reds' advantage of internal communications to summon Red Army reinforcements from the south and conscript every able-bodied man in the former capital under the slogan 'Death to the hirelings of foreign capital. Long live Red Petrograd!' In fourteen days, the Kronstadt sailors entered Gatchina, driving back Yudenich's force to Tsarskoye Selo and driving them out of there in four more days of bitter fighting in the snow. Yudenich's army was in headlong retreat under shelling and bombing by Red fliers who also released on the fleeing men millions of printed *laissez-passer* offers and incitements to mutiny like these:

> Soldiers of the army of Yudenich, Read, listen and think! The Red army does not fight against workers and peasants. Come over to our side. We shall treat you like brothers. Without landlords, capitalists, tsarist generals and bureaucrats, our country will live a peaceful and happy life. (signed) Leon Trotsky, President of the Military Revolutionary Soviet of the Republic.
>
> Military Order: All soldiers of the army of Yudenich are dismissed from duty on receipt of this order and ordered home. All officers resisting the

execution of this order are outlawed and every soldier is required to shoot them on the spot as enemies of the people.

Military Order: For all weapons delivered to any staff headquarters of the Red Army, the soldiers of Yudenich will be paid in full. Rifles 600 roubles. Machine guns 2,000 roubles. Cannon 15,000 roubles.

Military Order: Having lost working time on account of the criminal activities of Yudenich, his demobilised soldiers will retain as their [own] property their accoutrements and their utensils useful in peasant life.[189]

After retreating back into Estonia, Yudenich and his troops were evacuated on British ships, he heading for France, allegedly enriched with foreign subsidies he had kept for himself instead of using them to finance his army. He died in 1933 and was buried at Nice.

To the east in Siberia, near to Irkutsk on the shore of Lake Baikal, the Czech Legion was reluctantly allied with Admiral Kolchak's forces on the Trans-Siberian mainline, along which Kolchak was travelling with his Stavka on one of several armoured trains, aboard which was the Russian state treasury of gold and silver bullion that had been captured in Kazan, variously estimated to be worth between 409 and 651 million roubles. In September 1919 Kolchak's columns were being pushed eastwards by the Red Eastern Army Group and heading for Irkutsk, then under the control of the moderate socialist Political Centre Party, whose leaders refused to join either side in the Red v. White fighting. With his health deteriorating, the admiral was alarmed at the defection of most of his officer corps, who had decided that there was no longer any hope of beating the Reds. He opened negotiations to win over to his side a previous enemy, Grigory M. Semyonov, self-appointed *ataman* of the Baikal Cossacks, who were themselves allied with the Japanese based in Vladivostok. General Wrangel had described this mysterious character as:

a Transbaikalian Cossack, dark and thickset, and of the rather alert Mongolian type. His intelligence was of a specifically Cossack calibre, and he was an exemplary soldier, especially courageous when under the eye of his superior. He knew how to make himself popular with Cossacks and officers alike, but he had his weaknesses in a love of intrigue and indifference to the means by which he achieved his ends. Though capable and ingenious, he had received no education, and his outlook was narrow.

Semyonov was a larger than life character, whose favourite mistress was a Jewish cabaret singer. He had already fought in the Caucasus and southern Russia, been made Commissar for the Baikal region by the Reds and turned his coat to ally himself with the highest bidder, taking a division of Buryat fighters with him. Once armed and completely out of control, they raped and robbed their way across Central Asia. Semyonov's motive to join up with Kolchak had more to do with the treasure aboard the admiral's train than any political consideration. To get it, he was prepared to execute Kolchak's last-ditch plan to blow up some of the railway tunnels around Lake Baikal, through which the Trans-Siberian circumnavigated the vast inland sea, and thus prevent the Czechs from deserting. Had this been done, they would have been left on the wrong side of the break in the line, with no retreat to Vladivostok, but so would Kolchak, so it is hard to understand his reasoning. Maybe his serious morphine addiction had something to do with it.

The Political Centre government in Irkutsk demanded that Kolchak and the treasure be handed over to them, with the argument that Moscow had abolished capital punishment, so he would be given a fair trial. Under their own general Jan Syrový and a French general named Maurice Janin, the Czechs had had enough of Kolchak and handed the admiral over. Shortly thereafter, the Political Centre abandoned Irkutsk one step ahead of the Soviet Military Revolutionary Party marching in. Kolchak was interrogated and put on trial, the prosecutor accusing him of allowing his troops to commit a White Terror, burning down villages in the territory he occupied and mutilating the inhabitants by cutting off their ears and noses. The self-styled admiral defended himself, saying that his achievements were rather in the field of hydrography and polar exploration than on the battlefield, or even at sea. He added that he had given no orders for atrocities, although he understood that these things did happen in the heat of combat.

In January 1920 the Czechs signed an armistice with the Red forces: in return for being allowed to travel unmolested to Vladivostok, they renounced their claim to the gold in Irkutsk, although taking one wagon loaded with gold with them, and left Kolchak to face his fate. On 7 February, he was marched out of prison with one other officer to the river bank near a hole in the ice. The other officer accepted a blindfold; Kolchak refused one. A Cheka firing squad shot them both and shoved their bodies through the hole in the ice, to be carried away by the current. Kolchak's nemesis Semyonov was finally driven back to Vladivostok in October 1920. The following month he took ship for Japan, left there for the United States but had to leave that country too after accusations that his men had committed atrocities on American soldiers in Siberia. Allowed to travel to North China, he was given a small pension by his former allies in the Japanese occupation forces and schemed to restore the last emperor Pu Yi to his throne in Beijing. What exactly he did for the next twenty years is unclear, but in September 1945 he was arrested by Soviet paratroops in Manchuria. Belatedly charged with counter-revolutionary activities, he was found guilty and hanged on 29 August 1946.

The gold removed from Irkutsk was well guarded by the Czechs all the way back to their homeland after its independence from Austria. There, some of it was used to found their own bank called Legionárska Banka at a prestige address on Na Poříčí street in Prague, of which the imposing facade is unknowingly passed daily by hundreds of tourists looking for KFC and McDonalds outlets at the end of the street.

The defeat of the White armies was as much due to their generals' failure to offer any viable alternative to the Boshevik regime as to their geographical disadvantages. They offered no promise of a better future, only a return to tsarism with one of them sitting on the throne of the Romanovs. As to winning the hearts and minds of the Russian masses, their tactics of conscription, grain requisitioning, coercion and terror made it hard for ordinary people to choose between Red and White rule, so most civilians supported neither but gave in to whichever side was currently occupying their region.

In February 1918 General Semyon M. Budyonny created a Red cavalry unit. This grew into a regiment, then a brigade and finally into a division that performed successfully near Tsaritsyn (now Volgograd). Starting in the second half of June 1919 this Cavalry Corps under Budyonny's command, played the decisive role in the defeat of the main forces of Denikin's Caucasian Army on the upper reaches of the river Don. Units of the corps took Voronezh, closing a 100km gap in the Red Army's defense line on the route to Moscow and hastened the Whites' defeat in the Don region.

As late as 1920 there was still a small but viable White army in the Crimea, under Denikin's successor General Pyotr Wrangel, a Balt of

German origin with an enormous trademark moustache. Wrangel had a stroke of luck in the shape of the three-way war between Poland, Ukraine and the Bolsheviks, which obliged Trotsky briefly to take the pressure off the Crimean front. Wrangel's strict but fair rule in the White-occupied territory made it briefly seem that he was there to stay, but the Reds' cavalry under Budyonny eventually drove his rump army into a pocket on the Crimean peninsula.

There Wrangel held out long enough to evacuate 135,000 soldiers and civilian dependents, dubbed 'enemies of the Republic' by Trotsky, on 14 and 15 October 1920 in a flotilla of 126 French, American and Russian warships and merchant vessels from Sevastopol across the Black Sea to Turkey and onward to Yugoslavia, Bulgaria and elsewhere. Because London had not formally recognised Wrangel's regime a number of Royal Navy vessels stood by on a point of law without helping, to the disgust of many naval officers. Several hundred of Wrangel's officers and NCOs who subsequently found themselves stranded penniless in Constantinople accepted free passage on French ships taking them directly to North Africa, where they and Cossack and Polish cavalrymen were recruited wholesale to form the 1st Cavalry Regiment of the French Foreign Legion.

At the Tenth Party Congress in March 1921 Alexandra Kollontai and other speakers spoke for the Workers' Opposition faction in favour of greater involvement of the population in political affairs, but to no avail: Lenin's 'dictatorship of the proletariat' was there to stay for almost the next seven decades. The war with the Central Powers, the revolution and the subsequent fighting against the Whites and interventionists in which hundreds of thousands perished had led to a situation not unlike that which took the Russian Empire out of the First World War: widespread strikes, mutinies of garrison troops and peasant uprisings. One of a number of spontaneous rebellions against the Bolsheviks came in the Tambov region, 260 miles south-east of Moscow, where Lenin's *prodrazvyorstka* programme of forcible requisitions of grain and other foodstuffs was increased by 50 per cent in 1920. This meant death by starvation for many of the peasants who had produced the grain. On 19 August, after a Red Army unit applying the new regulations used exceptional violence against the population of a small town in the region, a political group calling itself Soyuz Trudovovo Krestyanstva, or Union of Working Peasants, set up an elected Duma that abolished Bolshevik power in the region, restored civil liberties and, most critically of all, returned the land and its crops to the peasants who had grown them. To fight off the Red Army, by October it had assembled 50,000 peasants, many of whom had military experience in the recent war, aided by many deserters from the Reds. This force was designated the Tambov Blue Army, to distinguish it from both Red and White forces. In January 1921 similar peasant revolts broke out in Samara, Saratov, Tsaritsyn and elsewhere. By then the Tambov army numbered 70,000 men and had successfully kept the Reds at bay for some months.[190]

Since the Polish-Soviet war had ended and General Wrangel's army gone, Trotsky was able to unleash 100,000 Reds on the Tambov rebels, using heavy artillery and armoured trains against men armed only with personal weapons. Frequent executions of civilians launched another Red Terror, in which special Cheka detachments used heavier-than-air poison gas to kill the guerrillas hiding in the forests. This chemical warfare continued for at least three months. Some 50,000 civilian 'enemies of the people' were interned in seven concentration camps with a very high mortality rate from malnutrition, but total deaths among the population of the area were estimated to be four or five times higher than this. The following month in Moscow the Central Committee announced the end of the punitive requisitions of *prodrazvyorstka*, replacing it with a less harsh policy of *prodnalog*. Derived from *prodovolstvenny* and *nalog*, meaning food tax, *prodnalog* left about one-third of the food produced in the hands of the peasants who had grown or raised it. Since they knew in advance how much they would have to hand over, the more energetic, or those with more fertile land, could work harder and produce a surplus, unaware they would be labelled *kulaki*, or fists, and later subjected to cruel punishment for this 'deviationist' activity.

In Soviet Russia, some people did not need to be labelled with any specific 'crime', except the belief that moral values were still important, even under the Soviet system. On 6 February 1922 the Cheka ceased to exist, Dzerzhinsky's organ of state terror becoming Gosudarstvennoye Politicheskoye Uprvalenie, or state political administration, still headed by him. Its officers kept the familiar name 'Chekisty' – as indeed they still are called today, after all the changes of initials for Soviet and Russian secret police and espionage arms. Some of the early victims included Lenin's list of intellectuals he had long planned to banish from Russian soil because their disappearance into the Gulag or death before a firing squad would have provoked reaction in the West. The necessary exit visas required were delayed in the Soviet bureaucratic machine. To speed up the process, disregarding Maxim Gorkys' protests, Lenin wrote from his sickbed, which would soon be his deathbed, on 16 September to Deputy Chairman of the GPU Unshlikht that 'these lackeys of capital, who think they are the brains of the nation … are not the brains. They're the shit.'[191] On 17 September Unshlikht's number two, Genrikh Yagoda, replied with a list of those arrested and in prison in Moscow or Petrograd, who would be leaving on 22 September. In fact, the process of expulsion lasted until the end of the year for some of them. Forced to board, in some cases international trains, but mostly ocean-going steamers in Petrograd harbour, carrying just two sets of clothing, plus what they were wearing, some books and other small mementoes, but no icons in their luggage, they were permitted to take with them only the equivalent of £25 per person, to start their new lives in exile.

Some tried to get money from abroad to smooth their expulsion from Russia, but it was illegal for Soviet citizens to have foreign currency and even friends who might have had some were too terrified to help. Prince Sergei E. Trubetskoy belonged to a noble family that had been famous as moral philosophers for generations. He was one of the few *expulsanty* who did receive friendly treatment, and later wrote:

> It was difficult to raise the money [to take with us]. Then, quite unexpectedly, my colleagues at the State Agricultural Institute came to my aid. My former boss, a man called Demchenko arranged back-pay for all the time I had been in prison, plus my salary for two months ahead – the entitlement for anyone made redundant. He took a considerable personal risk doing this and I begged him not to. He showed me there could be highly decent people among the Communists too. He and his staff threw me a party with 'best wishes for your new life' and only one Chekist and a few bourgeois worried for their own skins did not come.[192]

Since the *expulsanty* could not pay their fares, the GPU reluctantly paid for their travel. They were deposited in Central and Western Europe, the lucky ones re-emerging in the large Russian émigré community in Paris.[193]

On 30 December 1922, the four soviet republics created in 1918 united as the Union of Soviet Socialist Republics. The carefully chosen word *union*, which implied a voluntary association of equals, stopped three generations of Western liberals seeing that the USSR ruled from Moscow was the old tsarist empire re-created in five bloody years to deprive millions of ethnic identity and political freedom for three generations. The facts of the Tambov rebellion, ruthlessly suppressed for Trotsky by General Mikhail N. Tukhachevsky, were subsequently concealed in the Soviet Union until brought to light again by a local historian in 1982. Other peasant revolts in Samara, Saratov, Tsaritsyn, Astrakhan and elsewhere were crushed by a contingent of 30,000 Red Army soldiers, backed up, as a foretaste of Hitler's *Einsatzgruppen*, by Cheka extermination units using poison gas.

The Bolsheviks should have anticipated this sort of resistance to the agricultural policies that killed 7.5 million people living in some of the most fertile regions of Russia, but were shocked when the great heroes of the October Revolution – hailed as such by Trotsky – turned against them in March 1921. Some 10,000 sailors and 4,000 soldiers on the island fortress of Kronstadt – Peter the Great's bastion in the Gulf of Finland against a foreign attack on Petrograd – protested against the government's failure to provide food for the population, its restrictions on personal liberty and the placing of all workers under military discipline. In sympathy with widespread strikes and demonstrations against the famine and epidemics caused by the government's failure to provide basic food for the civilian population, for restricting political freedom and placing all workers under military law, on 26 February the crews of the battleships *Petropavlovsk* and *Sevastopol* sent a delegation across the Gulf to Petrograd, to report on the situation there. Two days later, the report of the delegates covered not only the motives of the strikers – with whom they sympathised – but also the Bolshevik government's harsh repression of them.

The result was a mass meeting in Kronstadt on 1 March of more than 15,000 servicemen and civilians *demanding* free elections to the soviets, freedom of speech and the press, freedom of assembly, freedom to travrel and freedom to organise trade unions. Other demands were for a reassessment of wages and the removal of Bolshevik roadblocks preventing peasant producers of food from bringing supplies into the cities. The only voices raised against the motion were those of two paid officials of

the Bolshevik Party. The meeting then voted to send a second delegation of thirty members to Petrograd, inviting strikers and others to visit
Kronstadt, but that delegation was arrested by the Bolsheviks immediately
on arrival in the city.

Another meeting of 303 delegates on 2 March in Kronstadt elected a
Provisional Revolutionary Committee of eventually twenty members to
organise the defence of the island after threats were made by the Bolshevik
officials there that this counter-revolutionary movement under Lenin's
slogan 'All power to the soviets' with the addition of the words 'and not
to parties' would be suppressed by armed force, although it was entirely
in the spirit of the two revolutions of 1917. The reply from Moscow was
that the Kronstadt movement was inspired by French intelligence officers and organised by former general Kozlovsky, Trotsky's representative
on the island. Had this been true, the uprising would have taken place a
few weeks later after the thaw due at the end of April when Kronstadt
was again a defensible sea-girt island that could have been reinforced and
resupplied from abroad by sea.

For a short time, Kronstadt was what the Bolsheviks had promised
Russia would become, with free trade unions and an elected Duma.
About 300 Bolsheviks who did not want to join the uprising were put
in prison but treated fairly, while the families of the garrison's soldiers
and sailors were taken hostage in Petrograd. Trotsky started organising
an attack with poison gas, only aborted by the defeat of the Kronstadters
before he could carry it out. On 5 March two anarchists named Emma
Goldman and Alexander Berkman offered to act as intermediaries
between the garrison and the government in a last-ditch attempt to prevent bloodshed – an offer that was completely ignored by the Bolshevik
Central Committee, which had already decided to suppress the uprising
as bloodily as possible – *'pour encourager les autres'* tempted by thoughts of
counter-revolution.

The Red assault on Kronstadt began on 7 March, with the first probes
failing as some Red Army soldiers defected to the insurgents and others
courageously suggested to their commissars that they should send spokes-
men to find out the Kronstadters' demands first. The assault dragged
on intemittently for ten days as more Red Army units arrived until
Trotsky had deployed an estimated 60,000 men commanded by Gen
Tukhachevsky. On the night of 16–17 March, 100 so-called agitators

in this force were arrested and seventy-four of them summarily shot by their own comrades. On the morning of 17 March, with party commissars manning machine-guns in the rear to force the attackers onto the ice swept by the garrison's machine-guns, about 8,000 rebels managed to escape in small groups across the ice to Finland, causing a major problem of asylum-seekers for the newly independent Finnish state, which had not yet decided on a policy of political asylum. Casualties were heavy on both sides, with many captured rebels summarily executed or sent to prison camps set up by Dzherzhinsky, where months later groups of them were still being shot by firing squads, which an otherwise loyal Bolshevik named Viktor Serge called a senseless and criminal agony. The newspaper of the Provisional Revolutionary Committee of the Sailors, Red Army men and Workers of the City of Kronstadt, also titled *Izvestiya*, referred to Trotsky as 'the bloody Field Marshal'.[194] Alexander Berkman, an American sympathiser with the Bolsheviks, noted in his diary: 'March 17 – Kronstadt has fallen today. Thousands of sailors and workers lie dead in the streets. Summary executions of prisoners *and hostages* [who had obviously not taken part in the rebellion] continue.'[195]

On the day following the defeat of the Kronstadt rebels, Lenin and the other Bolshevik leaders celebrated the fiftieth anniversary of the Paris Commune by renaming the battleship *Sevastopol* as *Paris Commune*.

More than 10,000 'heroic' Red soldiers were killed or wounded in the ten-day campaign, the wounded mostly dying of hypothermia, while left lying on the sea ice swept by sub-zero winds. How many rebels died in the fighting is unknown. Later communiqués disagreed on whether 6,528 or 10,026 were arrested after the taking of the fortress. Officially, 2,168 were summarily shot and 1,955 sent to labour camps, although 4,836 sailors were deported to Crimea and the Caucasus, perhaps to strengthen the Black Sea Fleet, then re-deported when Lenin heard of this to labour camps in the far less hospitable Far North. Their families who had been held hostage in Petrograd during the siege were also deported to Siberia. Whatever residents were allowed to remain on the island led a very different life under the Bolshevik troika imposed on them under a new military regime to make the point that 'All power to the soviets meant, All power to the Communist Party.'

As the Tambov rebels and the Kronstadt workers, sailors and soldiers learned too late, the Bolsheviks occupying all seats in the Soviet of People's

Commissars and key posts at every level of government made the Russian Soviet Federated Socialist Republic a dictatorship, as would be the Union of Soviet Socialist Republics. Trotsky's eventual victory over all the other elements in the civil war had little to do with popular support and was mainly due to the Red Army's brutally established control of European Russia and eventually Siberia also. This amazing military achievement for a civilian was ultimately the cause of Trotsky's assassination – since his prominence was perceived as a threat at first by Lenin and then by Stalin.

The uprising in March 1921 made Lenin realise that his rigid adherence to the doctrine of war communism had not only brought the national economy to the brink of total meltdown, in which workers had to be placed under military discipline, it also provoked a real danger of counter-revolution without any foreign intervention. Shortly afterwards, at the Tenth Party Congress he unveiled the New Economic Policy (NEP), involving the return of most agriculture, retail trade, and small-scale light industry to private hands, with the state retaining control of heavy industry, transport, banking, and foreign trade. Men and women who took advantage of this to start up small businesses and farms were known as *nepmen*. Money, which had been abolished under war communism, was also re-introduced the following year. The peasants were again allowed to own and cultivate land – and pay taxes for the privilege. What the public was not told, was that Lenin only intended this programme as a temporary expedient to re-boot the economy and give the party time to consolidate its power.

One way in which he did that was to dissolve Alexandra Kollontai's Workers' Opposition movement, which had for months been criticising the Bolsheviks' excesses. Although having some demands in common with many of the rebels across the former empire, she advocated supporting the Bolshevik government and working within the party to solve what she saw as temporary problems. Although the Workers' Opposition had actually supported the brutal crushing of the Kronstadt mutineers, Lenin now decided that even an open and loyal critic like Kollontai had no place in his Russia, where party solidarity under his rule was paramount because internal and external enemies were trying to exploit any disunity.

18

DECLARING WAR ON THE WORLD

Lenin's overriding obsession with a worldwide chain reaction of revolution in one country going viral and infecting the whole world took precedence over domestic Russian issues even during the civil war phase of the revolution. As early as 26 December 1917 *Izvestiya* announced that Sovnarkom had made an allocation of 2 million roubles to 'foreign representatives of the Commissariat of Foreign Affairs for the needs of the international revolutionary movement.'[196] It was a declaration of war on the capitalist democracies to realise a worldwide 'dictatorship of the proletariat' achieved by another invention of his, 'revolutionary morality', which meant:

[Resorting] to all sorts of cunning schemes and stratagems, to employ illegal methods, to evade and conceal the truth, in order to penetrate into the [foreign] trade unions, to remain in them and to conduct the Communist work in them at all costs. The struggle against [personalities and parties] of similar social type as our Mensheviks … must be waged without mercy, in the same manner as we have done it in Russia until all the incorrigible leaders of opportunism and of social chauvinism have been completely discredited and expelled from the trade unions.[197]

In a sense, the mission entrusted by Lenin to Béla Kun in Hungary was a trial run, for in the very month of March 1919 when Kun was proclaiming the Hungarian Soviet Republic in bloodshed and chaos, Lenin also inaugurated what seemed a brilliant way of instigating, assisting and controlling Communist revolutions outside Russia.[198] By careful manipulation, the bickering Socialist International was fatally weakened by being split into two opposing groups: parties which had supported their governments' war efforts versus those who had not. On 2 March 1919, Lenin made that organisation irrelevant by opening the First Communist International, abbreviated with his personal penchant for jargon, acronyms and neologisms to 'Comintern'. He chose the moment when only nineteen foreign parties had representatives in Moscow to approve or reject his ground rules, which suited him well. At the second Comintern congress in 1920, attended by delegates from thirty-seven countries, Lenin imparted the rules for Comintern members, the most important of which was his doctrine of 'democratic centralism'.

Like most of the dialectic, the term was defined as meaning the opposite of what it appeared to mean. 'Democratic' meant that each Moscow-approved party could send delegates to the Comintern meetings, provided they conformed to twenty-one conditions laid down by Lenin, which required them to model their structure on disciplined lines in conformity with the Soviet pattern and to expel all moderate socialists and pacifists, especially those who rejected violent tactics and Lenin's dictatorship. Whatever the believers wanted or pretended to believe, the Comintern was thus not a vehicle of international socialism, but a weapon of Russian foreign policy, which, throughout its 1,000 years of recorded history, was a process of continuous expansion. The catch, in any case, was that the approved foreign parties would have voting rights in the Comintern 'democratically' – which was defined as meaning in proportion to the size of their membership. Since the Russian Party was by far the largest, due to the many Soviet citizens who were *obliged* to join, it could always out-vote all the others, whose membership was voluntary, yet were bound to accept this 'democratic' majority vote. 'Centralism' actually meant from the top: Comintern headquarters were in Moscow and all power between the meetings lay with the permanent staff, controlled directly by the Kremlin.

With another touch of the political sleight of hand that confused many foreign observers as yet unaccustomed to Soviet double-talk, the 8th Congress of the Communist Party of the Soviet Union (CPSU) in March 1919 followed orders from the top to 'instruct' the Central Committee – usually referred to as 'Tseka', an acronym of its Russian title *tsentralny komityet* – to elect from its ranks a policy organ or Politburo of five members. Stalin was quietly gathering the reins of power into his hands while Lenin and Trotsky circled warily round each other politically, the advantage lying gradually with Trotsky as Lenin became more and more incapacitated with Kaplan's bullet or bullets, still lodged in his neck. The other two original Politburo members were Lev Kamenev, married to Trotsky's sister, and Nikolai Krestinsky. After Lenin's death, Stalin would murder Trotsky, Kamenev and Krestinsky because they knew too much about his past.

The declared justification of the Politburo was that questions of state too urgent to await the next meeting of the Central Committee needed to be resolved by a small permanent executive on a day-to-day basis. Effectively, the Central Committee thus became a rubber stamp for Politburo decisions, and so on down the line. Nobody in Russia now chanted 'All power to the soviets!' for the role of *soviety* was reduced to knee-jerk endorsement of orders from above on pain of imprisonment or worse. Because the party secretariat controlled the agenda of all meetings and also transmitted Politburo decisions to the rank-and-file, a critical post in this concentration of power was that of *otvetsvenny sekretar* – or responsible secretary. In 1922, when this post was translated into that of general secretary of the CPSU, abbreviated to *Gensek*, its first holder was Josef Stalin, who thereby became the Politburo's most influential member.

With at least 10 million people having died violently or prematurely during the revolution, the civil war and the devastation and dislocation that ensued, and millions more starving to death across the length and breadth of the Soviet empire, many of those displaced by events were desperately seeking parents, children or any other relative who had been torn from them hundreds or thousands of miles away. Bands of *besprizorny* – homeless children with no surviving adult relatives – wandered across the land, begging and stealing. Some apologists still argue that the vastness of the USSR prevented the CPSU leadership from learning the conditions it had brought about. Yet, on 19 March 1922, Lenin called on the Politburo for stronger measures, actually citing the famine with thousands of corpses along the roads and starving people driven to cannibalism.[199] Instead of alleviating the suffering he had caused the people he now ruled, Lenin had his eyes set on distant horizons, as though everything was perfect in the Soviet Union.

In his less monomaniacal moments, he may possibly have acknowledged to himself that even the October Revolution might not have taken place but for the catalyst of the First World War, during which the Western belligerents had suffered strikes, demonstrations, mutinies at the front and subsequently some short-lived revolutions, which had failed – in his view – because he was not controlling them. From there, a quantum leap of theoretical politics convinced him that Catherine the Great's dream of conquering the whole of Europe[200] lay within the grasp of the man in the Kremlin – i.e. himself – because there was a far more cost-effective way of inducing that unrest and using it to conquer the capitalist democracies than by going to war against them with bullets, bayonets and bombs. In his view, the personal liberties enjoyed by their citizens – such as free speech, the legal principle of habeas corpus, secret elections, free trade unions and unrestricted travel, none of which were allowed in the Soviet Union – were fatal flaws that could be exploited by politically trained agitators to bring down the democracies from within. If left alone, however, some might find socialist, national-socialist or other non-Communist ways of working out their own salvation. Even followers of Marx might have their own ideas about applying his theories – or they might, like Eisner and Kun, choose the wrong moment or lack the political sense or ruthlessness to mount a successful revolution and consolidate power afterwards.

To ensure that none of these things happened, Lenin decreed that it was imperative to inculcate into revolutionary socialists an unswerving discipline to the Soviet Party line and eliminate those who rebelled. The method was to train them in Russia, and finance their return to their own countries with generous funds to influence public opinion through propaganda, subversion of other political parties, and infiltration of trade unions. By controlling a country's workforce this way, Lenin was certain that a small number of disciplined activists could paralyse free-market economies as thoroughly as if a virus had been injected into the arteries of capitalism – which, in a sense, it had been.

If simultaneously all the fault lines based on class, sex, colour, religion and ethnic tensions in every democratic society were being ripped open by propaganda and political action, a disciplined pro-Soviet Communist Party would have the ruthlessness, the techniques, and the guidance from Moscow, to grab power in the subsequent civil disorder, and hang on to it by eliminating both rivals and allies. So long as all the foreign activists had it dinned into them that 'Moscow knows best', each post-revolutionary society would be based on the Soviet model and become a satellite of the USSR without the need for conquest by force of arms.[201]

With the Comintern acting as tradecraft school of a fifth column working throughout the non-Communist world by sabotage, subversion and infiltration of trade unions and other political parties, Lenin was effectively declaring a covert war on the same democratic governments with whom he claimed to desire normal diplomatic relations to get Russia back on its feet.

One could fill a library of books documenting completely his strategy for a Communist world centred on Moscow, but the Soviet fostering of Communism in Britain is a fair example. In 1920 a selection was made of the three socialist parties that had done their best to undermine the British government's war effort. The British Socialist Party, the Socialist Labour Party and Sylvia Pankhurst's Workers' Socialist Federation were welded into a new party: the Communist Party of Great Britain (CPGB). That required money, so veteran Communist activist Theodore Rothstein, who had been welcomed to Britain in 1891 as a 19-year-old refugee from tsarist Russia, became one of the early bagmen, bringing to Britain money, gold and jewels confiscated from Russians and foreigners who had fled after the revolution or been murdered, like the Romanovs. The proceeds were used to get the CPGB off to a flying start; the initial subsidy exceeded £50,000 – in modern terms, about £1 million[202] – this at a time when money was desperately needed to stave off famine in many parts of Russia.

CPGB founder member Bob Stewart wore a bulging money belt around his ample waist on his return from trips to Moscow. His comrade Jack Murphy also shuttled back and forth from Russia to Britain, carrying thousands of pounds in a money belt and accounting for every penny to his Soviet paymasters. On one documented trip, he brought in £12,600 – roughly £250,000 in modern value.[203] Another channel was CPGB's assistant general secretary Reuben Falber, who regularly collected shopping bags bulging with banknotes from a contact in London's Soviet Embassy. The job was not without risks: Comintern courier Michael Borodin was arrested while indoctrinating Scottish CPGB members and spent six months eating porridge in Glasgow's Barlinnie prison before deportation back to the land where his sentence for such activities would have been a miserable death.

There was no shortage of couriers and bagmen because in April 1920 the League of Nations appointed Norwegian philanthropist Fridtjof Nansen its high commissioner for the repatriation from Russia of a half-million German and Austro-Hungarian POWs. Lenin refused to recognise the League, but was prepared to deal with Nansen on a personal basis, with few people in the West apparently suspecting that the returnees included many like Béla Kun, who had been indoctrinated in captivity and came home hard-line Communists. Nansen was also appointed by the International Committee of the Red Cross to head an urgent famine relief programme in Russia. Although the Soviet government allowed him to open an office in Moscow, Lenin refused aid of food and other essentials from the American Relief Administration, which assisted war-ravaged European countries, because that revealed Western superiority to the recipients. Not until 1921 was the ARA allowed to open clinics in areas devoid of any medical care, and save uncounted thousands of Russians from starvation and sickness. Had it been allowed to commence operations earlier, it could have saved many more.

In a time when few working-class people had travelled abroad, except under mobilisation during the First World War, one of the perks for the foreign activists was expenses-paid trips to Moscow. CPGB activist Jack Murphy described after his first visit there how the foreign comrades from each country were brainwashed every night by Comintern staff specialising in that target country. No mean talker himself, Murphy commented, 'The Russians seemed incapable of exhaustion by discussion. We had got to learn that a Communist Party ... had to be disciplined, a party organised on military lines.'[204] Whenever comrades failed to agree, the mantra hurled at them was 'Moscow knows best'. As historian Francis Beckett commented in his well-documented history of the CPGB, 'it was an illusion that was to cost them much misery in the next seven decades.'[205]

Murphy was himself arrested in Moscow on suspicion of being a spy for the British police. Although he was cleared and released, it was a narrow escape. As he admitted dryly afterwards, 'The Russians have a method of dealing with police spies that does not leave any room for continued activity.'[206]

The degree to which Lenin controlled the foreign parties is exampled by feminist Sylvia Pankhurst being barred from the position in the CPGB merited by her previous political record because she argued with him over a number of issues. That hardheaded Scot Willie Gallagher, who had been convicted in 1916 under the Defence of the Realm Act for anti-war activities in the Clydeside dockyards, fell completely under Lenin's spell. But even he did not gain Lenin's seal of approval to become boss of the CPGB because he was also too independent to accept Comintern orders unquestioningly. Instead, Moscow selected 31-year-old boilermaker Harry Pollitt, a member of Pankhurst's Workers' Socialist Federation who had used cash brought from Moscow by Pankhurst for the 'Hands Off Russia' campaign to bribe London dockers not to coal up a ship carrying a cargo of munitions intended for Poland's war against its Soviet invaders.[207]

To ride herd on Pollitt, Moscow chose the brilliant, but embittered, 35-year-old academic Rajani Palme Dutt, the many chips on whose shoulders should have prevented him ever standing up straight. Son of a Swedish mother and an Indian father, Dutt hated everything about Britain, the British and their way of life. That it was flawed and exploitative of the working classes, no one would now disagree. That it was nowhere near as flawed and exploitative as the Soviet regime he worshipped was something to which Dutt shut his eyes resolutely. The third member of CPGB's governing trio was Harry Inkpin, who seems to have been chosen as a rubber stamp for the decisions of Dutt and Pollitt, under whom the party pursued its grimly pro-Moscow course for seventy-one years.[208] Inkpin's brother Albert was made General Secretary and became one of the first 'martyrs', imprisoned for six months in 1920 for publishing pro-Soviet propaganda and again in 1921 after police raided the party's premises in King Street, Covent Garden. Purchased with Soviet money, its sale was to save the discredited CPGB from insolvency half a century later.

To finance the CPGB, whose low membership came nowhere near justifying the expenses of its militantism, the Comintern sent millions in subsidies, which continued until the mid-1930s – and much later for the CPGB main organ, the *Daily Worker* newspaper,[209] thousands of copies of which were purchased in advance and flown to Moscow every day. Lenin in his mausoleum could congratulate himself that his blueprint was working when the CPGB managed to have three candidates elected to Parliament in the 1930s. Yet Dutt and his equally ruthless Estonian mistress Salme Murrik, an illegal immigrant who slipped into Britain in 1920, frequently antagonised their British comrades until Lenin summoned the Central Committee of the CPGB to Moscow for a lesson on the meaning of 'Moscow knows best'. A few years later, they would have disappeared into the Gulag or an unmarked grave but after their return to Britain pro-Moscow discipline inside the CPGB improved, although often disturbed by Dutt's paranoid suspicion of all his colleagues.

So powerful was their subsequent belief in Moscow-style Communism that it withstood the evidence of their own eyes and ears that the USSR was a tyranny, ruled first by Lenin and then by Stalin, where their own friends and trusted mentors could be imprisoned, tortured and executed without trial, and where those whom they had been taught to revere as gods in the Communist pantheon could be denounced with fatal results as capitalist spies, paid saboteurs and 'counter-revolutionary elements'. Perhaps one day some psychologist will explain why such dyed-in-the-wool atheists found in their contacts with the leadership of the CPSU what other believers would call a religious experience.

19

THE INADMISSABLE LETTER

An opera, they say, is not over until the fat lady has sung. A revolution is not complete until its leader has got rid of all his possible detractors, competitors and everyone who 'knows too much' about what really happened. Think no further than Fidel Castro and Che Guevara.

In April 1920 the Communist Party threw a big party for Lenin's fiftieth birthday, which was also celebrated by the publication of volume after volume of his *Collected Works*. Famous foreigners who came to shake his hand included Bertrand Russell and H.G. Wells from Britain. The latter went to Gosizdat, the state publishing house and asked for the royalties from all the millions of copies of his books published in Russia, only to learn that copyright was not recognised by the Soviet government, although they were quite happy to give him as much cash as he wanted to spend in Russia, on condition that not a single rouble left the country.[210] Another visitor to the Kremlin was Inessa Armand, by then in such poor health that Lenin sent her to a sanatorium in the Caucasus, where she died in a cholera epidemic that September, her body being buried beneath the Kremlin wall, genuinely mourned by her former lover. Alexandra Kollontai was also very ill, but took over the reins of Zhenotdel and was elected a member of the executive at the All-Russian Congress of Soviets on 8 December. At that congress, she joined the Workers' Opposition faction within the Bolshevik Party, fighting the increasing bureaucratisation of the Soviet state – a faction that would be banned with other groups at the Tenth Party Congress in March 1921. The poet Vladimir Mayakovsky progressed from being an ardent supporter of the CPSU to blowing out his brains in despair at what the revolution had become by 1930.[211]

Before the end of 1921 Lenin's health was also visibly failing, to the point where the Politburo ordered him to take a month's leave at his villa in Gorki, twenty miles south of Moscow, where Krupskaya and his sister could look after him in peace and quiet. He, however, felt so ill that he begged both his wife and Stalin to procure some cyanide so he could commit suicide. Instead, the Politburo brought eminent doctors, who could be relied upon to remain discreet, from abroad to examine him. Their opinions included the theory that Kaplan's bullets in his neck were giving him blood poisoning. In April 1922 the bullets were belatedly removed surgically, but the problems continued, leading some specialists to believe that he was suffering from syphilis while others – later proved right by autopsy after his death – considered that the most likely cause of his symptoms was arteriosclerosis. In May 1922 this led to his first stroke with temporary paralysis and loss of speeech, followed by a second one in December, which did not stop him demanding from his sick bed the death penalty for the leaders of the Socialist Revolutionary Party during their show trial. They were instead sent to prison until eventually falling victims to Stalin's great purges. The leading Mensheviks were likewise sent to concentration camps.

In 1922 Kollontai's voice was effectively silenced. Sent to serve with the Soviet legation in Oslo, from then until her retirement for health reasons in 1945, she was kept abroad as a diplomat while her work on the status of women was progressively sidelined in the USSR. This did not stop her being an effective ambassador to Norway and Sweden, a member of a trade delegation to Mexico, as a delegate to the League of Nations, and in the negotiations of the Finno-Soviet peace treaty of 1940. From 1946 until her death in 1952 at the age of eighty, she was an adviser to the Soviet Ministry of Foreign Affairs.

In December 1922 Lenin dictated *pismo k kongresu* – a composite letter to the congress, in which he attacked Trotsky, Kamenev, Bukharin, Zinoviev and others in the leadership for their individual failings, but also the people as a whole for their idleness, illiteracy, lack of punctuality and initiative. It was the letter of a grumpy old man. In it, he specifically recommended that Stalin be removed from the position of General Secretary of the Communist Party, arguing that:

Comrade Stalin, having become General Secretary, has concentrated excessive power in his hands and I am not convinced that he will manage to use this power with adequate care. Against this, Comrade Trotsky, as shown by his struggle with the Central Committee, is distinguished by his outstanding talents. He is certainly the most able person in the current Central Committee, but has an excess of self-confidence and preoccupation with burocracy.

At the beginning of January 1923, Lenin added:

Stalin is too crude, and this defect ... becomes unacceptable in the position of General Secretary. I therefore propose to the comrades that they should devise a means of removing him from this job and should appoint to this job someone else who is distinguished from comrade Stalin in all other respects only by the single superior aspect that he should be more tolerant, more polite and more attentive towards comrades, etc.

(signed) Lenin, 4 January 1923[212]

Lenin's wish was that this should be read out to all the delegates at the Twelfth Party Congress in April 1923, but his third stroke the previous month left him again paralysed and unable to speak. Hoping that he might recover, Krupskaya hid the letter for several months. After he fell into a coma and died at his home in Gorki on 21 January 1924 his body was transported to Moscow, to lie in state at the House of Unions under the gaze of hundreds of thousands of the party faithful shuffling past. Later it was embalmed against Krupskaya's wishes and placed in the specially constructed mausoleum on Red Square, like that of a pharoah in his pyramid. Several times re-embalmed as its condition deteriorated, and removed from Moscow during the Second World War, so that the Germans could not get their hands on it, the corpse became an unmissable stop on three generations of Communist visitors' tours of Moscow. The other great tribute was the renaming of Petrograd as Leningrad, which it remained until 1991, when the city reverted to its original name of St Petersburg.

Krupskaya rather ingenuously handed the 'letter to the congress' to the party's Central Committee Secretariat, with the request that it be read out at the Thirteenth Party Congress in May 1924. At that congress a version of Lenin's testament was read out after being edited by Stalin to exclude any criticism of himself, and particularly Lenin's recommendation that he should be replaced by Trotsky, 'despite [Trotsky's] arrogance and bureaucratic tendencies'.

When Krupskaya eventually managed to see Stalin and protest about this political sleight of hand, she threatened to tell the next congress herself what Lenin had actually written. Stalin had insulted her before, earning a reproof from Lenin. This time, he growled at her, 'Look here, old woman. If you don't behave yourself, I'll appoint another widow to Lenin.'[213] The complete contents of Lenin's 'letter to the congress' or political testament were not made public until the Twentieth Congress of the CPSU, thirty-two years after it had been written, when Nikita Khrushchev unveiled all Stalin's crimes, except those in which he had personally collaborated.

Defying Stalin after Lenin's death, Trotsky openly criticised his leadership, in response to which the Politburo launched a propaganda war against him. Stalin's dilemma was that Trotsky, although not much liked, was too well known and respected at all levels in the party to be assassinated or imprisoned. In 1925, however, he was fired from his post as Commissar for War on the grounds that the civil war phase was ended. In 1926 he was expelled from the Politburo, which was entirely under Stalin's thumb, and expelled from the party itself the following year, being exiled to Alma-Ata, then the capital of Kazakhstan in Central Asia. There, among other privations, the postal services withheld much of his incoming mail and did not forward many of his outgoing communications. On 2 June 1928 he wrote an open letter containing many complaints, of which this is an excerpt:

> One of my two daughters, Nina, is gravely ill with galloping [tuberculosis. She] is 26 years old, she has two babies, her husband is in exile. From the hospital my daughter wrote me on March 20 that she wished to 'liquidate' her illness in order to return to her job, but her temperature was high. Had I received this letter in time I could have telegraphed her and our friends to have her stay in the hospital. But the letter she mailed on March 20 was delivered to me only on June 1st. It was in transit for 73 days, i.e., it remained for more than two months in the pocket of a [Party] scoundrel corrupted by impunity. My oldest daughter Zina – she is 27 – has also been

"running a temperature" for the last two, three years. I should like very much to have her here but she is now taking care of her sister. Both of my daughters have of course been expelled from the Party and removed from their jobs, although my elder daughter, who used to be in charge of a Party school in Crimea had been transferred a year ago to a purely technical post. In a word, these gentlemen who smashed my secretariat are diligently occupying themselves with my family.[214]

After twelve months in Kazakhstan, Stalin exiled Trotsky entirely from the USSR. He first sought asylum with Russia's traditional enemy, Turkey, and was allowed to set up house on the Black Sea island of Prinkipo, where he devoted himself to writing a history of the revolution. Two KGB illegal agents, Romanian Zoya Zarubina[215] and her husband Yakov Blumkin, who had murdered Count Mirbach in 1918, were posted with false papers to Turkey. To finance their espionage work there Blumkin sold on the black market valuable Hassidic manuscripts looted from Russian museums and synagogues, but gave some of the money thus obtained to Trotsky. His wife denounced this deviation from orders to Moscow Centre, with the result that two Chekists were sent with orders to entice Blumkin on board a Soviet merchant ship in a Turkish port. Immediately on the ship's arrival in Russia, Blumkin was arrested and shot.[216]

Stalin implemented the docrine of *krugovaya poruka*, or collective responsibility, in Trotsky's case to include all his family. Forbidden treatment for her illness, Trotsky's daughter Nina died shortly after his letter quoted above. Her half-brother Sergei was brought from a labour camp in the Gulag to Moscow in 1937 and executed there by firing squad. Trotsky's other son died in Paris, in circumstances that closely resembled an NKVD Shmersh[217] assassination. But Stalin had eliminated *all* his political enemies inside the USSR and was not going to let Trotsky stay alive. In 1936, as the Spanish civil war began, he had been granted asylum in Mexico by President Lázaro Cárdenas and set up home with his second wife Natalya in a suburb of Mexico City called Coyoacán. Later, the grandson Seva was brought to Mexico to live with them. Unfortunately for Trotsky, Cárdenas also gave asylum after the Spanish civil war to many exiled Republicans. A group of twenty or so of these Spanish Communists, ordered by Moscow to break into the villa and kill Stalin's last surviving personal enemy, disguised themselves in Mexican police uniforms and were allowed to enter the fortified villa early on 24 May 1940[218] by an American guard, Robert Sheldon Harte, who had also turned off the alarm system. Overcoming the Mexican government guards, they sprayed the main bedroom with bullets from automatic weapons at waist height through the locked and barred door. Trotsky and his wife hid under the bed and miraculously survived. In the next bedroom, 13-year-old Seva was slightly wounded in one foot. The assailants and Harte departed in a hurry without checking that the target was dead. Harte, who 'knew too much' was later murdered by the Spaniards.

With Trotsky having allegedly signed a publishing deal with the American Hearst Corporation to write his potentially embarrassing history of the revolution, Stalin was furious at this failure and ordered Lavrenti Beria,[219] head of the NKVD, which was the current successor of the Cheka, to finish the job. Beria passed the job to Pavel Sudoplatov, deputy director of the NKVD's foreign service, who tasked the NKVD's North American spymaster Nahum Eitingon with the execution. This approach was more subtle: Eitingon gave the job to Ramón Mercader, whose mother Maria Caridad was a political commissar responsible for murdering at least twenty POUM[220] comrades during the Spanish Civil War and had trained her son in this bloodshed.

Posing as a Canadian businessman named Jacson [sic], Mercader was ordered to seduce Trotsky's virginal secretary Sylvia Ageloff. As her lover, Mercader arrived at the re-fortified villa on 20 August 1940 with an ice pick and a dagger hidden under his raincoat, despite the fact that it was a fine day. Recognising him, the guards allowed him to enter. Minutes later, the ice pick was buried in Trotsky's skull. He died the following day. At first Mercader refused to say why he had done the deed, but later told the police:

> I hit him [with the ice pick] just the once and he gave out a piteous, shattering cry at the same time as he threw himself onto me and bit my left hand, as you can see for yourselves by these three teeth marks. Then he took some slow steps back. As soon as they heard the cry, people arrived. I didn't try to escape.[221]

Roughed up by the guards, Mercader was arrested and sentenced to twenty years in prison – Mexico having no death penalty. Eitingon was rewarded with promotion by the grateful General Secretary of the CPSU. Released in 1960, Mercader sought asylum in the USSR under the name Ramón Lopez, but could not settle in Russia and re-emigrated, to live in Castro's Cuba, decorated with the medal of a Hero of the Soviet Union. After his death in Cuba, Mercader's ashes were buried under the name Lopez in Kuntsevo cemetery, outside Moscow.

A contributing factor in the execution was Trotsky's habit of telling everyone he met that a worldwide communist revolution was about to happen; Stalin wanted this too but preferred, as always, to work against the Western democracies in the shadows, while pretending, especially during the Second World War, that he was not their enemy.

Thus, on 21 August 1940, when Trotsky died in a Mexican hospital, the October Revolution could be said to be complete. Stalin had, in his customary manner, cut short the fat lady's song.

NOTES

1   It is generally agreed that he took twenty years to write it.

2   The word is thought to have originated under Servius Tullius, legendary sixth king of Ancient Rome (reigned 575–535 BCE), meaning a citizen of the lowest class, who served the state not with his property but only with his offspring, eventually able to fight. It was derived from *proletus* meaning 'one who has offspring'. *Oxford Dictionary of English Etymology* (Oxford, Clarendon Press 1966).

3   Originally named Herschel, he changed this to Heinrich on converting.

4   A title originally due to gas lamps lighting the main streets.

5   M. Evans, *Karl Marx* (London, Routledge 2007), pp. 32, 33, abridged.

6   18 March 1871–28 May 1871.

7   See D. Boyd, *The French Foreign Legion* (Thrupp, Sutton 2006) pp. 150–222.

8   A recent diagnosis suggests hidradenitis suppurativa.

9   Some sources say eleven mourners.

10   Calculated using the Bank of England inflation calculator.

11   D. Shub, *Lenin, a biography* (New York, Doubleday/Mentor 1948), p. 23. David Shub was a member of the Russian Social Democratic Party who knew Lenin and the other original Bolsheviks in their European hideaways. In September 1905 he returned to Russia, to join that year's revolution, but was arrested and exiled to Siberia. After escaping, he travelled to the USA, where he kept in touch for years with Lenin, Trotsky and the other leading figures while escaping the grim fate of most of his former comrades.

12   Of 7 roubles and 40 kopecks a month.

13   Shub, p. 33 (abridged).

14   Ibid, p. 36.

15   Ibid, p. 40.

16   Ibid.

17   Sometimes written in its original form as Braunstein.

18   Now known by its Ukrainian name Mykolaiv.

19   In Stuttgart, Germany.

20   R. Service, *Trotsky, a Biography* (London, Pan 2010), pp. 75–7.

21   Sometimes spelled 'Helphand', but Russian has no initial letter h. Hitler, for example, is spelled in Cyrillic 'Gitler'.

22   R. Bruce Lockhart, *Memoirs of a British Agent* (London, Putnam 1934), p. 237.

23   Lockhart, pp. 226–7 (abridged).

24   Ibid.

25   Quoted in Service, *Trotsky*, p. 93.

26   Ibid, p. 119 (abridged).

27   Later Soviet Commissar for Foreign Affairs.

28   Lockhart, p. 238 (abridged).

29   Stalin died 5 March 1953. Mikhail Gorbachev came to power just over thirty-two years later on 11 March 1985, but his relaxation of Stalinist repression took time to come into effect.

30   In Polish the name was written Dzierżyński.

31   Thought to be worth more than US $3 million in today's terms.

32   Shub, p. 61.

33   Which had also been used by Trotsky for one of his publications.

34   G. Kennan, *Memoirs 1925–1950* (New York, Pantheon 1967), p. 238 (abridged).

35   Ibid, p. 523.

36   See at length in D. Boyd *The Kremlin Conspiracy: 1,000 years of Russian expansionism* (The History Press 2014).

37   Ibid, pp. 67–8.

38   Consulted by the author in a private collection.

39   Boyd *Kremlin*, pp. 69–70.

40   Gen Hamilton noted in his scrapbook the shock he felt on seeing tall Caucasian (i.e. white) prisoners guarded by their short Japanese captors.

41   D. Shub, *Lenin* (New York, Doubleday/Mentor 1948), p. 12.

42   Service. *Trotsky*, p. 83.

43   Shub, p. 46.

44   L. Trotsky *Moya Zhizn* Vol. 1, p. 206 quoted in Service, *Trotsky*, p. 91.

45   Service, *Trotsky*, pp. 99–100.

46   Easily transported homes of Central Asian nomads, made of layers of felt from sheep wool fitted over a framework of bent lathes.

47   Then known by its Finnish name of Terijoki.

48   Shub, p. 65.

49   C. Clark, *The Sleepwalkers: How Europe Went to War in 1914* (London, Allen Lane 2012), p. 109.

50   An animated reconstruction of the events may be found on www.youtube. com by searching 'Film of Sarajevo Assassination'.

51   Quoted by J. Simpson in *Unreliable Sources*, Disc 1 (Macmillan Digital Audio 2010).

52   Ibid.

53   Ibid.

54   G. Elliot & H. Shukman, *Secret Classrooms* (London, St Ermin's Press/Little Brown 2002), p. 173.

55   W. Owen, *Anthem for Doomed Youth* (published privately 1920 by S. Sassoon in *Poems of Wilfed Owen*).

56   A comprehensive history of the war on the Russian fronts may be found in D. Boyd, *The other First World War* (Stroud, The History Press 2014).

57   M. Egremont, *Forgotten Land: Journeys among the ghosts of East Prussia* (New York, Farrar, Straus and Giroux 2011), p. 157.

58   A.W.F. Knox, *With the Russian Army 1914–1917* (London, Hutchinson 1921). A digitised version made available from University of Toronto may be downloaded from www. archive.org/details/with the russian army101knoxuoft.

59   Knox, pp. 113, 115, 134, 137, 232 (edited).

60   Lockhart, p. 137.

61   Stone, p. 52.

62   Knox, p. 45 (abridged).

63   Knox, pp. 184, 190.

64   Knox, pp. xx, xxi.

65   Ibid and p. 37 (abridged).

66   Russian calibres were calculated in *linii* meaning lines, not millimetres. This corresponded to 0.31 inches or 7.62mm.

67   Contracts existed licensing the Putilov engineering works in St Petersburg to produce these guns in Russia.

68   Knox, p. xxxiv.

69   Z.A.B. Zeman, *Germany and the Russian Revolution* (London, Oxford University Press 1958), p. 3

70   Zeman, pp. 140, 152.

71   Ibid, p. 3.

72   Ibid, p. 24.

73   J. Carmichael, *Russia: An Illustrated History* (New York, Hippocrene Books 1991), p. 193.

74   F. Farmbrough, *Nurse at the Russian Front* (facsimile edition London, Futura 1977), p. 92.

75   Ibid, p. 33 (abridged).

76   Ibid, p. 36 (abridged).

77   Ibid, pp. 74–8 (abridged).

78   From a number of such descriptions it is apparent that Bumby and his comrades had no clear idea where they were, which means that even their immediate officers had no maps – a situation all too frequent in the Russian lines.

79   Bumby account (abridged).

80   Bumby account (abridged). This is downloadable from *Dostupé z Metodického portal.*

81   Farmbrough, p. 88.

82   Stone, p. 184.

83   B. Moynihan *The Russian Century* (London, Random House 1994), p. 65.
84   Knox, p. 308.
85   Čestná vzpromínka 2005.
86   www.pamatnik.valka.cz (abridged).
87   Bumby account (abridged).
88   Knox, pp. 311–13, 317, 322–3 (abridged).
89   Dowling, p. 5; also N. Stone, *The Eastern Front 1914–1920* (London, Penguin 1998), p. 32.
90   Modern day Kaunas, Lithuania.
91   Stone, p. 186.
92   Knox, p. 328.
93   Now Narach, Belarus.
94   Farmbrough, p. 193.
95   Brusilov's *Vospominaniya* (memoirs) is downloadable in the original Russian without page numbers from miliera.lib.ru/memo.russian/brusilov/index.html.
96   Downloadable in Russian on museum/omskelekom.ru/ogik/Izvestiya_8/Eperina.html.
97   Ibid.
98   Ibid.
99   Brusilov *Vospominaniya* (abridged).
100 Extract from the diary on www.firstworldwar.com/diaries/carpathaianmemoir.htm.
101 Ibid.
102 Ibid.
103 Ibid (abridged).
104 R. Service, *Trotsky* (London, Pan 2010), p. 162.
105 Farmbrough, pp. 302–7 (abridged)
106 The letters are downloadable from www.alexanderpalace.org/letters/february17.html.
107 Ibid.
108 Ibid. Sources give different wordings but all include these sentences.
109 Ibid (abridged).
110 Vyborova subsequently denied this under Bolshevik interrogation, seeking to distance herself from the Tsarina.
111 E.N. Burdzhalov, *Vtoraya Russkaya Revolutsia* (Moscow, Nauka Press 1967), p. 147.
112 M. Wilson, *For them the War was not over: The Royal Navy in Russia 1918–1920* (Stroud, The History Press 2010), p. 15.
113 Ibid, p. 15 (abridged).
114 Ibid.
115 Ibid.
116 Neiberg and Jordan, p. 119.
117 Minute No. 29.

118 *Izvestia* of the Committee of Petrograd journalists No. 9, 4 March 1917/ Gregorian calendar 19 March (abridged).
119 Shub, p. 100.
120 Quoted in Shub, p. 103.
121 Carmichael, p. 193. Also, by googling 'photo of first meeting of petrograd soviet', a low-definition picture may be seen, with the banner clearly displayed at the back of the Duma hall.
122 Diary.
123 Extracts may be found on www.alexanderpalace.org.
124 M. Hughes, *Inside the Enigma* (London, The Hambledon Press 1997), pp. 102, 105.
125 Boyd, *Kremlin*, pp. 72–80.
126 Zeman, pp. 24, 92.
127 M. Pearson, *Inessa: Lenin's Mistress* (London, Duckworth 2001), p. 87.
128 M. Occleshaw, *Dances in Deep Shadows* (London, Constable 2006), p. 41.
129 M.S. Stănescu & C. Feneşan, *Lenin ş Trotski versus Ludendorff şi Hoffmann* (Bucharest, Editura Enciclopedică 1999), p. 77, quoted in S. Tănase *Auntie Varvara's Clients*, tr. A.I. Blyth (Plymouth, University of Plymouth Press 2010), p. 38 (abridged).
130 Shub, p. 108.
131 Shub, p. 110.
132 Original title: Vserossisskaya Chrezvychainaya Komissiya po borbe c kontrrevolutsiye i sabotazhem – the All-Russian Extraordinary Commission for Combating Counter-revolution and Sabotage – at first abbreviated to Vecheka and then simply Cheka.
133 Zeman, p. xi.
134 M. Hoffman *War diaries and other papers* (London, Secker 1929) Vol. 2, p. 117.
135 Quoted in Shub, *New International*, March–April 1950, and many other sources.
136 Shub's article in *New International* (abridged).
137 Ibid.
138 Neiburg and Jordan, p. 137.
139 Shub, p. 111.
140 R. Service, *Lenin* (London, Pan Macmillan 2011), p. 283.
141 Service, *Trotsky*, p. 175.
142 Ibid, p. 287.
143 For example *Soldatskaya Pravda* and *Okopnaya Pravda*.
144 2 July according to the Julian calendar.
145 It was commonly believed that Ekaterina Furtseva became Minister of Culture solely due to her relationship with Khrushchev.
146 G. Swain, *Trotsky and the Russian Revolution* (Abingdon, Routledge Seminar Studies 2014), pp. 44–5.
147 Quoted in Shub, p. 121.
148 Shub, p. 125.

149 *Source Records of the Great War*, Vol. 5, pp. 75–7.

150 Later, as Dean of Canterbury, Johnson was a governor of the Simon Langton Grammar Schol for Boys in Canterbury, where he was personally known to the author.

151 Lockhart, *Memoirs*, pp. 171–2 (abridged).

152 Quoted in Shub, p. 141 (abridged).

153 Zeman, p. 75.

154 L. Bryant, *Six months in Red Russia* (New York, Doran 1918), p. 145 (abridged).

155 *Source Records of the Great War*, Vol. 5, pp. 396–7 (abridged).

156 Text of telegram reproduced in Zeman, p. 117.

157 R. Service, *Stalin: A Memoir* (London, Pan 2005), p. 78.

158 L. Trotsky, *Moya Zhizn* (Moscow, Panorama 1991), Vol. 2, p. 90 (abridged).

159 Ibid, p. 154.

160 Telegram reproduced in Zeman, p. 117.

161 An acronym of Glavnoe Upravlenie Lagerei or Main Administration of the Camps.

162 Kennan, *Memoirs* (New York, Bantam Books 1967), pp. 562–3.

163 Complete title: Gosudarstvennoye Politicheskoye Upravlenie Narodnovo Komiteta Vnukhtrennikh Del.

164 A full account of his rounding them up and deporting those too important to murder may be found in L. Chamberlain *Lenin's Private War* (New York, St Martin's Press 2007).

165 Still then written in Arabic script.

166 Service, *Stalin*, p. 161.

167 Abridged, author's italics.

168 R. Service, *Trotsky*, p. 215 (abridged).

169 An account of the Dunsterforce campaign may be found in Boyd, *The Other First World War*, pp. 238–41.

170 Zeman, p.120.

171 Ibid.

172 See at greater length Boyd, *The Other First World War*, pp. 205–19.

173 Ibid, pp. 205, 207, 220, 222–8.

174 'At the gates of Kazan' in *The Military Writings of Leon Trotsky*, Vol. 1, 1918. Full text downloadable from marxists.org/archive/trotsky/quotes.htm.

175 *Bolshevitskye rukodovodstvo,* p. 156, quoted in D. Rayfield, *Stalin and His Hangmen* (London, Penguin 2005), p. 86 (edited).

176 Quoted in M. Kort, *The Soviet Colossus* (Abingdon, Routledge 2015), p. 131 (abridged).

177 Article in *Manchester Guardian*, 27 March 1933.

178 Ibid.

179 Article in *Manchester Guardian*, 25 March 1933.

180 Unlike true submarines, these vessels travelled on the surface and only submerged for the attack or if spotted by aircraft or enemy vessels.

181 A fuller account of the Allied interventions may be found in Boyd, *The Other First World War*, pp. 205–41.

182 Lockhart, p. 311, abridged.

183 A state company of stores licensed to trade with foreigners.

184 Documentation Centre of the Social Organisation of the Sverdlosk Region (DCSOSR) F. 41 Op. 1.D. 151, L. 10–22.

185 In March 1922 a number of people claimed that a patient in a North German mental hospital was the Grand Duchess Anastasia. Despite the Tsarina's brother, Grand Duke of Hesse Ernest Louis, employing a private detective who identified the patient as a Polish factory worker named Franziska Schanzkowska, who had a history of mental illness before the suicide attempt that had landed her in the asylum, some people who had known the Russian royal family did believe that she might be Anastasia, while others were unconvinced. Among those who believed that Anna Anderson, as she came to be called, was the Grand Duchess were composer Sergei Rachmaninov and a daughter and a son of the Tsar's physician Dr Botkin, who had played with the Tsar's children in the holidays. The successful film *Anastasia* starring Swedish actress Ingrid Bergman gave renewed publicity to her life and claims, but when she died in 1984, nearly seven decades after the murders in Ekaterinburg, tests on a lock of her hair did not match its DNA with that of the Tsar's daughters, although it did match that of a relative of Schanzkowska.

186 *Guardian*, 25 August 2007.

187 It was re-named the All-Union Communist Party in 1925 and finally became the Communist Party of the Soviet Union in 1952.

188 Rayfield, p. 80

189 H. Axelbank & M. Eastman, *Tsar to Lenin* (DVD published by Mehring Books 2015).

190 The Tambov rebellion is also referred to as 'Antonov's mutiny' or *Antonovschina* after Alexander Antonov, a socialist revolutionary leader of the movement.

191 Chamberlain, p. 126.

192 Quoted in Chamberlain, p. 128 (abridged).

193 The whole sad story is told in Chamberlain's book.

194 Shub, *New International*.

195 Ibid.

196 Shub, p. 166.

197 Quoted in Shub, pp. 171–2.

198 Service, p. 175.

199 N. Pokrovskii and S. Petrov, *Politburo i Tserkov* (Moscow, Gosizdat 1997), Vol. 1, pp. 141–2.

200 See Boyd, *The Kremlin Conspiracy*.

201 See Boyd, *Daughters of the KGB*.

202 F. Beckett, *Enemy Within: the rise and fall of the British Communist Party* (London, John Murray 1998), p.12.

203 Ibid, pp. 17–18.

204 Ibid, p. 13.

205 Ibid.

206 Ibid.

207 Ibid, pp. 28–9.

208 Ibid, pp. 27–9.

209 Title later changed to *Morning Star*.

210 Personal communication with the author by H.G.'s son Frank Wells.

211 Although there are some who thought he might have been murdered on Stalin's orders.

212 Abridged by the author.

213 M.S. Colley, *Gareth Jones: A Manchukuo Incident* (pub. Privately 2001), pp. xx, xxi.

214 Abridged by the author. The full text is downloadable from www.marxists. org/archive/trotsky/1928/06/alma-ata.htm.

215 She also used the names Liza Rosenschweig, Elizaveta Zarubina, Liza Gorskaya, Elizabeth Zubilin and Sara Herbert.

216 P. Sudoplatov, *Special Tasks* (London, Little Brown 1994), p. 189.

217 An acronym of *smert spionam* – death to spies.

218 Some sources say 21 May.

219 A fellow Mingrelian-speaker, Beria used to enjoy singing Georgian songs in Stalin's midnight singsongs, but eventually fell out with him, narrowly surviving Stalin's death, only to be murdered at a Politburo meeting shortly afterwards.

220 The Partit Obrer d'Unificació Marxista was a Catalan Marxist Party that did not accept Soviet commissars' dictates during the Spanish Civil War; its members were murdered by Moscow's commissars in Spain.

221 Article in *El Mundo*, July 1970, p. 17, entitled *Mi hermano Ramón no era un vulgar asesino*, quoted in Service, *Trotsky* (abridged).

FURTHER READING IN ENGLISH

Beckett, F., *Enemy Within: The Rise and Fall of the British Communist Party* (London, John Murray 1998)

Boyd, D., *Daughters of the KGB* (Stroud, The History Press 2005)

Boyd, D., *The Kremlin Conspiracy: 1,000 Years of Russian Expansionism* (Stroud, The History Press 2014)

Boyd, D., *The Other First World War – The Blood-Soaked Russian Fronts, 1914–1922* (Stroud, The History Press 2014)

Bruce Lockhart, R.H., *Memoirs of a British Agent* (London, Putnam 1934)

Chamberlain, L., *Lenin's Private War: The Voyage of the Philosophy Steamer and the Exile of the Intelligentsia* (New York, St Martin's Press 2006)

Farmborough, F., *Nurse at the Russian Front* (London, Futura 1977)

Fleming, P., *The Fate of Admiral Kolchak* (Edinburgh, Berlinn 2001)

Montefiore, Sebag S., *Stalin: The Court of the Red Tsar* (London, Orion Felix 2004)

Occleshaw, M., *Dances in Deep Shadows – Britain's Clandestine War in Russia 1917–20* (London, Constable 2006)

Pearson, M., *Inessa – Lenin's Mistress* (London, Duckworth 2001)

Rayfield, D., *Stalin and His Hangmen* (London, Penguin 2005)

Service, R., *Spies and Commissars – Bolshevik Russia and the West* (London, Macmillan 2011)

Service, R., *Stalin: A Biography* (London, Pan Macmillan 2005)

Service, R., *Trotsky: A Biography* (London, Pan Macmillan 2010)

D. Shub, *Lenin* (New York, Doubleday Mentor 1948)

Video

A fascinating montage of films shot at the time may be found in Hermann Axelbank's *Tsar to Lenin* (available on DVD, running time 63 minutes). Originally premiered in 1937 the film was suppressed by the Stalinist American Communist Party until reissued in 2012. See www.tsartolenin.com and an interesting collection of archive material may be found on the website www. alexanderpalace.org/palace.

INDEX

abdication 108–9
Ageloff, S. 206
Aims of Russian Socialism 23
Alexander II 21, 40
Alexander III 20, 40, 70
Alexander-Sinclair, Rear Admiral E. 161
Alexis I 46
All-Russian Congress of Soviets 120, 129–30, 132, 141, 148, 201
All-Russian Congress of Working and Peasant Woman 141
American intervention 153, 180, 185
American Relief Administration 198
anarchists 152, 163
Anderson, A. 174
Animal Farm 24
Anti-Semitism *see* Jews
Archangel 151–3, 161
Armand I 115–16, 141, 164, 201
Armeeoberkommando (AOK), Austrian high command 134, 145
Armistice 134–45
Austro-Hungarian Empire, forces 14, 55, 59, 63–4, 67, 69, 73, 80, 122, 146, 177
Axelrod, P. 22, 23

Balabanova, A. 116
Balkans 59–60

Baltic states 43, 44, 124, 127, 137, 145, 151, 182–3
Battleship Potemkin 45
Beckett, F. 198
Beria, L. 206
Berkman, A. 190, 191
besprizorny 195
Bizenko, A. 134–5
Black Hundreds, Black Squadrons 44–5, 51
Blanc, Louis 13
Blanquism 13
Bloody Sunday 44
Blumkin, J.G. 157, 160, 205
Bochkaryova, M. 100–1
Boevaya Organizatsiya 51
Bogdanov A. 36
Bogdanov, A.A. 25, 51
Bolshevik Military Organisation (BMO) 123–4, 126, 142
Bolsheviks 24–5, 28, 34, 36–8, 48, 53–5, 74, 99–100, 111, 115–16, 118–19, 121, 124, 126–8, 134, 142, 144, 146–7, 150, 154, 160, 182, 186, 189
Borutch, P. 22 *and see* Axelrod, P.
boyeviki 43
Brändström, E. 84–5
Brest-Litovsk 134–7, 141, 143–4, 148, 150, 152–4, 160

British intervention 107, 114, 120, 150, 152, 154, 161–2, 180
Bronstein, L.D. 26–7 *and see* Trotsky, Lev
Bruce, Major E.C. 162–3
Bruce Lockhart, R. 29, 71, 131–2, 161
Brusilov, General A. 91, 113, 122, 126
Bryant, L. 131, 133
Buchanan, Ambassador C. 110, 120
Buchanan, M. 106–7, 113
Budyonny, General S.M. 185
Bukharin, N. 148, 202
Bumby, J. 79–80
Burns, M. 16

Canadian intervention 161
Caridad, M. 206
Carpathians 75, 91, 95–8
Castro, F. 201
Catherine the Great 14, 26, 113, 196
censorship, *see* media
Central Asia 164, 184
Central Powers 65, 98, 133–4, 151, 186
Central Transcaspasian Dictatorship 150
Charkviani, Father 33
Cheka 35, 118, 143, 151–2, 157, 160–1, 163, 178–81, 184–5, 187, 189
Chekhov, A. 49
Cheminon, Major M. 43–4
Chernov, V. 111, 123, 180
chernozem 49
Chkheidze, N.S. 117, 125, 129
Chto dyelat' 23, 24, 27
Churchill, Sir W. 69
Clark, C. 63
Cold War 39
collectivisation and requisitions 24, 157–8, 177, 181, 186, 189
Comintern 193–4, 197, 199
Communist League 17
Communist Party of Great Britain (CPGB) 19, 197–200
Communist Party of Soviet Union (CPSU) 177, 194–7, 201–4
Condition of the Working Class in England 16
Constituent Assembly 54, 109, 134, 142

Cossacks 34–6, 46–7, 73, 77, 79, 105, 126, 154, 178, 180
Crimean War 45, 161
Critique of the Gotha Progamme 13
Cromie Cdr F. 161
Curzon Line, H. 157
Czech Legion 153–5, 157, 165–6, 174, 183–5

Daily Worker 199
Decembrists 47
Demuth, H. and F.L. 18
Denikin, General A.I. 162–3, 185
Deutsch-Französiche Jahrbücher 16
dictatorship of the proletariat 64, 193
Disconto Gesellschaft 120
Donskoi, B.M. 160
Dowling, T. 73
Duma 37, 51–3, 55, 92, 98, 102, 106–7, 109–10, 122, 177
Dunsterforce 150
Dutt, R.P. 199–200
Dzerzhinsky, F. 35, 118, 143, 151, 156, 160–1, 178, 180–1, 191
Dzhugashvili, B. 32–3
Dzhugashvili, J. 35
Dzhugashvili, J.V. 32–5 *see also* Stalin

Eichhorn, General H. 160
Eisenstein S. 45
Eisner, K. 181, 196
Eitingon, N. 206
Ekaterinburg 165–74
Engels, Friedrich 16–19
expulsion of intellectuals 144, 188

Falber, R. 197
famine 49, 105, 198
Farmborough, F. 74–5, 76–80, 91, 100–1, 128
FBI 37
female soldiers 100–1
field post 70, 92–4
Finland 44, 48, 52, 54–5, 142, 145, 152, 191
First World War 37, 59, 63–69, 186, 196

Franco-Prussian war 18
Franz Ferdinand, Archduke 59–62
French intervention 162–3

gas, poison 93–4, 187, 189–90
Geladze, K. 32–3
Gelfand, I.L. aka Alexander Parvus
    28–9, 48, 52, 54, 73–4
Gensek 195, 202–3
George V 109
Georgia 32–6, 44, 164, 178
German Empire, forces 63, 69, 73, 80,
    88, 101
German subsidies 65, 74, 118–20, 125,
    128, 132–3, 142–3
Goldman, E. 190
Golytsin, Prince 106
Gorky, M. 133, 187
GPU 144, 187
Grey, Sir E. 63
Grigoriev, General V. 88–9
Guevara, C. 201
Gul, R. 30

Hamilton, General I. 44
Hardinge, Ambassador C. 44
Harte, R.H. 206
Hearst Corporation 206
Hitler, Adolf 32
Hoffmann, General M. 119, 137, 144
Hungarian Democratic (or Soviet)
    Republic 181, 193

independence movements 124
Inkpin, A. and H. 199
internal exile 22, 27, 34, 36–7, 47, 116,
    191, 204
International Women's Day 103
Irkutsk 27, 28, 34, 37, 154, 183–5
Iskra 23, 24, 28, 48, 55
Ivan the Terrible 39
Izvestiya 36, 52, 109, 142, 173, 191, 193

Janin, General M. 184
Japan-China war 40
Japanese intervention 153

Jewish Social Bund 24
Jews 21, 26, 51, 137, 149, 163
Johnson, H. 131
'July Days' 123–4

Kamenev, L. 34, 55–6, 99, 110, 121,
    124, 135, 195, 202
Kaplan, F. 160, 178, 195, 202
Kazan 21, 47, 154–5, 180, 183
Kennan, G. 38–9, 144
Kerensky, A. 111–13, 118, 121–3,
    125–8, 132, 153, 182
KGB 21
Khabalov, General S.S. 103, 106
Khrushchev, N. 204
Kitchener, General H. 64
Knox, Colonel A. 69–73, 90, 101, 107,
    130
Kolchak, Admiral A. 180, 183–5
Kollontai, A. 116, 125, 164, 186, 192,
    201–2
Kornilov, General L. 123, 126–8, 161–2
Kovno 88–90
Krassin, L. 132
Krestinsky, N. 195
Kronstadt/personnel 53, 107, 125, 129,
    142, 161, 182, 189–191
Kropotkin, Prince P. 51
Krupskaya, N.K. 22–3, 25, 51, 115–16,
    121, 152, 164, 202–4
Kühlmann, Baron R. 132–3, 137
kulaki 158–9, 187
Kun B 181, 193, 196, 198
Kuropatkin, General A.N. 44–5, 55,
    91, 94

League of Nations 198
Lenin, V.I. 22–5, 27–32, 35–8, 48, 51,
    53–6, 64–5, 98, 112, 114–16,
    118–21, 123–6, 128–30, 132, 134,
    136, 141–5, 148–50, 152, 156–8,
    160, 177–8, 180–2, 186–8, 191,
    193–7, 200–4 *see also* Ulyanov V.I.
Leningrad 203 *see also* Petrograd, St
    Peterburg
Levine, D. 38

lice 95
Locker-Lampson, Commander O. 161
Ludendorff, General E. 89, 119, 126–7, 136–7
Lvov, Prince G.E. 109, 125

Makhno, N. 162–3
Manchester Guardian 62, 131, 158–9
Manifesto der Kommunistischen Partei 13, 19
Manifesto of 30 October 53, 116
March Revolutions 14
Martov, J. 22, 34, 51
Marx, H. 16
Marx, K. 13–19, 21, 24, 27, 34, 136, 196
Marx, J. 16–19
Marxism 21, 22, 24, 28–9, 55, 143
Marxism-Leninism 143
Masaryk, T. 120
Materialism and Empirio-criticism 36
Maugham, S. 131
Mayakovsky, V. 201–2
media, censorship 15, 17, 54, 133–4, 142
Mendelssohn & Co. 118–19
Mensheviks 25, 28–9, 34–7, 51, 74, 121, 124, 133, 157, 160, 180, 193, 202
Mercader, R. 206–7
Mikhail, Grand Duke 106, 108
Milyukov, P. 124
Mingrelian language 32, 34
Molotov, V.M. 110, 157
Montgomery, Gen B. 91
Moscow 40, 46, 48, 51, 54, 122, 124, 127, 131, 141, 145, 148, 151–2, 156, 162–3, 196, 199–200, 203
Moya Zhizn 137
Muggeridge, M. 158–9
Mukden battle 43, 45
Murmansk 151–3, 161
Murphy, J. 198
Murrik, S. 200
Muslims 126, 164
mutiny 45, 48, 51, 53, 98, 101, 103, 105–7, 122–5, 196

Nachalo 52
Nansen, F. 198

Napoleon 47, 77
Narodnaya Volya 20, 21, 50–1
Neue Rhenische Zeitung 17
New Economic Policy 192
Nikolaev 26–7
Nikolai I 47
Nikolai, Grand Duke 52, 70, 71, 89, 91, 173
NKVD 37
Nya Banken 118, 120

Oberste Heeresleitung (OHL) German high command 63, 68, 80, 115, 123, 134–6, 144–5, 152
Odessa 26–7, 48, 163
Okhrana 21, 22, 27, 34–8, 50, 53–6, 104, 115, 121
Omsk 92, 180
Orgburo 157
Orlov, A. 37–8
Outlines of a Critique of Political Economy 16

Pale of Settlement 21, 26, 50
Paléologue, Ambassador M. 73
Pankhurst, S. 129, 197, 199
Paris Commune 18–19
Parvus *see* Gelfand
Peter the Great 39, 53
Petrograd 70, 99, 102–6, 109, 115, 117, 122–4, 128, 130–1, 136, 142, 148, 151–2, 180, 182 *see also* St Petersburg, Leningrad
Plekhanov, Georgi 22–4, 28, 111
Poland 44, 66–7, 75–83, 101, 137, 145, 186
Politburo 132, 157, 195, 202, 204
Pollitt, H. 199
Port Arthur 41, 43, 45–6
Potresov, A. 24
POUM 206
POWs 45, 68, 79–80, 99, 101, 122, 198
Pravda 36–7, 120–2, 134, 142, 145
Princip G. 62
Protopopov, A.D. 106
provisional government 106, 109–13, 115, 119, 121, 123–5, 127–9

Pskov 108–9
Pugachoff, Y. 47
Putilov works 102–3, 125, 180

Ransome, A. 131
Rasputin 70, 89, 98–9, 106
Razin, S. 46–7
Red Army 30, 153, 155, 157–8,
    161, 163–4, 179, 181–3, 185–7,
    189–90, 192
Red Cross 198
Red Guards 133, 155
Red Terror 178, 181, 187
Reed, J.S. 131
Rennenkampf, General P. 68
Revolution of 1905 44, 51, 55, 98, 107
Revolution, February 103–7, 110, 112,
    118
Robins, Colonel R. 143
Rodzianko, M.V. 102, 105–6, 108
Romanov children 70, 103–4, 112–13,
    165, 167–73, 175
Romanov massacre 166–173
Roosevelt, President T. 46
Rosenfeld, L. *see* Kamenev
Rothstein, T. 197
Royal Navy 109, 161
Rozhestvensky, Admiral Z. 43, 45
RSFSR 156–7, 192
Russell, B. 201
Russian Empire 19, 40, 42, 46, 71, 74,
    98–9, 177, 186
Russian Social Democratic Labour
    Party (RSDLP) 37, 53
Russo-Japanese war 35, 37, 40, 43,
    45–6, 48, 66
Ruszki, General N.V. 103, 106, 108

Samara 21
Samsonov, General A. 68, 73
Savinkov, B. 126
Schlieffen Plan 66
'sealed train' 114–17
Second World War 39, 43, 163
Sedova, Natalya I. 28–9, 48, 52, 54–5,
    99–100

Semyonov, G.M. 183–5
Serbia 59, 60
serfdom 46–8, 71
Service, R. 100, 121, 149
Shelepina, Y.P. 131
Shlyapnikov 110
Shub, D. 119
Shushenskoye 22
Siberian Bank 120
Simbirsk 20–1 *and see* Ulyanovsk
Sisson, E. 143
Social Democratic Labour Party
    (SDLP) 28, 34–5, 115, 146
Socialist International 55, 112, 194
Socialist Revolutionaries 51, 111, 115,
    120, 124, 133–4, 151, 154, 157,
    159–60, 180, 202
Sokolnikoff, G. 149
Sokolovskaya, A.L. 27, 28, 133
Sophie, wife of Franz Ferdinand 59–60
Soviet of Worker's and Soldiers'
    Deputies 109–11, 117–18, 126,
    128–9, 167
Soviet of Workers' Deputies 52
Sovnarkom 30–1, 130, 134, 142, 145,
    149, 156, 193
Soyuz Borby 22
St Petersburg 20–2, 44, 48, 51–3, 175
    see also Petrograd, Leningrad
Stalin, J.V. 32, 36, 38, 55, 110–11, 120,
    129–30, 132, 141, 144–5, 156–8,
    162, 164, 180–2, 192, 195, 200,
    202–7 *see also* Dzhugashvili, J.V.
Stalingrad/Volgograd/Tsaritsyn 163, 185
Stavka – Russian high command 66–8,
    80, 89, 91, 94, 101, 104, 106, 135
Stewart, B. 197
Stinnes, H. 65, 74
Stolypin, P.A. 55
strikes 44, 48, 50, 52–3, 56, 98–9,
    136–7, 179–80, 186, 189, 196
students 50–1
Sudoplatov, P. 206
Sukhomlinov, V. 73, 88
surrender of Central Powers 162, 164
Svanidze, E. 35–6

Sverdlov 110
Sverdlovsk Archeological Inst 175

Tambov rebellion 186–7, 189, 191
Tannenberg battle 68
Tatar-Mongol Yoke 71
Tchaikovsky, N.V. 152
Temporary Laws 21
Times 44, 62–3
Trans-Caspasian Provincial Gov't 164
Trans-Siberian railway 40–1, 43, 44,
    153–4, 165–6, 183
Triple Entente 63
triple intervention 41
Trotsky, L. 25, 28–32, 35, 48, 51–5,
    98–100, 120, 123–5, 127, 128–30,
    132–4, 136–7, 141, 144–5, 149,
    153, 155–8, 162–4, 177–8, 180–2,
    186–7, 189, 190, 192, 195, 202–7
    see also Bronstein, L.B.
Trotsky, sons, daughters L., N., S. and
    Z. 204–5
Tsar Nicholas II 41, 51–3, 55, 70, 89,
    91, 94, 98–9, 102–13, 116, 122,
    132–3, 165, 167–73, 175
Tsarina Alexandra 41, 70, 89, 98–9, 102,
    104–6, 112–13, 165, 167–73, 175
Tsederbaum, J. *see also* Martov, J.
Tukhachevsky, Marshal 38, 189
Turkey 59, 205

Ukraine 14, 26, 82, 122, 124, 137,
    144–5, 164, 177, 186
Ukrainian Black Army 162
Ulyanov, A.I. 20
Ulyanov, I.N. 20
Ulyanov, V.I. 20–2 *see also* Lenin
Ulyanova, M.A. 20–1, 23, 25
Ulyanovsk 20
Union of Working Peasants 186
universities 51
Uritsky, M. 160
USSR 32, 143–4, 189, 192, 195–7, 205

Verkholensk 27
Victoria, Queen 41

Vladivostok 40, 151, 153, 161, 183
von Bethman-Hollweg, T. 114
von Bismarck, O. 62
von Czernin, O. 136
von Hindenburg, General P. 82, 136
von Hutier, General Oskar 127
von Mirbach, Ambassador W. 142,
    150–1, 157, 160, 205
von Moltke, Field Marshal 66
von Plehve, V. 50–1
von Westphalen, Jenny *see* Marx, Jenny
Voroshilov, K.E. 35, 162
Vostochnoye Obozrenie 27
Vyrobova, A. 106

Walpole, H. 131
war communism 177–8, 192
Warburg, M. 65, 74
Warsaw/salient 66–8, 79–81, 83, 85,
    88, 90, 94
Wells, H.G. 201
Western Allies 63, 144, 150–1, 153
White Terror 163, 181, 184
White Volunteer Army 162–3
Wilhelm II 114
Winter Palace 129
Witte, Count S.Y. 40, 44, 48, 50, 52–3
Women's Death Batallion 101, 120, 129
Workers' Opposition 186, 192, 201
Wrangel, General P.N. 162–3, 185–7

Yagoda, G. 188
Yeltsin, B. 174, 175
Yoffe, A. 134, 149
Yudenich, General N. 182–3
Yurovsky, J.M. 166–73

Zarubina, Z. 205
Zemlyatchka, R. 181
Zhenotdel 164, 201
Zhivoye Slovo 121
Zhordania, N. 178
Zimmermann, A. 74
Zinoviev, G. 35, 55–6, 114, 116, 121,
    124–5, 202
Zvyozda 37